Disciplinary Discourses

Disciplinary Discourses

Social Interactions
in Academic Writing

Ken Hyland
University of London

MICHIGAN CLASSICS EDITION

The University of Michigan Press
Ann Arbor

2014 2013 2012 2011   5 4 3 2

ISBN 0-472-03024-8

Library of Congress Cataloguing-in-Publication

Hyland, Ken.
    Disciplinary discources: social interactions in academic writing / Ken Hyland
Michigan classics ed.
        p.   cm.
    Includes bibliographical references and index.
    ISBN 0-472-03024-8 (pbk.)
        1. Authorship—Social aspects. 2. English language—Discourse analysis.
3. Scholarly publishing—Social aspects. 4. Academic writing—Study
and teaching. 5. Academic writing—Social aspects. I. Title.

PN146.H94   2004
302.2'244—dc22   2004047984

Foreword

As I write this short foreword on a chilly November weekend in Ann Arbor, I reflect briefly on some of the events of the previous week. On Monday evening, I taught my 'Writing for Publication' class; in that class, I spent some time going over with my international doctoral students Ken Hyland's chart showing how reporting verbs change from field to field. Engineers *report*, but philosophers *argue!* On Tuesday afternoon, I met with some of the first-year undergraduates taking my freshman seminar on 'Academic Discourse', three of whom are writing their final projects on textbooks. Omar is examining how textbook writers from three fields 'engage with their readers'; Jee-Hon is comparing a psychology textbook published in 1971 with one published in 2001; and Alex is analysing the forms and functions of exemplification in the opening chapters of textbooks from physics and chemistry. All three have been reading Chapter 6 of *Disciplinary Discourses,* along with other papers about textbook discourse written by Alison Love and Greg Myers.

On Thursday, Christine Feak and I gave a workshop organized by the University of Michigan's Graduate School on 'Writing the Literature Review' to 80 or so students from across the university. Throughout, the discussions and illustrations involved felt such a sense of disciplinary differences in style and rhetoric that I am sure Ken Hyland would have approved. Finally, on Friday Chris and I went to the university's Sweetland Writing Center to give a seminar for graduate student instructors destined to teach disciplinary-specific writing courses in the winter semester. Our main chosen text was a one-page introduction written by a Chinese doctoral student from the School of Natural Resources and the Environment. This text led to sharply different views, with those from the humanities attacking what they considered to be its heavy use of bland parenthetical references, while the graduate students from biology and psychology came to the text's defense.

These little stories from a particularly busy week point, I believe, to two conclusions. First, for all of us involved in teaching academic writing—whether to undergraduates, graduates or researchers, and irrespective of the first languages of those individuals—the issues around the linguistic and rhetorical expression of disciplinary conventions and expectations are becoming more and more central. Second, we have come increasingly to realise how important in this regard have been Ken Hyland's publications over the last decade or so. The capstone of these is his *Disciplinary Discourses*, which was originally published in 2000. It is a capstone book for several reasons: its complex methodology (corpus linguistics, move analysis, interview transcripts from disciplinary informants, and text-based responses from experts), its coverage of a wide range of genres, its fluent writing style, and its careful and subtle articulation of a social constructionist approach.

There was a real chance that this important volume would have gone out of print much before its time, and so I salute the University of Michigan Press for seizing an opportunity to republish it and, by doing so, making it easily available to present and future practitioners and researchers in our field. For it is indeed an important volume; the last time I looked at the *Social Science Citation Index,* there had already been 38 references to *Disciplinary Discourses* in the less than three years since its original publication.

John M. Swales
Ann Arbor, 2003

Contents

Preface

This book makes a new appearance in the colours of the University of Michigan Press following a relatively short, but agreeably visible, life in Chris Candlin's Applied Linguistics and Language Studies series with Longman. While this is not a new edition of *Disciplinary Discourses*, its republication in a new imprint is a result of the mysterious manoeuvres of academic publishing and highlights how closely a central area of academic life is coupled to market imperatives. This republication therefore offers something of a vivid illustration of the thesis presented in the final chapter of this book, suggesting one way in which dominant social discourses regulate interactions and practices in other domains. The fact that the book has been taken up by another publisher, of course, also shows the influence of wider interests in publishing and how individual editors can make a difference. As I said, a mysterious place to be.

This second incarnation, however, offers me a brief opportunity to situate this book more generally in the field of English for Academic Purposes, a field which has grown enormously in the past twenty-five years and which has continued to develop rapidly since the book's original publication four years ago. In an era of globalisation, English is now established as the world's leading language for the dissemination of academic knowledge. Whether we see this as a facilitative lingua franca or a rampaging *Tyrannosaurus rex* (Swales, 1997), the dominance of English has transformed the educational experiences and professional lives of countless students and academics across the planet. Fluency in the conventions of English academic discourses is now virtually essential as a means of gaining access to the knowledge of our disciplines and navigating our careers. It has also reshaped the ways that teaching and research are conducted in higher education, not only creating the multi-million dollar enterprise of EAP, but leading to the recognition that native English speakers also benefit from an explicit understanding of the arcane and alien discourses of their fields.

This expansion, both of English and the linguistic and cultural heterogeneity of students in higher education, means that support for student writing is often embedded in the mainstream curriculum at universities. Writing is now an integral feature of many university courses and professional development programmes, and this has led, in turn, to a more urgent need to understand what these discourses of the academy are and what counts as 'good writing'. Until fairly recently faculty, students and often writers themselves, saw academic writing as monolithic and homogeneous, a set of decontextualised skills which were transferable across domains and disciplines. It was also seen as something that students brought with them from their school backgrounds or, more often, did not. Recent research, including the research which appears in this book, has consistently shown, however, that the discourses of the academy are enormously diverse, and that this diversity has important implications for writers as they interact with their teachers and peers, and as they write themselves into their disciplines.

Research into disciplinary writing has begun to provide important insights into the structures and meanings of texts in a range of fields and to show how different academic contexts place demands on communicative behaviours which are likely to be unfamiliar to disciplinary novices. It has, moreover, helped us to see the ways disciplines are constantly re-created through the ongoing social and discursive practices of individuals as they negotiate and reconfirm their membership in academic communities.

This research has also had important implications for writing instruction, grounding teaching and learning in an understanding of the cognitive, social and linguistic demands of specific academic disciplines. Beyond this, by exploring what is involved in writing across the disciplines, it has also begun to promote an 'academic literacies' view of writing (Lea and Street, 1998), which recognises the complexities of contemporary modular and multi-discipline courses and demonstrates a concern with issues of identity, epistemology, interaction and power relations. This approach helps decouple university language teaching from the focus on grammar, literature or 'personal writing' approaches of earlier days and moves it towards developing new kinds of literacy so learners are better placed to critically engage with the values of institutional goals and practices.

This brings us to the book you hold in your hands, which embraces all these issues in various ways. Its main aim, however, is to pull together a range of apparently disparate topics to offer an account of social interactions in published academic writing. It takes the view that it is largely through texts that individuals collaborate with others, both to create knowledge and define their academic allegiances, and goes on to show how this is accomplished in a range of genres and disciplines. My purpose is to provide a series of analyses with a common thread. By examining a range of pragmatic features, through the use of corpus and interview data, I seek to reveal how writers from different disciplines typically position themselves and their work in relation to other members of their professional communities. I then attempt to situate this approach within the related issues of research, teaching and the social forces of power and discourse change.

As a result, *Disciplinary Discourses* looks at academic writing in a way that may be unfamiliar to some readers. This is because we often see academic discourse in a way which privileges its ideational function, how it works to construct a particular experience of the world. Clearly, how academics label, categorise, and show relationships in the phenomena they study are central aspects of academic perception and communication. But, as in any other domain of language use, they also select their words to engage with others and to present their ideas in ways that make most sense to their readers. This involves what Halliday refers to as the interpersonal function of language, and it is encoded in every sentence we write. Readers must be drawn in, influenced, and persuaded by a text that sees the world in similar ways to them, employing accepted resources for the purpose of sharing meanings in that context. In other words, academic writing is an interactive, as well as cognitive, project.

A central aspect of this view is that academic writing is not a unitary or stable object. Although certain features of writing that we commonly recognise as 'academic' may be widespread, writers act as members of groups which see the world in different ways and which change over time. It is as individuals that we make contributions to the disciplinary communities of which we are members and it is only here that, as insiders, we construct meanings. Within disciplines, writers speak to colleagues in recognisable discursive spaces in recognisably acceptable ways, shaping their actions to the presumed understandings and needs of their readers. Only in relation to these communities are meanings validated, and they only receive validation to the extent they are compatible with the understandings and practices of these communities.

There are two main ways we can study social interactions in writing. We can examine the actions of individuals as they create particular texts, or we can examine the distribution of different genre features to see how they cluster in complementary distributions. In this study I have followed the second route. My approach steps back from particular authors or readers to reveal interaction as a collection of rhetorical choices rather than as specific encounters of people with texts. To see how writers behave as members of social communities means going beyond the decisions of individual writers to explore the regularity and repetition of the socially ratified forms which represent preferred disciplinary practices. Writers are oriented to more than an immediate encounter with their text when composing; they also conjure up institutional patterns which naturally and ideologically reflect and maintain such patterns. These can only be seen by viewing activity as socially and culturally constituted modes of praxis.

This book is, then, an elaboration and demonstration of these ideas. In it I give close attention to specific features in a corpus of 1.5 million words supported by interviews with subject specialists concerning their communication practices. The analyses involve 1,400 texts from five genres in eight disciplines covering a deliberately broad cross-section of academic practice. Table 1 gives an overview of the genres. Molecular biology and magnetic physics represent the pure sciences, and mechanical engineering and electronic engineering the applied sciences. Philosophy and sociology are often categorised as either humanities or social sciences, while marketing and applied linguistics might be regarded as more applied social sciences.

Table 1. The texts

Genre	Texts	Number of disciplines	Total words
Reasearch articles	80	8	500,000
Book reviews	160	8	160,000
Scientific letters	90	3	143,000
Abstracts	1,040	8	156,000
Textbook chapters	56	8	481,000
Totals	**1,426**		**1,440,000**

The book begins by discussing the issues I have raised above in more detail, providing an outline of the significance of academic writing and reviewing the main linguistic approaches to written social interactions. Chapter 1 therefore outlines a converging body of theory that suggests academic texts reflect discipline-specific knowledge-making practices. In particular, I make considerable use of the insights originating from the work of Swales, Berkenkotter and Huckin, and Geertz, to highlight the importance of academic texts and their role in constructing both an understanding of what disciplines are, and the ways they go about creating knowledge.

This survey is followed in Chapter 2 by a more detailed discussion of one way in which writers in different fields work to create a context for their research, examining the use of citation. This is a central means by which writers establish the credibility and novelty of their claims by situating them in an appropriate disciplinary framework. Citation is seen as a set of practices which reflects both social and epistemological understandings and provides a way of characterising disciplines in terms of the different ways they see the world, formulate research and structure arguments. In this chapter then, I not only argue that citation is a key feature of knowledge-making, but seek to provide a framework for understanding the various genres and features examined in subsequent chapters.

In Chapter 3 I examine book reviews, focusing on the ways that writers manage interpersonal relationships through the expression of praise and criticism. More than in other academic contexts, this genre carries considerable risks of contestation and personal conflict, as judgements are public and may reflect personally on the work of a specific author. Social interactions therefore involve a careful balance of critique and collegiality as writers walk a line between honest evaluation and professional respect. I show how this is accomplished through a range of interpersonal strategies at different levels of the text.

Chapter 4 focuses on the scientific letter, or quick report, a relatively new genre restricted to a few rapidly moving scientific fields where a fast publication time is needed to announce new breakthroughs. Here we find interactions geared to relatively hard-sell persuasive goals and reconstruction of a disciplinary consensus. Successfully staking a claim in this fast-moving world of modern science involves both promotion and mitigation, emphasising the novelty and significance of a piece of research in a restricted space while simultaneously displaying appropriate sensitivity to community expectations of negotiation and professional humility on one hand, and potential opposition from colleagues with alternative positions on the other.

In Chapter 5 I examine the ways that information is presented in article abstracts and the strategies writers use to demonstrate credibility and membership by addressing the community from within recognised and legitimate academic boundaries. Persuasion is essentially an ability to convince one's peers both that one's research and interpretations are sound, and that one has the competence to address issues and colleagues as a disciplinary insider. This involves deploying a range of rhetorical strategies, both at clause level and in the cognitive structuring of the texts.

In Chapter 6 I move from peer communication to explore the ways that academic writers interact with students in both representing the knowledge of their fields and communicating the values and literacy practices of their particular communities. Here I focus on metadiscourse features in seven textbooks in eight disciplines, exemplifying some of the major ways that writers represent themselves, their views and their audience in constructing both a perspective of a disciplinary consensus and an identity as an 'expert'. My argument in this chapter is that meanings in the textbook genre are essentially created for two audiences simultaneously, involving the writer in orientating both learners and colleagues to accept a body of representative knowledge and a professional insider identity.

Chapter 7 examines some of the implications of the approach for both teaching and research. Here my intention is to offer something of a justification for the method and a practical guide for its extension. First I briefly set out what a social orientation to texts might look like and consider the two main methodologies of approaching texts in this way. I then provide a detailed overview of the research methodology I have adopted in this book. Next I explore the pedagogic ramifications of viewing texts as discipline- and genre-specific forms of social interaction in ESP and EAP settings, seeking to encourage a view which focuses both on texts and on individuals acting as members of groups. I conclude the chapter by pointing to some important areas of relative neglect in the study of academic discourse, and go on to suggest a number of directions that teachers, researchers and students may like to follow.

Finally in Chapter 8 I attempt to draw connections between the social interactions of community members and wider issues of institutional power and disciplinary authority. Here I explore the kinds of hierarchically structured social organisation that are maintained by these interactions and examine some of their social and political consequences. In particular, I look at how disciplinary communities accommodate to the pressures of political and market forces, how they work to promote a particular world view and how they help to entrench a particular distribution of power, status and material resources. In this final chapter I also look at issues of social and discursive change, touching on the modes and possibilities for resistance and revision to these dominant valorized genres.

ADDITIONAL REFERENCES

Lea, M. and Street, B. V. (1998). Student writing in higher education: an academic literacies approach. *Studies in Higher Education,* **23** (2), 157–172.
Swales, J. (1997). English as *Tyrannosaurus rex. World Englishes,* **16** (3), 373–382.

Acknowledgements

I owe a debt to my colleagues, friends, informants and family who have given me a great deal of intellectual and personal help in writing this book.

First, there would have been no book without the help of my specialist informants, whose thoughtful views on their practices and insightful commentaries on various texts were invaluable. Among these informants I would like to mention Mark Gaylord, John Bishop, Bill Roberts and Bruce Richardson. I am grateful for their time, patience and ideas.

The book has also grown out of the context of conversations and discussions with many people over many years. These are too numerous to name, but I would especially like to mention Chris Candlin, series editor for the original publication of this book, for his warm support and critical reading of my chapters, and Vijay Bhatia, Malcolm Coulthard, Ann Johns, Sue Hood and John Swales, whose collective sense I've always recognised and appreciated but not always followed. I hope they are not too disappointed by how their views are borrowed and mangled in these pages. I am also grateful to John Milton for advice on corpus issues, and to Ulla Connor, Minna-Ritta Luukka and Michel Perrin for guidance on research on academic writing outside English.

More immediately, I am indebted to Kelly Sippell, the ESL editor at the University of Michigan Press, for her vision and support in moving this book into the University of Michigan stable. Her assistance smoothed the transfer process immensely.

As ever, I want to express my deepest thanks to Fiona Hyland for her care, encouragement and thoughts on academic writing. For always being there to discuss ideas, offer advice, read drafts and patiently sympathize during the trials of writing, this book is for her.

Finally I would like to acknowledge Oxford University Press for permission to reprint an earlier version of Chapter 2 which appeared as 'Academic attribution: citation and the construction of disciplinary knowledge' in *Applied Linguistics*, vol. 20, no. 3, pp. 341–367 (1999).

Chapter 1

Disciplinary cultures, texts and interactions

This book is a study of social interactions in published academic writing, looking at why members of specific disciplines use language in the ways they do. It focuses on texts as the outcome of interactions and explores the view that what academics do with words is to engage in a web of professional and social associations. The book, therefore, is essentially about relationships between people, and between people and ideas. I seek to show that in research articles, abstracts, book reviews, textbooks, and scientific letters, the ways writers present their topics, signal their allegiances, and stake their claims represent careful negotiations with, and considerations of, their colleagues. Their writing therefore displays a professional competence in discipline-approved practices. It is these practices, I suggest, and not abstract and disengaged beliefs and theories, that principally define what disciplines are.

Successful academic writing depends on the individual writer's projection of a shared professional context. That is, in pursuing their personal and professional goals, writers seek to embed their writing in a particular social world which they reflect and conjure up through particular approved discourses. Here then, I follow Faigley's (1986: 535) claim that writing 'can be understood only from the perspective of a society rather than a single individual' and Geertz's (1983) view that knowledge and writing depend on the actions of members of local communities. Looking at writing in this way evokes a social milieu which influences the writer and activates specific responses to recurring tasks.

Rather than regarding linguistic features as regularities of academic style, or the result of some mental processes of representing meaning, I examine them for traces of social interactions with others engaged in a common pursuit. To do this we need to see academic writing as collective social practices, and to focus on published texts as the most concrete, public and accessible realisation of these practices. These texts are the lifeblood of the academy as it is through the public discourses of their members that disciplines authenticate knowledge, establish their hierarchies and reward systems, and maintain their cultural authority. To study the social interactions expressed through academic writing is not only to see how writers in different disciplines go

1

about producing knowledge, it is also to reveal something of the sanctioned social behaviours, epistemic beliefs, and institutional structures of academic communities.

This view is not new, of course, and strong foundations for it are provided in the work of Berkenkotter and Huckin (1995), Bazerman (1988), Myers (1990) and others. In fact, it is perhaps a truism that writing involves interactions. Writers and readers clearly consider each other, try to imagine each other's purposes and strategies, and write or interpret a text in terms of these imaginations. While it might be obvious that writing is interaction, it is not at all evident just what a particular text tells us about that interaction or about those who participate in it. What motivates interactions in academic writing? What linguistic features realise these interactions? What strategies are involved and what principles are employed? What do these tell us about the beliefs and practices of the disciplines?

These are by no means trivial questions for the analysis of discourse, the understanding of disciplinary communities, or the teaching of academic writing. We need to understand these transient regularities and why particular features seem to be so useful to writers that they become regular practices, often institutionalised as approved disciplinary literacies. An improved awareness of such interactions is, then, the key to understanding how academic discourse works in English, whether seen as professional training or as published emblems of scholarship. Such an understanding, in turn, allows users to question both prevailing discursive practices and the relations they express, offering teachers, novices and expert writers greater alternatives in their choice of discourse forms and in their ability to negotiate and establish a plurality of cultural norms in disciplines.

This, then, provides the starting point, a theoretical and pedagogical imperative which urges us to research texts, their contexts and their ideologies – to see how genres are written, used and responded to as part of the wider social and intellectual culture of a particular group and historical period. First, I want to provide some theoretical background as a context for what follows in subsequent chapters. I shall do this by highlighting four central themes of the book: the notions of academic writing, knowledge-construction, disciplinary cultures, and social interactions.

THE IMPORTANCE OF ACADEMIC WRITING

The written genres of the academy have attracted increasing attention from fields as diverse as philosophy, sociology of science, history, rhetoric, and applied linguistics. There is, however, a clear consensus on the importance of written texts in academic life – a recognition that understanding the disciplines involves understanding their discourses. There are two main reasons for this.

The first reason is that disciplinary discourse is considered to be a rich source of information about the social practices of academics. Kress (1989:

7), for example, argues that discourses are 'systematically-organised sets of statements which give expression to the meanings and values of an institution'. Texts, that is, are socially produced in particular communities and depend on them for their sense. As Bazerman (1993: vii) observes:

> ... everything that bears on the professions bears on professional writing. Indeed, within the professions, writing draws on all the professional resources, wends its way among the many constraints, structures, and dynamics that define the professional realm and instantiates professional work.

In academic fields this means that texts embody the social negotiations of disciplinary inquiry, revealing how knowledge is constructed, negotiated and made persuasive. Rather than simply examining nature, writing is actually seen as helping to create a view of the world. This is because texts are influenced by the problems, social practices and ways of thinking of particular social groups (Kuhn, 1970; MacDonald, 1994). In other words, discourse is socially constitutive rather than simply socially shaped; writing is not just another aspect of what goes on in the disciplines, it is seen as *producing* them.

The second reason for the attention given to academic writing is the fact that what academics principally do is write: they publish articles, books, reviews, conference papers and research notes; they communicate with colleagues by e-mail, reprint requests, and referee evaluations; they communicate with students by handouts, study guides and textbooks; they contribute to electronic lists and to university reports; and they submit applications for grants and equipment. Latour and Woolgar (1979), for example, have suggested that the modern research lab devotes more energy to producing papers than to making discoveries, and that scientists' time is largely spent in discussing and preparing articles for publication in competition with other labs. The popular view of the 'academic' as a solitary individual experimenting in the laboratory, collecting data in the field or wrestling with ideas in the library, and then retiring to write up the results, is a modern myth. Research is essentially a *social* enterprise, both in the sense that it is an immediate engagement with colleagues and that it is mediated by the social institutions within which it occurs. It is hardly surprising, therefore, that the written communications of academics express this social imperative.

But while disciplines are defined by their writing, it is *how* they write rather than simply *what* they write that makes the crucial difference between them. An article may discuss garlic proteins, motherese or the existence of truth without people, but we see more than differences of content when we start to read them carefully. Among the things we see are different appeals to background knowledge, different means of establishing truth, and different ways of engaging with readers. Scholarly discourse is not uniform and monolithic, differentiated merely by specialist topics and vocabularies. It is an outcome of a multitude of practices and strategies, where what counts as convincing argument and appropriate tone is carefully managed for a particular audience. These differences are a product then of institutional and interactional forces, the result of diverse social practices of writers within their fields.

One reason for these differences in disciplinary discourses is that texts reveal generic activity (e.g. Reynolds and Dudley-Evans, in press; Swales, 1990). They build on the writer's knowledge of prior texts and therefore exhibit repeated rhetorical responses to similar situations with each generic act involving some degree of innovation and judgement. This kind of typification not only offers the individual writer the resources to manage the complexities of disciplinary engagement, but also contributes to the stabilisation of reproduction of disciplines. Our attention is therefore directed towards textual variation, not only in the content of the texts we examine in a particular discipline, but in the structure of those texts and the kinds of rhetorical strategies they allow. By focusing on the stereotypical and the commonplace we catch a glimpse of what is largely unattended to by writers themselves, the pragmatic expectations and beliefs which are taken for granted in their naturalness. Thus, because these textual regularities apparently reflect the unremarked and automatic practices of disciplinary situated writers, they offer insights into the routine understandings which guide social interactions in those disciplines.

Until recently these disciplinary variations were often obscured by the practicalities of preparing learners for academic studies in English – an enterprise that has tended to emphasise genre rather than discipline and similarity rather than difference. A purely formal view of academic writing tended to dominate early practice in English for Academic Purposes (EAP). This was a view which largely took for granted the academy's perception of its texts as objective, rational and impersonal, and set out to provide students with the generic skills they needed to reproduce them. By ignoring context it was possible to ignore variation and to marginalise language itself as simply a set of skills for clearly communicating ideas from one person to another. Moving away from a process approach to writing, and with little research to help them, teachers were principally concerned to offer second language students survival training in universities where English was the medium of instruction. Textbooks and materials thus emphasised 'common core skills' such as describing, summarising, expressing causality, and so on as general principles of a universal academic literacy (e.g. Murray, 1989; Spack, 1988).

Only in the last ten years has the importance of a more socially situated analysis of genres been fully understood. This social conception of academic writing has been illuminated from a number of directions. The most important of these have been the theory of language developed by Halliday (1978, 1994) which emphasises the mutually constituting relationship of language and context; Miller's (1984) notion of genre as typified rhetorical action; and Toulmin's (1958) conception of disciplinary-specific argument forms. Together these perspectives have led to a view of genre as a means of routinely representing information in ways that reflect the social contexts of their construction and the beliefs of their users, providing insights into the norms, epistemologies, values and ideologies of particular fields of knowledge (e.g. Candlin and Hyland, 1999a). However, while genres develop from repeated situations, thereby helping to stabilise participants' experiences and give them a sense of solidarity, we must not see them as frozen artefacts. Genres are also in a state of constant evolution as members respond to professional and private exigencies in new and innovative ways (e.g. Bhatia, 1999).

The importance devoted to academic writing has not been entirely restricted to English. In recent years greater attention has been given to the rhetorical conventions of academic exposition in a number of different languages and genres. Rhetorical patterns of academic writing in the humanities in Czech (Čmejrková, 1996), the sciences in Malay (Ahmad, 1995), linguistics in Bulgarian (Todeva, 1999) and sociology in Russian (Namsaraev, 1997), for instance, differ considerably from those described for English. There has been a strong tradition of research into Languages for Specific Purposes in Scandinavia and Central Europe over the past 25 years, exemplified by the collection in Lundquist et al. (1998) and in the reviews by Schröder (1991) and Gunnarsson (1995). Academics writing in German (e.g. Schröder, 1995; Ylonen et al., 1993), Finnish (e.g. Luukka, 1995), and French (e.g. Eurin Balmet and Henao de Legge, 1992; Gambier, 1998; Lerat, 1995) have also paid considerable attention to professional and academic discourse, although much of the European work has tended to focus on terminological issues rather than generic description.

Writing, therefore, is not simply marginal to disciplines, merely an epiphenomenon on the boundaries of academic practice. On the contrary, it helps to create those disciplines by influencing how members relate to one another, and by determining who will be regarded as members, who will gain success and what will count as knowledge. Texts therefore contain traces of disciplinary activities in their pages; a typical clustering of conventions – developed over time in response to what writers perceive as similar problems – which point beyond words to the social circumstances of their construction. They offer a window on the practices and beliefs of the communities for whom they have meaning.

THE SOCIAL CREATION OF KNOWLEDGE

To a large extent disciplinary discourse has evolved as a means of funding, constructing, evaluating, displaying and negotiating knowledge. Merton's view that the goal of science is to add to a body of certified knowledge has also been adopted as a dominant practice in the humanities and social sciences. It is the display of this ideology which distinguishes academic discourse from other kinds of writing, and allows us to examine variations between academic disciplines. Examining texts as disciplinary practices moves us from the individual to the collective, from the boundaries of the page to the activities of social beings. Because of this, such writers as Geertz (1983) and Bruffee (1986) reject a representational view of knowledge and instead argue that knowledge emerges from a disciplinary matrix. In Rorty's (1979: 170) words, it is 'the social justification of belief'.

Social constructionism has undermined an earlier, objectivist, model which regarded writing as a means of simply dressing the thoughts that one sent into the world, and which saw texts as channels of communicating independently existing truths. The basic premise of constructionism is that academics work within communities in a particular time and place, and that the intellectual climate in which they live and work determine the problems they investigate, the methods they employ, the results they see, and the ways they write them up. In the words of Knorr-Cetina (1981), all they do is 'theory impregnated'.

In this view, academic knowledge is both situated and indexical, 'inextricably a product of the activity and situations in which it [is] produced' (Brown et al., 1989: 33); that is, it is embedded in the wider processes of argument, affiliation and consensus-making of members of the discipline. As Weimer (1977: 5) observes, all reporting occurs within a pragmatic context and in relation to a theory which fits 'observation and data in meaningful patterns. … Theories argue for a particular pattern or way of seeing reality'. Similarly, Toulmin (1972: 246) states that 'nature has no language in which she can speak to us on her own behalf', while the eminent theoretical physicist Stephen Hawking (1993: 44) notes that all our notions of the universe are based on models:

> A theory is a good theory if it is an elegant model, if it describes a wide class of observations, and if it predicts the results of new observations. Beyond that it makes no sense to ask if it corresponds to reality, because we do not know what reality is independent of a theory.

Thus it is naïve to regard texts as accurate representations of what the world is like because this representation is always filtered through acts of selection, foregrounding and symbolisation; reality is seen as constructed through processes that are essentially social, involving authority, credibility and disciplinary appeals.

So from the perspective of the social constructionist, academic texts do more than report research that plausibly represent an external reality, they work to transform research findings or armchair reflections into academic knowledge. This knowledge is not a privileged representation of non-human reality, but a conversation between individuals and between individuals and their beliefs. This is not to fall into a world of idealism divorced from the physical world. Scientists and sociologists need their sensory experience of the world, but this experienced reality *under-determines* what they can know and say about it. They must therefore draw on principles and orientations from their cultural resources to organise it. We cannot step outside the beliefs or discourses of our social groups to find a justification for our ideas that is somehow 'objective'.

The acceptance of theories is located in the discourse community and the constraints on justifiable belief are socially constructed among individuals. The model is of 'independent creativity disciplined by accountability to shared experience' (Richards, 1987: 200). 'Objectivity' thus becomes 'consensual intersubjectivity' (Ziman, 1984:107), as methods and findings are coordinated and approved through public appraisal and peer review. We are then concerned with knowledge and knowing as social institutions, with something collectively created through the interactions of individuals.

The importance of social factors in transforming research activities into academic knowledge is perhaps most clearly illustrated by the socio-historical variability of rhetorical practices. The conventional linguistic means for securing support for scientific knowledge are not defined by a timeless idea, but developed in response to particular rhetorical situations. The work of Robert Boyle and his colleagues in the 1650s, for example, was crucial in establishing rules of discourse to generate and validate facts and create a 'public' for experimental research (Shapin, 1984). Boyle laid down literary and social means of verifying facts by a multiplication of the witnessing experience, stating how writers should reproduce the phenomena in their texts and establish themselves as providers of reliable testimony. An appropriate moral and interactional posture were therefore essential to the process of gaining assent to one's results from the beginning.

Atkinson (1996) similarly observes that research writing in the seventeenth and eighteenth centuries was substantially influenced by author-centred norms of genteel conduct, and that these were gradually transformed by changing social conditions and the growing professionalism of research communities. Using a cluster analysis of features, Atkinson found that papers steadily became less affectively and 'narratively' focused and more 'informational' and abstract over this period, shifting to an 'object-centred' rhetoric organised around specific community-generated research problems rather than around the experiencing gentleman-scientist. Halliday (1988, 1998) has also shown how the use of nominalisation and strings of nominal groups has increased in science to allow writers to package complex phenomena into single semiotic entities. Forms such as '*the rate of glass crack growth depends on the magnitude of the applied stress*' have become a powerful resource for constructing and communicating increasingly complex concepts. This practice serves to 'semiotically reconstruct' experience and bring into being a new construction of knowledge and new ways of seeing the world.

In other words, today's rhetorical situation has emerged from the *political* establishment of a scientific community and increasingly refined over the centuries to reflect a changing audience and material conditions. As publication became essential to research, a network of scientists evolved which required institutionalised standards of public debate. Changes in argument, referencing and length of research articles in physics, for example, appear to reflect increasing knowledge and changes in audience requirements (Bazerman, 1988). More recent changes have been tracked by Berkenkotter and Huckin (1995) who see the emergence of a news-oriented text schema in biological research articles since 1944. They argue that this increasing promotion of results in research papers has developed to accommodate the increasingly selective reading patterns of researchers swamped by the explosion of information in the sciences.

What is regarded as 'truth' is thus a 'best guess', relative to a particular time and community, and what may appear as self-evident in the practices we find today simply contributes to the illusion that these conventions are somehow natural. Persuading readers to accept a particular observation as a fact, or at least as a worthwhile contribution to disciplinary knowledge, involves relying on situated assumptions concerning what issues to address and how best to contextualise results. Knowledge claims are the outcome of socially agreed-upon ways of discussing academic problems that are always subject to dialectical revision (Prelli, 1989; Bizzell, 1992). The persuasiveness of academic discourse, then, does not depend upon the demonstration of absolute fact, empirical evidence or impeccable logic, it is the result of effective rhetorical practices, accepted by community members. Texts are the actions of socially situated writers and are persuasive only when they employ social and linguistic conventions that colleagues find convincing.

Considerable evidence shows that academic papers are written to provide an account that reformulates research activity in terms of an appropriate, but often contested, disciplinary ideology (e.g. Gilbert and Mulkay, 1984; Myers, 1990). It has been argued, for example, that in the sciences research articles are constructed to conceal contingent factors, downplaying the role of social allegiance, self-interest, power and editorial bias, to depict a disinterested, inductive, democratic and goal-directed activity. This is, moreover, a perspective that occasionally receives support from within the disciplines themselves.[1] In sum, the discursive practices which certify knowledge rely more on subjective decisions of plausibility than universal principles of rationality. Rational argument is a social matter, governed by disciplinary norms and oriented to achieving an intersubjective consensus through persuasive means. Notions of what counts as convincing argument, appropriate theory, sound methodology, impressive logic and compelling evidence are community-specific.

DISCIPLINARY CULTURES

The view that knowledge is constructed within social communities draws attention to the homogeneity of disciplinary groups and practices. Each discipline might be seen as an academic tribe (Becher, 1989) with its particular norms, nomenclature, bodies of knowledge, sets of conventions and modes of inquiry constituting a separate culture (Bartholomae, 1986; Swales, 1990). Within each culture individuals acquire specialised discourse competencies that allow them to participate as group members. These cultures differ along social and cognitive dimensions, offering contrasts not only in their fields of knowledge, but in their aims, social behaviours, power relations, political interests, ways of talking and structures of argument (Toulmin, 1972; Whitley, 1984). Through the code of their specialised languages, these tribes consecrate their cultural privilege (Bourdieu and Passeron, 1996).

Academics talk to each other within the frameworks of their disciplines and generally have little difficulty in identifying the most central journals, main grant-awarding agencies, essential conferences, leading figures and most prestigious departments in their fields. The notion of *discourse community* has therefore proved useful here as it seeks to locate writers in particular contexts to identify how their rhetorical strategies are dependent on the purposes, setting and audience of writing (e.g. Bruffee, 1986). Bizzell (1982: 217), for example, has discussed them in terms of 'traditional, shared ways of understanding experience' including shared patterns of interaction, and Doheny-Farina (1992: 296) refers to the 'rhetorical conventions and stylistic practices that are tacit and routine for the members'. Killingsworth and Gilbertson (1992: 7) make the interesting point that communities are actually a kind of communication media in that they affect the manner and meaning of any message delivered through it.

The concept, however, has not found universal favour. Harris (1989), for example, argues that we should restrict the term to specific local groups, and labels other uses as 'discursive utopias' which fail to state either their rules or boundaries. Chin (1994), Cooper (1989) and Prior (1998) more pointedly view the term as altogether too structuralist, static and deterministic, giving too much emphasis to a stable underlying core of shared values which removes writing from the actual situations where individuals make meanings. Clearly there is something in this. If we see communities as real, stable groups conforming to rules and values and upholding a consensus we are clearly obscuring the potentially tremendous diversity and variation of members' roles, allegiance and participation in their disciplines. We are also neglecting the innovation and momentum that is possible in disciplines – which I have discussed briefly in the last section.

The fact is, of course, that discourse communities are not monolithic and unitary. They are composed of individuals with diverse experiences, expertise, commitments and influence. There are considerable variations in the extent to which members identify with their myriad goals, methods and beliefs, participate in their diverse activities, and identify themselves with their conventions, histories or values. In addition to committed researchers, influential gatekeepers and high profile proselytisers, communities comprise competing groups and discourses, marginalised ideas, contested theories, peripheral contributors and occasional members. The student neophyte, the laboratory research assistant, the professorial theorist and the industrial applied scientist interact with and use the same texts and genres for different purposes, with different questions and different degrees of engagement. Disciplines are, in short, human institutions where actions and understandings are influenced by the personal and interpersonal, as well as the institutional and sociocultural.

Questioning the construct of community, however, has sharpened some of its meaning. Killingsworth (1992) thus distinguishes between local groups of readers and writers who habitually interact, and global communities defined exclusively by a commitment to particular actions and discourses. Porter (1992) understands a community in terms of its *forums* or approved channels of discourse such as publications, meetings, and conferences which carry traces of its orientations and practices. The view that academic groups might be constituted by their characteristic genres of interaction, of how they get things done, rather than existing through physical membership has also attracted Swales (1993). In other words, an individual's engagement in its discourses can comprise his or her membership of that discipline – an idea Swales (1998) elaborates as a 'textography of communities'.

So while it remains a contested concept, the notion of community does foreground what is an important influence on social interaction. It draws attention to the fact that discourse is socially situated and helps to illuminate something of what writers and readers bring to a text, emphasising that composition and interpretation both depend on assumptions about the other.

The equally powerful, and equally inexact, metaphor 'communities of practice' has also been employed to avoid a strong reliance on a shared core of rather abstract knowledge and language. Here the central aspect of disciplinary groups is the emphasis on situated activity and 'a set of relations among persons, activity, and world, over time and in relation with other tangential and overlapping communities of practice' (Lave and Wenger, 1991: 98). This shifts the focus from language or social structure to the situated practices of aggregations of individuals; to communities strongly shaped by a collective history of pursuing particular goals within particular forms of social interaction. Irrespective of whether we choose to label disciplines as tribes, cultures, discourse communities or communities of practice, these concepts move us from a concern with the abstract logicality and substance of ideas of academic writing to the world of concrete practices and social beliefs. They put community decision-making and engagement at centre-stage and underline the fact that disciplinary discourse involves language users in constructing and displaying their roles and identities as members of social groups.

The idea of disciplinary cultures therefore implies a certain degree of interdisciplinary diversity and a degree of intradisciplinary homogeneity. Writing as a member of a disciplinary group involves textualising one's work as biology or applied linguistics and oneself as a biologist or applied linguist. It requires one to give a tangible and public demonstration that one has legitimacy. There are then disciplinary constraints on discourse which are both restrictive and authorising (Foucault, 1972), allowing one to create successful texts which display one's disciplinarity, or tacit knowledge of its expectations, for the practical purposes of communicating with peers. This points to the power relations hidden in text, the unspoken assumptions of a largely undiscussed world which is the basis for cooperative action (Bourdieu, 1980: 269).

Sullivan (1996) argues that there are four central elements of such disciplinary constraints: an ideological perspective of the discipline and the world; assumptions about the nature of things and methodologies; a system of hierarchical power relationships; and a body of doctrinal knowledge of external reality. Nevertheless, while such factors help draw the boundaries of cooperative action among disciplinary members, we might be cautious in emphasising the degree to which a consensus exists and how far the authority of a single overarching disciplinary paradigm determines behaviour. Instead, as I noted earlier, disciplines might be seen as systems in which multiple beliefs and practices overlap and intersect.

Most disciplines are characterised by several competing perspectives and embody often bitterly contested beliefs and values. Rauch (1992), for instance, highlights the very different, and largely incompatible, values and assumptions underlying a debate between conservation biologists on the species status of the red wolf. In other fields empiricists contest the same ground with phenomenologists, cognitivists with behaviourists, existentialists with Freudians, and relativists with realists. Communities are frequently pluralities of practices and beliefs which accommodate disagreement and allow subgroups and individuals to innovate within the margins of its practices in ways that do not weaken its ability to engage in common actions. Seeing disciplines as cultures helps to account for what and how issues can be discussed and for the understandings which are the basis for cooperative action and knowledge-creation. It is not important that everyone agrees but members should be able to engage with each others' ideas and analyses in agreed ways. Disciplines are the contexts in which disagreement can be deliberated.

While all academic discourse is distinguished by certain common practices, such as acknowledging sources, rigorous testing, intellectual honesty, and so on, there are differences which are likely to be more significant than such broad similarities. The ways that writers chose to represent themselves, their readers and their world, how they seek to advance knowledge, how they maintain the authority of their discipline and the processes whereby they establish what is to be accepted as substantiated truth, a useful contribution and a valid argument are all culturally-influenced practical actions and matters for community agreement.

These practices are not simply a matter of personal stylistic preference, but community-recognised ways of adopting a position and expressing a stance. 'Doing good research' means employing certain post-hoc justifications sanctioned by institutional arrangements. As a result, the rhetorical conventions of each text will reflect something of the epistemological and social assumptions of the author's disciplinary culture. In the sciences, for example, this often requires a public commitment to experimental demonstration, replicability and falsification of results. In philosophy it may involve narratives containing 'twin-Earth fantasies', 'imaginary conversations' and argumentative point scoring (Bloor, 1996).

In sum, disciplinary communicative practices involves a system of appropriate social engagement with one's material and one's colleagues. The writing that disciplines produce, support and authorise can therefore be seen as linked to forms of power in those organisations. They are representations of legitimate discourses which help to define and maintain particular epistemologies and academic boundaries. Because texts are written to be understood within certain cultural contexts, the analysis of key genres can provide insights into what is implicit in these academic cultures, their routine rhetorical operations revealing individual writer's perceptions of group values and beliefs. Genres are not therefore only text types but imply particular institutional practices of those that produce, distribute and consume them (Fairclough, 1992: 126). Individual and social purposes interact with discourse features at every point of choice and in every genre, and to analyse these is to learn something of how each discipline views knowledge and defines itself.

TEXTS AS SOCIAL INTERACTION

This discussion of academic texts, disciplinary cultures, and the social construction of knowledge, highlights the interactive and rhetorical character of academic writing. It leads us to see writing as an engagement in a social process, where the production of texts reflects methodologies, arguments and rhetorical strategies designed to frame disciplinary submissions appropriately. Creating a convincing reader environment thus involves deploying disciplinary and genre-specific conventions such that 'the published paper is a multilayered hybrid *co-produced* by the authors *and* by members of the audience to which it is directed' (Knorr-Cetina, 1981: 106). Textual meanings, in other words, are socially mediated, influenced by the communities to which writers and readers belong.

If texts are a means of studying social negotiations between academics, how is this achieved in particular texts? For what reasons? What are we looking for? From the discussion so far it is clear that academic writing is broadly concerned with knowledge-making and that this is achieved by negotiating agreement among colleagues. In most academic genres then, a writer's principal purpose will be persuasive: convincing peers to assent to a knowledge claim in a research paper, to fund a project in a grant-submission, to accept an evaluation in a review, to acknowledge a disciplinary schema in a textbook, and so on. These shared purposes both help us to identify what is similar in these genres and what is disciplinarily distinctive, and also suggest some areas where common practices will involve social interactions.

In knowledge-creating genres such as the research article, for example, these practices will include (at least) the need to:

- establish the novelty of one's position
- make a suitable level of claim
- acknowledge prior work and situate claims in a disciplinary context
- offer warrants for one's view based on community-specific arguments and procedures
- demonstrate an appropriate disciplinary ethos and willingness to negotiate with peers.

The means by which academics present knowledge claims and account for their actions thus involves not only cognitive factors, but also social and affective elements, and to study these necessarily moves us beyond the ideational dimension of texts to the ways they function at the interpersonal level.

Both are involved in the interactions needed to secure peer agreement because the writer's ability to influence the reader's response is severely restricted. If 'truth' does not lie exclusively in the external world, there is always going to be more than one credible interpretation of a piece of data and more than one way of looking at a certain problem. This plurality of competing interpretations, with no objective means of absolutely distinguishing the actual from the plausible, means that while readers may be persuaded to judge a claim acceptable, they always have the option of rejecting it. All statements require community ratification, and because readers are guarantors of the negatability of claims this gives them an active and constitutive role in how writers construct them.

In other words, the social interactions in academic writing stem from the writer's attempts to anticipate possible negative reactions to his or her persuasive goals. The writer will choose to respond to the potential negatability of his or her claims through a series of rhetorical choices to galvanise support, express collegiality, resolve difficulties and avoid disagreement in ways which most closely correspond to the community's assumptions, theories, methods and bodies of knowledge.

Opposition to statements can come from two principal sources (Hyland, 1996a, 1998a). First, readers may reject a statement on the grounds that it fails to correspond to what the world is thought to be like, i.e. it fails to meet *adequacy conditions*. Claims have to display a plausible relationship with 'reality' (the discipline's epistemological framework), and writers must take care to demonstrate this satisfactorily by using the specialised vocabularies and argument forms of the discourse community. Here writers have to encode ideational material, establish relationships, employ warrants, and frame arguments in ways that the potential audience will find most appropriate and convincing. Thus what writers choose to emphasise from among the array of physical and conceptual phenomena in their fields, their decision to adopt an attitude of systematic doubt or personal conviction, and their choice of reasoning, are part of their strategic skill in establishing authority and credibility.

Second, statements have to incorporate an awareness of interpersonal factors, addressing *acceptability conditions*, with the writer attending to the affective expectations of participants in the interaction. Rhetorical strategies for social interaction are employed here to help the writer to create a professionally acceptable persona and an appropriate attitude, both to readers and the information being discussed. This means representing one's self in a text in a way that demonstrates one's flawless disciplinary credentials; showing yourself to be a reasonable, intelligent, co-player in the community's efforts to construct knowledge and well versed in its tribal lore. Critical here is the ability to display proper respect for colleagues and give due regard for their views and reputations. In this sense linguistic choices seek to establish an appropriate, discipline-defined balance between the researcher's authority as an expert-knower and his or her humility as a disciplinary servant (Myers, 1989). This is principally accomplished through a judicious balance of tentativeness and assertion, and the expression of a suitable relationship to one's data, arguments and audience.

In sum, the interactions of academic writing indicate the writer's acknowledgement of the community's epistemological and interpersonal conventions and connect texts with disciplinary cultures. Academic knowledge is not simply a databank of general, and generally agreed upon, facts, but networks of values, beliefs and routines that guide practice and define disciplines. The academic writer must make assumptions about the nature of the world and about how it will best be received by a particular audience, the question of adequacy corresponding to the objective negatability of a proposition and acceptability to its subjective negatability. Texts thus reveal how writers attempt to negotiate knowledge in ways that are locally meaningful, employing rhetorical skills which establish their credibility though an orientation towards arguments, topics and readers.

APPROACHES TO ACADEMIC INTERACTIONS

Theorists have sought to account for the social interactions in texts in two main ways, focusing on either models of actors or models of social structures. The former, notably Grice's (1975) Cooperative Principle and Nystrand's (1989) Reciprocity Principle, posit general principles of interaction based on what people are believed to be like, examining linguistic features for evidence of the operation of these principles. More structural approaches, influenced in particular by Foucault and taken up by Kress and Hodge (1993) and Fairclough (1992, 1995), seek to establish links between discourse and society by focusing on aspects of context such as power and ideology. Both views assume then that discourse is socially embedded and has social consequences, although they look at this from different directions.

Grice's (1975) well-known Cooperative Principle has been very fruitful for those seeking a theoretical model of interaction. This is built on the idea that readers understand texts by drawing on both their knowledge of the context and their belief that writers will consider their interpretive needs. Thus, when approaching a text we assume communication will be shaped by various universal maxims of cooperation, most generally that what we find will be consistent with the accepted purpose of the discourse. Anticipating that such maxims are being observed, we interpret apparent violations of expected relevance, informativeness, honesty and clarity as meaningful, i.e. as conveying pragmatic 'implicatures'. Particular importance has been given to the reader's ability to recover contextual relevance from a text (e.g. Sperber and Wilson, 1986). Once again this is principally a philosophical theory which does not systematically elaborate the idea of context, it is clear, however, that the reader's ability to supply assumptions about the relevant social institutions and relationships are likely to be a crucial dimension of interpretation.

Nystrand (1989) similarly develops an approach to interaction based on the writer and readers' 'mutual co-awareness' and the social group's taken-for-granted rules of conduct. For him, an effective text is one which 'balances the reciprocal needs of the writer for expression and the reader for comprehension' (1989: 81) and where participants draw on certain 'elaborations' in texts to overcome interpretive difficulties.

Importantly, then, linguistic choices are seen to work as a result of the way participants attribute to each other the intention to communicate, and the principles these writers propose are seen as culturally and contextually variable means of systematising the process of inferencing. Both Nystrand and Grice (indirectly) posit an interactive connection between writers and readers that makes communication possible, linking them together via principles that allow texts to be interpreted in relatively stable and predictable ways. Participants are seen as interactants who engage in strategic reasoning to determine a consistent purpose in rhetorical choices. Rationality is therefore attributed to exchanges based on a collective commitment to conduct discourse in a certain way, drawing on the community as a kind of normative framework for interpretation.

This approach tends to emphasise the ways that writers imagine readers' expectations, knowledge and interests in constructing their texts, deciding what to include, what to highlight and how to show the relationships between elements. It is 'information-oriented' (Thompson and Thetela, 1995) in the sense that linguistic choices are based on the clarification of meaning. This, however, omits a great deal of what writers do when they directly engage with others to influence their response by conveying an attitude to the text or to the readers themselves. In other words, for a fuller picture we need to fill out this view of interaction with an interpersonal dimension.

Such a dual perspective has formed the cornerstone of many genre accounts of writing and has perhaps received its most explicit realisation in Brown and Levinson's (1987) politeness model of interaction. Brown and Levinson seek to explain variations in linguistic features as politeness strategies rationally selected to accomplish communicative goals. Modifying Goffman's (1967) concept of face as the desire to be approved of (positive face) and to act without being impeded (negative face), Brown and Levinson argue that writers are motivated to protect both aspects of their own face and that of their readers. In this theory the need to balance face needs is a consequence of the fact that interaction is seen as inherently imposing, involving numerous Face Threatening Acts (FTAs). In academic settings, Myers (1989) has argued that knowledge claims, criticisms and denials of claims constitute FTAs, both against readers engaged in the same research area and a wider disciplinary audience, and that we can reconstruct the reasoning behind linguistic choices such as hedges and solidarity pronouns as strategies to mitigate threats to face.

Politeness is thus used to explain why academic writers might deviate from the strictly utilitarian principles of communication suggested by Grice and Nystrand. The approach has been extremely useful in repositioning discourses which are apparently autonomous, impersonal and informational as socially grounded. It highlights, in other words, competitive and cooperative interactions which are conducted through features often seen as merely conventions of academic style.

The view that certain assumptions of conversational behaviour serve to motivate strategy choices in knowledge-creating discourse may be suggestive, but it is not entirely satisfactory. Conversation, generally, is not argument, and the model neglects significant differences in purposes and consequences between these registers, generalising the avoidance of imposition in phatic contexts to the regularities of academic discourse. Clear distinctions can be drawn between these discourses, however, not only because these communicative sites have distinct purposes, but also because they generally have very different consequences for participants. There is more at stake in most academic encounters as, for most writers, their careers ride on successful participation in them.

The impositions of conversation are not those entailed in presenting a claim or an evaluation in a research article because these writing practices not only seek to legitimate the views of their holders, but also their rights to employment, prestige and material support. Communication is the key cognitive and social impetus in academia and as such reflects central aspects of disciplinary cultures, representing the point where knowledge is advanced, reputations are gained and merit is bestowed. Engagement in disciplinary forums therefore involves norms of interpersonal behaviour which are underpinned by the sanctions inherent in a system of academic recognition and rewards that hinges on publication (Hyland, 1997). Although writers may well calculate the impositional impact of their statements, politeness cannot explain the full significance of their rhetorical choices.

Brown and Levinson's model, while an interesting theory of how linguistic features might represent strategic choices, is insufficiently grounded in social structures to account for the motives, roles and conventions of disciplinary interaction. It is undoubtedly correct that academic writers engage in conflict avoidance and that they weigh up the effects of their statements when communicating with their peers, but this is not to say that interaction is based on individual judgements of imposition or entitlements to deference. If we seek to reconstruct interaction from the features of texts based on assumptions about the strategic accomplishments of model actors, then we also need to locate these actors in particular physical, social and economic realities. We need to recognise their behaviour as influenced by their pursuit of goals in given institutional contexts, and to see that these behaviours have real consequences. In other words, an adequate framework for the study of facework must be based on a more complex understanding of social life, and in particular for disciplinary discourse, on the ambitions, constraints and rewards of academic engagement.

Accounts of discourse as interaction which focus more explicitly on the social structures of language use, attempt to provide just such an understanding of social life, seeking to fill in the causal relations between language and society that social actor models leave implicit. Approaches associated with the work of writers such as Kress and Fairclough problematise the cooperative model of discourse sketched above by highlighting the often asymmetrical distribution of discoursal and social rights. This view criticises such models for exaggerating the extent to which strategic actions are cooperatively negotiated and failing to identify the power relations in texts, leaving unexamined *who* actually defines interactional concepts like 'truth', relevance', 'informativity' and so on (Fairclough, 1995: 47). These writers therefore adopt what is widely termed a 'critical approach' and set themselves the task of revealing how social structures impinge on the ways that discourse is created and interpreted. These structures are seen as being principally ideological, and so to study discourse is to study the ways in which meaning ideologically serves to sustain relations of power (Thompson, 1984).

Ideologies serve to link individuals and groups, providing ways to maintain communities and structure common purposes and beliefs; they help, in other words, to constitute what is real. All knowledge, including disciplinary knowledge of the world and members' knowledge of the social practices of their communities, is contingent upon social structures; neither the content of natural knowledge nor the practical knowledge of investigation and reporting can be separate from the social processes that produce it (Dant, 1991; Thompson, 1984). Importantly, then, both language and the ways it is used have meanings only in virtue of the discursive formations in which they occur. Disciplinary discourses assist solidarity, facilitate coordinated activities, offer frameworks to achieve personal goals, and contribute to the successful reproduction of communities. In using language, however, we engage in reinforcing our relations with others and in sustaining the asymmetrical relations of power of those contexts.

At the community level, academics write as group members. They adopt discoursal practices that represent an authorised understanding of the world (and how it can be perceived and reported) which acts to reinforce the theoretical convictions of the discipline and its right to validate knowledge. In the hard sciences, for example, discourse functions to convey ideological representations which help to impart an authority to a discipline-defined epistemology based on a detached attitude to an external reality of objective facts. This discourse has been spectacularly successful in gaining credibility, influence and prestige for its practitioners, providing a standard of rhetorical inquiry which other disciplines have not always imitated sufficiently successfully to gain similar respectability. Ideologies thus serve to define disciplines and to establish their status and power in a wider social structure, offering members an identity based on a set of typical practices, norms and objectives, and building the authority of the group, both in relation to society and to other groups. The fact that ideologies often become naturalised and unnoticed disguises their inherently social functions.

At a more individual level, disciplinary ideologies commit members to engage cooperatively in approved discoursal practices as a way of securing personal goals. Success often involves a display of disciplinary competence and members must present a narrative that is perceived by the community as persuasive both in terms of the propositions that the writer sets out and the credibility of the *persona* he or she seeks to convey. Engagement in a rhetorical forum that is discursively adversarial, and where there are always multiple plausible interpretations for any given phenomenon, encourages writers to accommodate their textual practices to those that readers, particularly journal editors and referees, are likely to find most convincing. Studies focusing on the process of peer review, for example, have shown the influence of disciplinary gatekeepers on revision practices in order to secure publication (Berkenkotter and Huckin, 1995; Myers, 1990). In these ways, the conventions of the research article are shaped by the ideological assumptions of the discipline and reinforced by both routine use and the customary procedures of academic quality control.

Participation in the social interactions of academic discourse, therefore, involve writers in discoursal practices that are largely argumentative and competitive. In Brown and Levinson's terms, the imposition of strategies is going to be high, but attributing them to politeness fails to give sufficient importance to the ideological/institutional constraints which distinguish the allowable from the doubtful. The social actor approaches remind us that people and actions are at work within texts: that writers and readers are aware of each other's aims and have common assumptions about how texts function. However, they fail to make explicit the connections between social norms and linguistic conventions, and how wider social practices and beliefs are embedded in the rhetorical features of texts.

While we can learn about texts by studying social action, we cannot just read off social action from texts. Participants may not always act strategically and they always have the option of adopting a personal or idiosyncratic relation to the text. So while we might point to possible norms and conventions as reflecting ideological behaviour, we must always recognise that the social world is not always a stable and predictable place. Moreover, as we have seen, this view of writer–reader interaction is largely a theoretical construct, devised to explain how individuals make decisions while writing, rather than an account of the various purposes and uses that the completed text may actually fulfil in the hands of the consumers. The important point is, however, that texts reflect writers' expectations of how they will be read, and therefore provide clues to the wider understandings underlying their creation.

I am, then, interested less in specific occasions of writing than in what this writing tells us of how writers shape their ideas by directing them beyond the immediate situation to the expectations of a disciplinary audience. Specific individual experiences or goals may impinge on the settings of composition, but it is the writer's ability to project from these immediate contexts to a perceived social reality that is important in determining disciplinary structures and meanings. From intensive study of large numbers of texts it is possible to see how much academic writing is the result of situated choices, and how writers typically select the forms and patterns that are most likely to help them to negotiate their purposes with an anticipated audience.

In sum, the notion of writer–reader interaction provides a framework for studying texts in terms of how knowledge comes to be socially constructed by writers acting as members of social groups. It offers an explanation for the ways writers frame their understandings of the world and how they attempt to persuade others of these understandings. But while the norms and ideologies that underpin these interactions provide a framework for writing, they are, essentially, a repertoire of choices rather than sets of binding and immutable constraints. As Mulkay (1979: 72) observes, norms should be seen

> not as defining clear social obligations to which scientists generally conform, but as flexible vocabularies employed by participants in their attempts to negotiate suitable meanings for their own and others' acts in various social contexts.

The resulting texts constitute a social and institutional code, both rhetorical and interpersonal, for achieving agreement.

These issues form the background and the motivation for what follows, and many are revisited there. In the ensuing chapters I shall try to give concrete expression to these ideas through a series of linked studies, each examining particular discoursal features and informants' accounts of their practices in selected genres. Because my goal is to explore the social interactions expressed in the features of texts, I give priority to published writing as the principal sites of academic engagement. It is here that writers most significantly interact with their peers, their students and their disciplines.

NOTE

1. An interesting insider's narrative of how chance, competition and self-interest are often disguised in the published account is offered in James Watson's (1968) discussion of the events leading to the discovery of the structure of DNA.

Chapter 2

Academic attribution: interaction through citation

This chapter explores one of the most important realisations of the academic writer's concern for interactions with an audience: that of reporting, or attributing propositional content to another source. Citation is central to the social context of persuasion as it can provide justification for arguments and demonstrate the novelty of one's position (Gilbert, 1977; Dubois, 1988). By acknowledging a debt of precedent, a writer is also able to display an allegiance to a particular community or orientation, create a rhetorical gap for his or her research, and establish a credible writer ethos. But while the literature recognises the rhetorical weight of citation, we know little about its relative importance, rhetorical functions or realisations in different disciplines. In this chapter I shall explore the conventions of citation behaviour in a range of academic fields and, through interviews and corpus analysis, seek to reveal some of the interactional purposes embedded in those conventions. First, I need to provide a context for the chapter by establishing some intertextual linkages of my own.

CITATION AND INTERTEXTUALITY: SOME PRELIMINARIES

The construction of academic facts is a social process, with the cachet of acceptance only bestowed on a claim after negotiation with editors, reviewers and readers. The final ratification is granted, of course, with the citation of the claim by others and, eventually, the disappearance of all acknowledgement as it is incorporated into the literature of the discipline. This process of ratification clearly suggests that writers must consider the reactions of their expected audience, for it is ultimately one's peers who provide the social justification which transforms beliefs into knowledge. As I noted earlier, the absence of any objective means of distinguishing observation from presumption means that there is generally always more than one plausible interpretation for a given piece of data, necessitating a delicate process of negotiation for a claim. One consequence of this is that writers are obliged to situate their research in a larger narrative, and this is most obviously demonstrated through appropriate citation.

Myers (1990) and Berkenkotter and Huckin (1995) have traced the passage of research articles through the review procedure and see the process as one of essentially locating the writer's claims within a wider disciplinary framework. This is achieved partly by modifying claims and providing propositional warrants, but mainly by establishing a narrative context for the work through citation. One of Myers' case study subjects, for example, increased the number of references from 57 to 195 in a resubmission to *Science* (Myers, 1990: 91). Myers and Berkenkotter and Huckin see academic writing as a tension between originality and humility to the community, rhetorically accommodating laboratory activity to the discipline. So while Berkenkotter and Huckin's scientist subject sought to gain acceptance for original, and therefore significant, work, the reviewers insisted 'that to be science her report had to include an intertextual framework for her local knowledge' (ibid: 59).

Academics generally tend to see research and rhetorical activity as separate issues. However, appropriate textual practices are crucial to the acceptance of claims. Explicit reference to prior literature is a substantial indication of a text's dependence on contextual knowledge and thus a vital piece in the collaborative construction of new knowledge between writers and readers. The embedding of arguments in networks of references not only suggests an appropriate disciplinary orientation, but reminds us that statements are invariably a response to previous statements and are themselves available for further statements by others. Fairclough (1992), extending Bakhtin, refers to these intertextual relations as 'manifest intertextuality' which he distinguishes from 'constitutive intertextuality':

> In manifest intertextuality, other texts are explicitly present in the text under analysis; they are 'manifestly' marked or cued by features on the surface of the text such as quotation marks...The constitutive intertextuality of a text, however, is the configuration of discourse conventions that go into its production.
>
> (Fairclough, 1992: 104).

I shall primarily be concerned with manifest intertextuality in this chapter although the two are clearly related in academic discourse. Overt reference to specific other texts, and the response of writing to prior writing, is an important constitutive feature of research articles, contributing to how we identify and evaluate research writing in different disciplines.

The importance of citation as a constitutive element of the modern academic paper can be seen in its increasingly prominent role in the ways writers seek to construct facts through their communicative practices. Historical research on scientific texts has demonstrated the gradual emergence of the Discussion section to replace Methods as the dominant basis of persuasion (Atkinson, 1996; Bazerman, 1988). While partly due to the standardisation of experimental procedures, this is largely the result of the increasing contextualisation of scientific work in disciplinary problems. Bazerman found, for example, that the number of items in reference lists had risen steadily this century from about 1.5 per article in the *Physical Review* in 1910 to more than 25 in 1980.

The inclusion of explicit references to the work of other authors is thus seen as a central feature of academic research writing, helping writers to establish a persuasive epistemological and social framework for the acceptance of their arguments. References, however, have not only increased quantitatively, they have become more focused, pertinent and integrated into the argument, responding to the fact that 'common theory has become an extremely strong force in structuring articles and binding articles to each other' (Bazerman, 1988: 157). Citation helps to define a specific context of knowledge or problem to which the current work is a contribution, and therefore more references are now discussed in greater detail throughout the article.

In sum, new work has to be embedded in a community-generated literature to demonstrate its relevance and importance. For this reason both the incidence and use of citation might be expected to differ according to different rhetorical contexts, influenced by the ways particular disciplines see the world and tackle research.

CITATION SIGNALS

We need, then, to look at the different ways in which reports are 'manifestly marked' in academic writing. These ways are generally seen as relatively unproblematic due to the highly developed conventions prescribed in the official manuals of such authorities as the *American Psychological Association, Modern Humanities Research Association, American Chemical Society* and *Council of Biology Editors*. But while they provide a relatively stable rhetorical context for communication, these guides also convey the impression that writing is mainly a matter of applying established rules. The fact that different citation choices carry different rhetorical and social meanings complicates this picture considerably.

The literature reveals the availability of a wide range of signalling structures and reporting forms which offer options beyond the simple choice of 'direct speech' or 'indirect speech' found in traditional grammars (e.g. Thomas and Hawes, 1994; Thompson, 1996). One strand of research has sought to demonstrate the rhetorical effects of different syntactic features, emphasising the influence of thematic position, tense and voice on the reported information. Shaw (1992), for example, suggests that past tense and active voice tend to be associated with reporting detail, while passive-perfect verbs often initiate new subtopics. Malcolm (1987) argues that writers exploit temporal reference to strategically manipulate generality, while Swales (1990: 154) suggests that the present simple-present perfect-past scale, which covers over 90 per cent of finite reporting verbs, represents increasing distance of various kinds from the reported finding.

Two important attribution features of interest to researchers have been the distinction between integral and non-integral structures and the role of different reporting verbs. Integral citations are those where the name of the cited author occurs in the citing sentence, while non-integral forms make reference to the author in parentheses or by superscript numbers (Swales, 1990: 148). The use of one form rather than the other appears to reflect a decision to give greater emphasis to either the reported author or the reported message.

The use of a reporting verb to introduce the work of other researchers is also a significant rhetorical choice. Hunston (1993) points out that verb selection ascribes information as 'received knowledge' and thus influences its evaluative status, while Tadros (1993) shows how this choice enables writers to detach themselves from a proposition, predicting their later declaration of their own position. Thomas and Hawes (1994) and Thompson and Ye (1991) have sought to categorise the ways in which this variation of commitment to reported information is realised in particular reporting verb selections, detailing the choices as a network of writer options. The importance of these verbs therefore lies in the fact that they allow the writer to convey clearly the kind of activity reported and to distinguish precisely an attitude to that information, signalling whether the claims are to be taken as accepted or not.

In the research reported in this chapter I wanted to be sure to cover all instances of citation irrespective of surface realisation. I therefore computer searched the research article corpus for canonical citational forms such as a date in brackets, a number in square brackets, and Latinate references to other citations (for example, op cit., ibid.). This sweep, however, left a number of citations unaccounted for, particularly in the philosophy papers where renewed or extended discussion of a previously mentioned author often occurred without the repetition of a reference. A concordance was therefore made on all the names in the bibliographies of these articles, of third person pronouns and of generalised terms for agents, such as 'these researchers'.

Possessive noun phrases, such as 'Pearson's r' and 'the Raleigh–Ritz procedure', which did not integrate prior content were excluded, while those which legitimately referred to textual objects and attributed material to other sources (eg. 'Gricean strictures', 'Davidson's argument') were counted. References to schools or beliefs, such as 'Platonists argue ...', were only included if they referred to a specific author, as in 'Platonists like Bolzano argue ...'. Finally, it should be noted that I was only concerned with references to the work of other writers and shall exclude discussion of self-citation in this chapter. The latter is far less central to academic argument than other-citation and, I suspect, differs considerably from it in terms of motivation and disciplinary distribution.

Next I distinguished how authors were referred to syntactically and examined how citations were incorporated into the article, as quotation, summary or generalisation from several sources. Finally, I scanned the citations again to quantify the use of all main verbs associated with the authors identified through the above procedures, categorising cases according to a modified version of Thompson and Ye's (1991) taxonomy of reporting verbs in article introductions. Note that in the following discussion I also adopt Thompson and Ye's useful convention of referring to the person citing as the 'writer' and the person cited as the 'author'.

AN OVERVIEW OF ACADEMIC CITATION

There are clear disciplinary differences in both the extent to which writers rely on the work of others in presenting arguments and in how they choose to represent such work. Table 2.1 indicates the importance of citation in academic writing, with an average of almost 70 per paper, and also the degree of disciplinary variation. The figures broadly support the informal characterisation that softer disciplines tend to employ more citations, with engineering and physics well below the average, although the frequencies for molecular biology seem to differ considerably from this general picture.

Table 2.1   Rank order of citations by discipline

Rank	Discipline	Av. per paper	Per 1,000 words	Total citations
1	Sociology	104.0	12.5	1040
2	Marketing	94.9	10.1	949
3	Philosophy	85.2	10.8	852
4	Biology	82.7	15.5	827
5	Applied linguistics	75.3	10.8	753
6	Electronic engineering	42.8	8.4	428
7	Mechanical engineering	27.5	7.3	275
8	Physics	24.8	7.4	248
	Totals	67.1	10.7	5372

Table 2.2 shows that there was far less variation in the ways disciplinary communities refer to sources, with all but philosophy displaying a distinct preference for non-integral structures.

Table 2.2   Surface forms of citations (%)

Discipline	Non-integral	Integral	Subject	Non-subject	Noun-phrase
Biology	90.2	9.8	46.7	43.3	10.0
Electronic engineering	84.3	15.7	34.2	57.6	8.2
Physics	83.1	16.9	28.6	57.1	14.3
Mechanical engineering	71.3	28.7	24.9	56.3	18.8
Marketing	70.3	29.7	66.9	23.1	10.0
Applied linguistics	65.6	34.4	58.9	27.1	14.0
Sociology	64.6	35.4	62.9	21.5	15.6
Philosophy	35.4	64.6	31.8	36.8	31.4
Overall averages	67.8	32.2	48.3	32.7	19.0

Integral forms tend to give greater prominence to the cited author and only the articles in philosophy, which typically consist of long narratives that engage the arguments of other writers, consistently included the cited author in the reporting sentence[1]:

(1)   Davidson ascribes to Dewey the view that ...   (Phil)

      ... some can be analysed in the manner suggested by Lewiss, ...   (Phil)

      Sherin (1990) argues that police agencies establish triage systems whereby ...
                                                                                         (Soc)

In the physical sciences, of course, journal styles often require numerical-endnote forms which reduces the prominence of cited authors considerably:

(2)   However, as has been analysed in a recent paper [17] dealing with the spin–spin
      ...   (Phy)

      The latter has been the subject of debate [13, 14].   (Phy)

      Refs [12–19] work out the theory of spatial kinematic geometry in fine detail.
                                                                                         (ME)

Within integral sentences, greater emphasis can be given to authors by choice of syntactic position and, once again, there seems to be a broad division between the hard and soft disciplines with the former tending to favour reporting passive or adjunct agent structures (e.g. according to ...). Philosophers once more differed in their greater use of noun phrases and possessive forms, which are often accompanied by more than a hint of evaluation:

(3)   If I guess correctly that the Goldblach conjecture is true, ...   (Phil)

      We can usefully start with Stalnker's pioneering sketch of a two-stage theory.
                                                                                         (Phil)

      ... according to Davidson's anomalous monism, our mental vocabulary ...   (Phil)

      ... on a par with Aristotle's famous dictum that ...   (Phil)

These forms are far less common in the sciences, and also differed in function, largely acting as shorthand references to procedures rather than a means of introducing an authors' work:

(4)   The Drucker stability postulate in the large regains ...   (ME)

      Using the Raleigh–Ritz procedure, i.e. making it stationary with respect to ...
                                                                                         (Phy)

      ... are evaluated with 8×8=64 two-dimensional Gaussian quadrature formula.
                                                                                         (ME)

      Matthei's equations [17, 19] were first used as a starting point in the scale
      model ...   (EE)

In sum, we tend to find a marked overall disposition towards non-integral and non-subject citation forms in the science and engineering papers.

Another aspect of reporting which has interested researchers is how source material is used in the writer's argument (Dubois, 1988; Thompson,

1996). Clearly the ways writers choose to incorporate others' work into their own, ranging from extended discussion to mandatory acknowledgement, can have an important impact on the expression of social relationships in the collaborative construction of a plausible argument. Choices here largely concern the extent to which the report duplicates the original language event, the options being use of short direct quotes (up to six or eight words), extensive use of original wording set as indented blocks, summary from a single source, or generalisation, where material is ascribed to two or more authors.

There appears to be little disciplinary variation in the framing of imported messages. Table 2.3 shows that citations were overwhelmingly expressed as summary, with generalisation comprising most of the remainder. Direct quotation was minimal and did not occur in any science papers. These results are clearly related to the discoursal conventions of journals and the fields they represent, ultimately pointing to the persuasive purposes of academic citation in different traditions. As the way information is presented is crucial in gaining acceptance for a claim, writers will tend to express the original material in their own terms. This entails employing the cited text in a way that most effectively supports their own argument. Summary and generalisation are obviously the most effective ways of achieving this as they allow the writers greater flexibility to emphasise and interpret the comments they are citing. In most cases the original author's words are only likely to be carried into the new environment when writers consider them to be the most vivid and effective way of presenting their case.

Table 2.3   Presentation of cited work (%)

Discipline	Quote	Block quote	Summary	Generalisation
Biology	0	0	72	38
Electronic engineering	0	0	66	34
Physics	0	0	68	32
Mechanical engineering	0	0	67	33
Marketing	3	2	68	27
Applied linguistics	8	2	67	23
Sociology	8	5	69	18
Philosophy	2	1	89	8

Finally, I examined the choice of reporting verbs in the corpus. Over 400 different verbs were used in citations, although the seven forms in the totals column in Table 2.4 constituted over a quarter of all cases, and nearly half of the forms occurred only once. The ratio of reporting/non-reporting structures was fairly uniform across disciplines, although philosophers tended to employ more report verbs and physicists used fewer. As can be seen, there were substantial differences between disciplines, both in the density of reporting structures and in the choice of verb forms. The table shows an enormous variation between disciplines and suggests that writers in different fields almost draw on completely different sets of items to refer to their literature. Among the higher frequency verbs, almost all instances of *say* and 80 per cent of *think* occurred in philosophy, 70 per cent of *use* in electronics, 55 per cent of *report* in biology, and 53 per cent of *examine* in applied linguistics. Verbs such as *argue* (100 per cent of cases), *suggest* (82 per cent), and *study* (70 per cent) were favoured by the social science/humanities writers while *report* (82 per cent), *describe* (70 per cent), and *show* (55 per cent) occurred mainly in the science/engineering articles.

Table 2.4   Reporting forms in citations

Discipline	Reporting structures		Most frequent forms
	Per paper	**% of citations**	
Philosophy	57.1	67.0	say, suggest, argue, claim, point out, propose, think
Sociology	43.6	42.0	argue, suggest, describe, note, analyse, discuss
Applied linguistics	33.4	44.4	suggest, argue, show, explain, find, point out
Marketing	32.7	34.5	suggest, argue, demonstrate, propose, show
Biology	26.2	31.7	describe, find, report, show, suggest, observe
Electronic engineering	17.4	40.6	propose, use, describe, show, publish
Mechanical engineering	11.7	42.5	describe, show, report, discuss
Physics	6.6	27.0	develop, report, study
Totals	28.6	42.6	suggest, argue, find, show, describe, propose, report

Following Thompson and Ye (1991) and Thomas and Hawes (1994), I classified the reporting verbs according to the type of activity referred to. This gives three distinguishable processes:

1. Research Acts, referring to real-world activities, which occur in statements of findings (*observe, discover, notice, show*) or procedures (e.g. *analyse, calculate, assay, explore*).
2. Cognition Acts, concerned with mental processes (*believe, conceptualize, suspect, view*).
3. Discourse Acts, which involve verbal expression (*ascribe, discuss, hypothesize, state*).

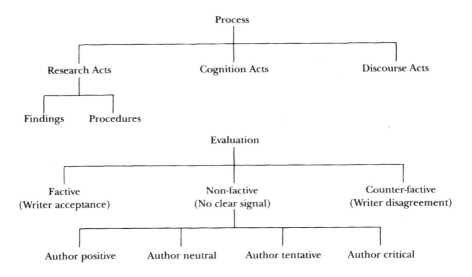

Figure 2.1   Categories of reporting verbs

In addition to selecting from these process categories, writers also exploit the evaluative potential of reporting verbs. The taxonomy employed here diverges from Thompson and Ye's rather complex multi-category system but retains their insight that writers can vary their commitment to the message by adopting an explicitly personal stance or by attributing a position to the original author. Thus, the writer may represent the reported information in one of three ways: as true (*acknowledge, point out, establish*); as false (*fail, overlook, exaggerate, ignore*); or non-factively, giving no clear signal. This last option allows the writer to ascribe a view to the source author, reporting him or her as positive (*advocate, argue, hold, see*), neutral (*address, cite, comment, look at*), tentative (*allude to, believe, hypothesise, suggest*) or critical (*attack, condemn, object, refute*). These process and evaluative options are summarised in Figure 2.1.

There is a fairly clear division in the process categories corresponding to the traditional division between hard and soft disciplines (Table 2.5). Broadly, philosophy, sociology, marketing and applied linguistics largely favoured discourse activity reporting verbs, and the engineering and science papers displayed a preference for research-type verbs.

Table 2.5   Classification of process category verbs (%)

Denotation	Bio	Phy	EE	ME	Mkt	AL	Soc	Phil	Totals
Research	43.1	56.0	55.2	47.0	31.2	30.5	29.1	23.5	33.5
Cognition	7.2	6.1	2.9	1.7	7.3	10.5	6.9	14.7	8.9
Discourse	49.7	37.9	41.9	51.3	61.5	59.0	64.0	61.8	57.6

The evaluative verbs, on the other hand (Table 2.6), showed broadly similar distributions, with verbs expressing the writer's belief in the reliability of the information (factives) exceeded by those withholding judgement (non-factives) in all disciplines. Only humanities/social science papers contained examples which were explicitly critical (counter-factive). The presentation of material using non-factive verbs again revealed disciplinary distinctions with writers in the soft disciplines up to four times more likely to report authors as expressing either a positive or a negative stance.

Table 2.6   Classification of evaluative category verbs (%)

Evaluation	Bio	Phy	EE	ME	Mkt	AL	Soc	Phil	Totals
Factive	26.7	15.1	16.1	27.3	19.6	20.0	16.3	15.4	19.0
Counter-factive	0.0	0.0	0.0	0.0	1.8	1.9	3.0	2.8	1.6
Non-factive	73.3	84.9	83.9	72.7	78.6	78.1	80.7	81.8	79.4
Author positive	16.7	8.9	8.2	8.2	29.2	32.2	30.1	31.0	25.7
Author neutral	60.9	76.8	69.9	76.5	35.0	48.3	47.7	39.2	49.2
Author tentative	22.4	14.3	21.2	15.3	33.5	17.6	16.8	21.0	21.1
Author critical	0.0	0.0	0.7	0.0	2.3	1.9	5.4	8.8	4.0

HARD v SOFT KNOWLEDGE AND COMMUNITY PRACTICES

The extensive use of citation underlines the fact that, in academic writing, the message presented is always embedded in earlier messages. However, while all writers drew intertextual links to their disciplines, they did so to different degrees and in different ways, which reflect clear disciplinary distinctions. The differences are meaningful because citation plays such an important role in mediating the relationship between a writer's argument and his or her discourse community. Differences in rhetorical conventions can therefore suggest characteristic variations in structures of knowledge and intellectual inquiry. The regularities therefore point to 'stereotypical social actions' (Miller, 1984) and offer insights into the knowledge-constructing practices of disciplinary communities. Broadly speaking, these differences, like others we shall examine later in this volume, correspond to the traditional distinctions between the sciences and engineering as hard knowledge, and the social sciences/humanities as soft disciplines.

The concept of hard and soft domains of knowledge is obviously not without problems, partly because these are everyday terms which carry connotations of clear-cut antithetical divisions. As a result, the use of these terms to characterise academic disciplines by types of knowledge forms clearly runs the risk of reductionism, or even reification, by packing a multitude of complex abstractions into a few simple opposites. Moreover, for some the terms may seem ideologically loaded, privileging a particular mode of knowing based on the structural perspectives, symbolic representations and model-building methods of the natural sciences. However, the hard–soft scheme is more directly related to established disciplinary groupings than some more abstract categorisations (Becher, 1989). Moreover, evidence from a questionnaire survey of academics (Biglan, 1973) and from psychometric tests of students' learning strategy preferences (Kolb, 1981) suggest that it may actually represent actors' own perceptions of the areas in which they are engaged.

Obviously such broad distinctions cannot capture the full complexity of disciplinary differences, and may only be acceptable at a general level of analysis, but they do provide a useful basis for identifying dimensions of variability between these fields. If the hard–soft distinction is conceived as a continuum rather than as unidimensional scales, I believe it offers a convenient way of examining general similarities and differences between fields without positing rigidly demarcated categories.

Reference to prior research clearly plays a more visible role in the humanities. Together the articles in philosophy, sociology, marketing and applied linguistics comprised two-thirds of all the citations in the corpus, twice as many as the science disciplines. Writers in these fields were also more likely to use integral structures and to place the author in subject position, to employ direct quotes and discourse reporting verbs, and to attribute a stance to cited authors. Writers in the hard sciences on the other hand were, with the exception of biology, less extensive in their citation practices and tended to downplay the role of the author. These differences, I suggest, are closely bound to the social activities, cognitive styles and epistemological beliefs of specific disciplinary communities.

CONTEXTUALISATION AND THE CONSTRUCTION OF KNOWLEDGE

An important cognitive feature of hard knowledge is its relatively steady cumulative growth, where problems are typically seen as determined by the imperatives of current interests and new findings are generated by a linear development from an existing state of knowledge (Kolb, 1981; Kuhn, 1970). While perhaps an ideological artefact of practitioners, such ontological representations nevertheless have important epistemological and rhetorical consequences. My scientist informants, for example, saw themselves as inhabiting a relatively discrete and clearly identifiable area of study and their research as proceeding along well-defined paths. The conception that their work occurs within an established framework of theoretical knowledge is reflected in scientists' routine discourse practices, as it means that writers can presuppose a certain amount of background, procedural expertise, theoretical understanding and technical lexis. In particular, such shared assumptions allow research to be coordinated by reporting experiments using a highly formalised and standardised code in place of an extensive system of references to previous work (cf. Bazerman, 1988).

Because new ideas must be situated in relation to assimilated disciplinary knowledge, the most influential new ideas are often those that most closely follow the old ones. Peer review practices which seek to eliminate the shoddy or unimportant also help to sustain an essentially conservative disciplinary consensus as reviewers judge work according to their own current interests. Because of this, writers working in new areas, such as early chaos theory where no literary context existed, had to use radical rhetorical strategies such as exemplars, equations, and longer introductions to establish common ground (Paul and Charney, 1995). Paul and Charney's analysis of readers' think-aloud responses to this work demonstrates a principal concern with relating their reading to their prior knowledge and their own research. Readers thus attended more 'to the context-setting information than to the description of the new project' (ibid.: 428), demonstrating the importance of a solid communal basis for the interpretation and validation of scientific writing.

This kind of direction and predictability is relatively rare in the humanities and social sciences however. Here new knowledge follows altogether more reiterative and recursive routes as writers retrace others' steps and revisit previously explored features of a broad landscape. In addition, issues are more diverse and detached from immediately prior developments (Becher, 1989). Writers draw on a literature which often exhibits greater historical and topical dispersion, being less governed by current imperatives and less dependent on a single line of development. As my informants noted,[2] in these circumstances research cannot be reported with the same confidence of shared assumptions:

> *I often cite from social psychology or organisational behaviour and other fields that my readers may not be familiar with, so I need to build a basis for what I'm saying. I don't just have to show my reasoning is dependable but also that my scholarship is too.*   (Mkt interview)

> *I'm conscious that my work may be read by both academics and teachers and so I often lay out the background carefully. To fit maybe different audiences.*   (AL interview)

More importantly, the literature is open to greater interpretation, findings are more frequently borrowed from neighbouring areas, and there are not the same clear-cut criteria for establishing or refuting claims. Together these differences mean that readers cannot be assumed to possess the same interpretive knowledge. Writers therefore often have to pay greater attention to elaborating a context through citation, reconstructing the literature in order to provide a discursive framework for their arguments and demonstrate a plausible basis for their claims. The more frequent citations in the soft texts therefore suggest greater care in firmly situating research within disciplinary frameworks and supporting claims with intertextual warrants.

These two broad conceptions of knowledge also result in different views about what constitutes a pertinent contribution and, indirectly, who can be cited. Scientific claims, if accepted, are generally regarded as discoveries which augment an orderly and coherent sequence of explanations in a given problem area, each fitting another block in the incremental completion of a research puzzle. This implies the assimilation of prior claims by new. As a result, a reader is unlikely to find Einstein, Oppenheimer or Planck cited in a physics paper:

> *This knowledge is assumed. It is not that we reject them but it is just well known facts. My personal view of science is of a huge volcano and lava is flowing down and I'm at the end of one stream of lava. Nobody cites volcanoes in their papers.*   (Phy interview)

Citation in the hard disciplines is therefore a means of integrating new claims into current knowledge while drawing on it as supporting testimony, situating the new work in the scaffolding of already accredited facts. References, particularly in physics, therefore tend to be tightly bound to the particular research topic under discussion, which closely defines a specific context of knowledge and contributes to a sense of linear progression. Intertextuality provides persuasive support by demonstrating the current work as 'valid science': the precedent providing a forceful warrant for current innovation.

In the humanities and social sciences, on the other hand, the fabric of established understandings has a wider weave. Problem areas and topics are generally more diffuse and range over wider academic and historical territory, and there is less assurance that questions can be answered by following a single path. Thus the substantial differences in citation rates between broad academic fields partially reflect the extent to which a context can be confidently assumed to be shared by readers. In soft domains, on the other hand, old ground is re-crossed and reinterpreted rather than suppressed. The process of coming to terms with the complexity of human behaviour is perceived as less obviously progressive and therefore less likely to discard older ideas as obsolete or irrelevant. As my sociology informant observed, 'good theory doesn't date ... Durkheim is a cottage industry. People promote or pan his ideas but he's still there because we can't say for sure whether he's right or wrong'. As a result, disciplinary giants are frequently encountered in the soft papers, particularly in 'pure' knowledge fields, where the pathfinders' stocks of relevance are clearly greater:

(5)   Marx located barricades at the core of conspiratorial movements ...   (Soc)

The first is derived from Durkheim's (1938) notion that there is a general ...

(Soc)

However, both Piagetian and Vygotskian thinking involve constructivist ...   (AL)

Wittgenstein insists that what is true or false is what people say, ...   (Phil)

Aristotle had a point when he defined humans as language users.   (Phil)

AGENCY AND EPISTEMOLOGY IN CITATIONS

The findings I presented above can also be explained in terms of disciplinary dispositions to either acknowledge or suppress the actions of humans in constructing knowledge. Once again, what constitutes valid claims and admissible reasoning differs between disciplines, and these values and epistemologies are instantiated in aspects of a community's genre conventions. An important aspect of the positivist-empirical epistemology that characterizes a great deal of scientific endeavour is that the authority of the individual is subordinate to the authority of scientific procedure. While these procedures may often be named after their originators (as in (4) above), this does not directly acknowledge the role of individuals in creating knowledge, but functions as an insider code to situate current work within a framework of shared methodological understandings.

Although many scientists may have perceived the achievement of absolute truth to be an illusory goal, their discursive practices are nevertheless guided by empiricist beliefs. Articles in the hard sciences still suggest that knowledge is accomplished by the correct application of prescribed procedures, and that nature reveals itself directly through scientific method. In this perspective, human judgement as a mediating link in the interpretation of data is downplayed, descriptions of phenomena are depicted as representing a reality independent of the observer, and empirical methods are reified in the conventions of scientific narrative. Scientists act as if they see themselves as discovering truth, not making it.

The conventions of impersonality in science articles play an important role in reinforcing this ideology by portraying the legitimacy of hard science knowledge as built on socially invariant criteria. While seeking to establish their own reputations through publication and the recognition bestowed by citation, writers routinely (and often unreflectingly) also subscribe to the assumption that the person who publishes a claim is largely immaterial to its accuracy. The author is merely 'a messenger relaying the truth from nature' (Gilbert, 1976: 285). This not only helps to account for the relatively low incidence of citation in the physics and engineering corpus, but also for the predominance of non-integral structures and perhaps also the overwhelming use of the footnote format:

(6)   Furthermore, it has been shown [103] that the fundamental dynamic range of
      ...   (EE)

      As already observed by others [17], T1 was found to be ...   (Phy)

      ...power gradient linearity in Ref (1) may be partly due to the choice of target
      fields...   (Phy)

      ... has been summarised by various authors (2, 8,16) and is still being re-
      analysed.   (ME)

The suppression of authors as agents has also blurred Swales' (1990) original integral v. non-integral distinction and led to the emergence of a variant form of reporting structure. Examples such as these are fairly common in the corpus:

(7)   According to ref. [11] the coupling parameters in the free electron ...   (Phy)

Ref. [9] developed finite formulations and corresponding code.   (Phy)

...using the highly efficient techniques described in [22], [23], and [25].   (EE)

...properties of a line trajectory in spatial motion are researched by Refs [21–23], ...   (ME)

Reference [20] presents a unified theory of kinematic synthesis to solve the problem.   (ME)

References [4, 5] reveal points with special kinematic meanings in the main body.   (ME)

While not all my scientist informants were comfortable with this hybrid pattern, its frequency testifies to a certain acceptability, particularly in physics and mechanical engineering. Its use also underlines the considerable variation in how reporting verbs are used in different disciplines.

Thus, together with relatively low citation rates and high use of non-integral forms, these kinds of patterns help to convey epistemological assumptions which give little space to those whose contributions are cited. Removing the agent helps remove the implication of human intervention, with all the influences of personal interest, social allegiance, faulty reasoning and other distorting factors beyond the empirical realm which that might suggest. These citation practices therefore help maintain the legitimacy of scientific knowledge as built on non-contingent pillars such as strict procedures, replication, falsification, and rigorous peer review in the process of publication.

OWNERSHIP AND MEMBERSHIP IN DISCIPLINARITY

Molecular biology differs significantly from these fields. Although it is a 'hard' science, and presumably shares the ethos and commitments sketched above, it has the greatest density of citations in the corpus, with three times as many attributions as physics, and also the highest proportion of author subjects among the sciences. While the reasons for these differences are unclear, they appear to reflect the distinctive ways that biology pursues and argues problems and understands the scientific endeavour (cf. Chargaff, 1974).

In many ways molecular biology is neither fully established nor prototypically 'scientific'. It is a relatively new discipline, with perhaps less cohesive research networks, and its methods are more descriptive, relying to a greater extent on 'beautiful models' than either physics or chemistry (Kellenberger, 1989). Its particular flavour is partly a consequence of its subject matter, the complex results of evolutionary change and exact geometrical replication of organisms over millions of years. This allows less abstraction and certainty than other sciences, but there is another strong reason for its distinctiveness.

The personalities of biology, the creators of its speculations and discoveries, have also tended to assume greater importance than in other hard sciences, both inside and outside the discipline (Judson, 1995; Watson, 1968).

Darwin, Bragg, Pauling, Luria and Crick are perhaps among the most well-known academics of any field. Halloran (1984) has argued that this is the result of an entrepreneurial spirit in the discipline, a notion of scientific knowledge as private property which originated with Watson and Crick's seminal 1953 paper, which simultaneously offered a model of DNA and a model of the scientist:

> Both argumentatively and stylistically Watson and Crick put forward a strong proprietary claim to the double helix. What they offer is not the structure of DNA or a model of DNA, but Watson and Crick's structure or model.
>
> (Halloran, 1984: 75)

The proclivity for citation in molecular biology, and for the exceptional scientific emphasis on integral reporting structures, might therefore be seen as an indication of a disciplinary ethos which emphasises proprietary rights to claims. Admittedly this claim is purely speculative and more research is required to account for this difference. However, my data suggests that constructing knowledge in biology seems to involve rhetorical practices which give greater weight to *who* originally stated the prior work, rather than the traditional conventions of impersonalisation still observed in the other hard disciplines studied here.

Writers in marketing also appear to give significant recognition to the ownership of ideas. Their texts contain large numbers of reporting verbs and author names in subject position. A marketing professor admitted that there was a certain self-advocating tendency among practitioners: 'Some people really promote their work and the area of research that they are in, both behind the scenes and in their papers.' While it is difficult to draw strong connections, this may be related to the involvement of large numbers of marketing academics in corporate consultancies, a source of increasing influence on research.

> *A lot of the research we do comes from real-world or corporate problems and even if it doesn't originate there, the ultimate goal is that it should end up there.* (Mkt interview)

Such dual interests increase the possibility of overlap between research and commercial values, with attribution practices becoming influenced by the norms of ownership and competition more typically associated with the marketplace.

The effects of professional and workplace contexts on academic literacy practices are largely unknown, but are clearly pertinent. Writing is collective, cooperative persuasion and occurs within communities bound together by shared assumptions about the nature of the world, how to hold ideas, and how to present them to peers. This social basis of knowledge means that its authority originates in the groups who comprise the audience for texts, who both shape this knowledge and render it intelligible. The participation of academics from applied fields such as engineering, applied linguistics, and marketing in their respective public arenas of communication is therefore likely to have consequences for their discursive behaviours. Academic 'forums of competition' (Toulmin, 1958), within which new concepts are appraised, become blurred with those of a more applied orientation as members are influenced by the problems, procedures and criteria of evaluation which emerge from, and are relevant to, workplace concerns and practices. The effects of such interactions on citation conventions remains to be studied.

Another discipline with high author visibility is philosophy, where citation plays a very different role to the one it plays in the hard sciences. Here knowledge is constructed through a dialogue with peers in which perennial problems are recycled through personal engagement:

> *Citing allows you to debate with others, the questions have been around a long time, but you hope you are bringing something new to it. You are keeping the conversation going, adding something they haven't considered. ... You know most of them anyway, you read them and they read you.* (Phil interview)

Bloor (1996: 34) refers to philosophical rhetoric as essentially 'mind-to-mind combat with co-professionals', a characterization which my informant amusedly accepted. In this context the extensive use of citation helps to achieve a high degree of personal involvement among protagonists. Many citations are repeated references in a protracted debate or draw on the reader's shared knowledge of an author's views without referring to a specific text. To emphasise the immediacy of the argument and its relevance to current concerns, they are usually presented in the present tense. These few random extracts give some flavour of this:

(8)   I disagree sharply with Rawles on the matter of ...   (Phil)

My main critique of Maudlin's solution is that ...   (Phil)

Nor can I see how Donnelan's syntactically simpler paradigm and my example three differ...   (Phil)

Davidson and Wittgenstein are alive to this possibility.   (Phil)

This conventional dispute structure often goes beyond the writer's response to the paraphrased arguments of an adversary to an imagined dialogue where claims are provided on their behalf. In the absence of an actual counter-argument, philosophers may strengthen their position by inventing one and attributing it with a hypothetical citation:

(9)   It might be suggested (perhaps by someone like René Descartes) that the problem ...   (Phil)

Wittgenstein would argue that this term expresses ...   (Phil)

Now Rawls could say that his concern, too, is distributive justice ...   (Phil)

If Churchland intends to say that. ...   (Phil)

Clearly these citation practices are not supporting the writer's claim to be extending the thread of knowledge from what has been previously established, but are helping to position the writer in relation to views that he or she supports or opposes. Scollon (1994) has argued that citing the work of others is not simply an issue of accurate attribution, but also a significant means of constructing an authorial self. Writing in the humanities stresses the individual creative thinker, but always within the context of a canon of disciplinary knowledge. Foregrounding the names of those whose work we engage with enables us to establish a professional persona. This was mentioned explicitly as a reason for citing by the sociologist:

> *I've aligned myself with a particular camp and tend to cite people from there. Partly because I've been influenced by those ideas and partly because I want them to read my work. It's a kind of code, showing where I am on the spectrum. Where I stand.* (Soc interview)

ETHOS AND EVALUATION: THE USE OF REPORTING VERBS

The distribution of reporting verbs in the corpus also shows that there are broad community-based preferences, both for specific items and the implications carried by particular semantic categories. More work needs to be done in this area, but once again it is possible that these choices serve to reinforce the epistemological and social understandings of writers by conveying an orientation to a particular ethos and to particular practices of social engagement with peers.

The finding that the humanities and social science articles contained far more, more varied, and more argumentative reporting verbs is partly a function of their greater need to elaborate a shared context. As discussed above, research in any field has significance only in relation to an existing literature, and citation helps to demonstrate accommodation to this community knowledge. In the soft fields, convincing readers that an argument is both novel and sound may often depend on the use of reporting structures not only to build a shared theoretical basis for one's arguments, but to establish a common perspective on the reliability of the claims one reports. Writers have to construct an epistemic as well as a disciplinary context. The different epistemological structure and social organisation of the hard sciences, on the other hand, often allow writers to assume more common ground with readers, requiring less need to demonstrate the relevance and reliability of prior studies using reporting verbs.

In addition to a heavier rhetorical investment in contextualisation, the greater use of reporting verbs in the soft fields also reflects the more discursive character of these disciplines. Briefly, reporting verbs fit more comfortably into an argument schema which more readily regards explicit interpretation, speculation and complexity as legitimate aspects of knowledge. The soft disciplines typically examine relationships and variables that are more numerous, less easily delineated and more subject to contextual and human vagaries than those studied in the hard sciences. Causal connections, conclusive demonstration, and depictions of feature are less easily established in the humanities (Kolb, 1981). One reason for the use of a wider repertoire of cita-tion verbs therefore is simply that they facilitate qualitative arguments which rest on finely delineated interpretations and conceptualisations, rather than systematic scrutiny and precise measurement. What appear at first sight to be stylistic proclivities for uniform choices in the hard sciences then, may actu-ally reflect the different procedures, subject matter, epistemological understandings and research perspectives which characterise those fields.

The scientific ideology which perceives laboratory activity as impersonal, cumulative and inductive also helps to explain the relatively high frequency of 'research' verbs found in the science/engineering corpus. These com-prised about half of the denotation choices in biology, physics and the engineering disciplines, and between a quarter and a third of those in the soft disciplines. This emphasis on real-world activities helps to convey the experimental explanatory schema typical of the sciences, where knowledge is more likely to be represented as proceeding from laboratory activities than the interpretive operations or verbal arguments of researchers.

(10) Edson et al. (1993) <u>showed</u> processes were induced only after the cells were treated...   (Bio)

... linear and non-linear distraction <u>observed</u> in LC delay lines [2].   (EE)

... a 'layer' coupled-shot finline structure was <u>studied</u> by Mazur [7] and Tech et al. [8] ...   (Phy)

... <u>using</u> special process and design [42], or by <u>adding</u> [101], or <u>removing</u> [83] a mask.   (EE)

References [7, 8] <u>developed</u> instantaneous invariance via point coordinates for the ...   (ME)

This emphasis was particularly evident in the physics and engineering papers, which together contained only nine cognition verbs, thereby camouflaging the role of author interpretation in the research process. Applied linguists and, in particular, philosophers, however, used such verbs extensively, under-scoring the part that reasoning and argument play in the construction of knowledge:

(11) Acton (1984) <u>sees</u> preparing students psychologically as a ...   (AL)

Parry <u>concluded</u> that by reading less, this student was encountering fewer new words. ...   (AL)

Some writers, e.g. Adams (2), <u>think</u> that ...   (Phil)

Donnelan <u>believes</u> that for most purposes we should take the demonstatum to be ...   (Phil)

Report verbs, however, do not simply function to indicate the status of the information reported, but the writer's position in relation to that informa-tion. The selection of an appropriate reporting verb allows writers to signal an assessment of the evidential status of the reported proposition and demonstrate their commitment, neutrality or distance from it. There was, however, little difference in how writers used verbs from the major categories in this corpus, although only soft disciplines employed counter-factive verbs, representing reported material critically:

(12) His revisionist interpretation of Twiggy <u>overlooks</u> historical research ...   (Mkt)

In addition, he <u>fails</u> to fully acknowledge the significance of ...   (Soc)

Lillian Faderman has also probably <u>exaggerated</u> the pervasiveness of ...   (Phil)

Churchland did not simply <u>misuse</u> the word 'theory'.   (Phil)

Generally writers in all fields tended to indicate their positions to cited material more indirectly, by ascribing an attitude to authors. These imputed positions showed clear disciplinary variations, with scientists and engineers overwhelmingly representing authors as conveying a neutral attitude to their findings. This conveys a detached and impartial reporting style to these papers, reflecting the need to build a convincing argument by simply displaying an awareness of prior or parallel research without appearing to corrupt it with personal judgement :

(13) ... the relevant theory was <u>developed</u> by Bruno [11].   (Phy)

These ornamentations were <u>described</u> by Schenck et al. (1984) as ...   (Bio)

Yeh et al [7] <u>reported</u> that a typical force ...   (EE)

Paiva and Venturinit (9) <u>presented</u> an alternative formulation ...   (ME)

Writers in the soft disciplines, on the other hand, were far more likely to depict authors as adopting a particular stance towards their work, either presenting their view as true, false or tentatively correct:

(14) Baumgartner and Bagozzi (1995) strongly <u>recommend</u> the use of ...   (Mkt)

Law and Whitley (1989) <u>argued</u>, for instance, that ...   (AL)

However, both Davidson and Wittgenstein explicitly <u>disown</u> the view ...   (Phil)

Kubiak <u>hints</u> that the Polish tradition ...   (Soc)

They were also more likely to evaluate this attributed position by adding adverbial comment, although this was largely restricted to philosophy:

(15) He argues there, <u>correctly</u> to my mind, that ...   (Phil)

Churchland <u>correctly</u> rejected this move ...   (Phil)

As Dipankar Gupta <u>correctly</u> asserts ...   (Soc)

Clearly these explicitly evaluative strategies are better suited to the more disputational style of argument favoured by the humanities, as they allow writers to open a discursive space within which to either exploit their opposition to the reported message or to build on it. Establishing intertextuality by attributing a view to another also allows this to be done dialogically, by engaging the scholarship of the discipline through a discourse with those who have created it. Once again, then, we find that textual conventions point to distinctions in how knowledge is typically negotiated and confirmed within distinct academic communities, facilitating the different means by which writers are able to link their local contributions into a wider disciplinary framework of expectations.

CONCLUSIONS

Reference to previous work is virtually mandatory in academic articles as a means of meeting priority obligations and as a strategy for supporting current claims, but how writers choose to present information is as important as the information they choose to present. The disciplinary differences discussed here indicate that the imperatives motivating citations are contextually variable and are related to community conventions of effective argument. Discoursal decisions are socially grounded, influenced by the broad enquiry patterns and knowledge structures of the disciplines. How writers choose to frame their studies for colleagues, whether they rely on a sprinkling of citations to invoke a set of common understandings or provide an elaborate scaffold of supporting references, will to some extent be influenced by their themes. More centrally, however, such decisions will crucially depend on the community they address.

Such practices cannot, of course, be seen as entirely determined; as language users are not simply passive recipients of textual effects, but the impact of citation choices clearly lies in their cognitive and cultural value to a community, and each repetition helps to instantiate and reproduce these conventions. The broad distinctions explored in this chapter therefore provide support for the view that our routine and unreflective writing practices are deeply embedded in the epistemological and social convictions of our disciplines. In the next chapter I shall examine this view in a very different context.

NOTES

1. Text extracts are coded as Phil (philosophy), Soc (sociology), Mkt (marketing), AL (applied linguistics), Bio (biology), Phy (physics), EE (electronic engineering) and ME (mechanical engineering).
2. The quotes I have included in the text often occurred in much longer stretches of talk and it has proved impossible to provide a full context without inflicting serious and incoherent digressions on my argument. They are therefore presented as representative 'soundbites' which best reflect insiders' views.

Chapter 3

Praise and criticism: interactions in book reviews

In the previous chapter I focused on the most visible and celebrated genre of the academy, the academic paper, and on one of the ways that writers reach out to ground their research in the understandings of their communities. In this chapter I want to explore the links between communicative practices and the structures of social and institutional relations in academic texts in a very different genre and through very different means. Here I examine the strategies of praise and criticism in a somewhat neglected genre: that of published peer reviews.

Like the research article, the book review is a crucial site of disciplinary engagement, but it is a site where the interpersonal stakes are much higher. The notion of site, or context of interaction, is an important variable here as it helps to determine the accepted form and the pragmatic force of the evaluation employed. Different conventions are observed in these two distinct sites. Book reviews are more interactively complex than research papers as they do not simply respond to a general body of more-or-less impersonal literature. Instead there is a direct, public, and often critical, encounter with a particular text, and therefore of its author, who must be considered as a primary audience of the review. While writers of research articles commonly avoid critical references, reviews are centrally evaluative. Intertextuality thus carries greater risks of personal conflict, for while most academic genres are evaluative in some way, the book review is most explicitly so. Here we see the workings of the peer group in perhaps its most nakedly normative role, where it publicly sets out to establish standards, assess merit and, indirectly, evaluate reputations.

Judgements can therefore carry significant social consequences and criticism becomes a potential source of friction because it can represent a direct challenge to a specific author. Negotiating social interactions therefore involves charting a perilous course between critique and collegiality, minimising personal threat while simultaneously demonstrating an expert understanding of the issues.

This, then, is a genre not only where arguments are scrutinised and responded to by disciplinary colleagues, but where interpersonal considerations are likely to be critical. The interactional conventions of the genre facilitate a careful balancing act which reflect both ideational and interpersonal orientations and demonstrate, once again, the various ways that writers and readers are linked through their participation in the same discipline. For students, the genre is important for learning to express the standards of evaluative comment which exist in their fields, and as a model for the wide use made of article critique assignments in a range of graduate programmes.

THE BOOK REVIEW GENRE

Book reviews have been a part of the academic landscape for almost 2000 years (Orteza y Miranda, 1996), but their evolution as a modern genre really began in the mid-seventeenth century, when the output of books, and thus new knowledge, increased enormously. Initially they served to summarise and chronicle uncritically the explosion of learning in the sciences for the reading public, and journals such as the *Analytical Review* and the *Monthly Epitome* emerged which were devoted entirely to this purpose (Roper, 1978). The widespread practice of simply recording published scholarship was abandoned in favour of more selective and critical writing with the introduction of *The Edinburgh* in 1802. The style of reviews also underwent a rhetorical shift with the publication of this journal. The common practice of transcribing long passages from the reviewed text without comment was now replaced with the reviewer's own opinion, often conveyed at length and with little connection to the original (ibid.: 45).

This tension between partiality and recount continues to be part of the review genre today, although the books they critique may have diminished in their influence in some fields. For example, in his diachronic study of the *Physical Review* from 1893 to 1980, Bazerman (1988: 158) notes the disappearance of the mention of new books from the journal around the 1930s. The principal source of academic novelty and learning in research physics from that time became, first, the article, and, more recently, the letter.

However, while the research article is often considered to be the key genre of modern knowledge-creation, it has not entirely replaced books as a vehicle for publishing new work and building an academic reputation. UNESCO (1992) reports that 842,000 academic titles were published in 1990, almost 20 per cent more than ten years earlier and over 60 per cent more than in 1970. Much of this growth, of course, has been in the softer disciplines. In the social sciences and humanities, for example, books are the major means of communicating research (Steig, 1986), but they have not completely disappeared as a means of presenting new results in the physical sciences. Griffith and Small (1983) point out that:

> The journal article is, for many parts of social science, a poor vehicle of communication, ill-suited to discuss extremely complex issues. Books are, in fact, the medium through which change is really affected.

Whitley (1984) attributes this to the greater 'technical task uncertainty' of

these disciplines, the need to elaborate ambiguous results and justify interpretations based on criteria that are less fixed, shared and uniformly applied
than those employed in the sciences. Becher (1989), also notes that books
are more characteristic of 'rural research areas', where topics are less narrowly focused, slower moving, and less competitively researched.

Because of this, book reviews continue to play a significant role in the
scholarship of the soft disciplines, often consuming a considerable amount of
journal space. They also appear in a number of hard knowledge journals,
despite the fact that book publication accounts for only a fraction of research
output in these disciplines. Steig (1986), for example, suggests that book
publication is perhaps ten times greater in history than in the sciences.
Consequently, reviews in the hard fields are often considerably shorter. My
corpus of 20 published reviews in each of the eight disciplines[1] varied in their
average length between 1,700 words in philosophy and 400 in electronic
engineering. The engineering and science reviews in fact amounted to only
31 per cent of the total corpus length, presumably because these disciplines
afford books less importance than the soft fields.

Neither strictly a 'research-process' genre, nor one of Swales's (1996)
'occluded' genres of academic life, the book review seems to have largely
escaped applied linguistic scrutiny. Paul Theroux suggests that literary book
reviews are actually a kind of public correspondence between reviewer and
reviewed that no one else reads. This might at first blush seem an even more
apt description of academic book reviews. After all, they are less widely dis-
seminated, less crucial in influencing purchases or prizes, and less significant
in accumulating merit for their writers. A lengthy piece in a prestigious peri-
odical such as the *New York Review of Books* or the *Times Literary Supplement*, for
example, allows considerable room for the writer to craft a review with reflec-
tion and imagination, and this might subsequently be regarded as a work of
scholarship which contributes to his or her reputation. In the academic
world, in contrast, reviews are often tucked away at the back of the journal
and give neither space nor prominence to their writers.

However, while a somewhat unsung genre of the academy, it nevertheless
plays an important role in supporting both the manufacture of knowledge
and the social cohesiveness of disciplinary communities. Reviews are highly
visible and often carefully considered; all my informants, for instance, read
reviews regularly for news about titles and more general information on the
area covered by the review. Very much a public discourse, book reviews contribute to the dissemination and evaluation of research while providing an
alternative forum in which academics can set out their views. It thus not only
offers a means by which junior academics can gain institutional credit and a
publication profile, but allows established writers a rhetorical platform. Here
they can signal their allegiance to a particular orientation or group, and pro-
claim a position without engaging in the long cycle of inquiry, review and
revision involved in a full-length paper.

Despite their length and distinct purpose, however, reviews are nevertheless rhetorically and interactionally complex and represent a carefully crafted

social accomplishment. In most fields, then, a good review needs not only to offer a critical and insightful perspective, drawing on considerable knowledge of the field, but at the same time respond to the complex demands of this delicate interactional situation, displaying an awareness of the appropriate expression of praise and criticism.

In this chapter I shall focus on praise and criticism to elaborate some of the main semantic resources that writers use to negotiate judgements and valuations in reviews. Following Holmes's (1988) characterisation of compliments, praise is defined as an act which attributes credit to another for some characteristic, attribute, skill, etc., which is positively valued by the writer. It therefore suggests a more intense or detailed response than simple agreement. Criticism, on the other hand, I regard as the expression of dissatisfaction or negative comment on the volume. Clearly book reviews are not only catalogues of positive and negative speech acts but also include neutral descriptions of aims, organisation and content, and also provide writers with a discursive space in which to elaborate their own views. Consequently, it is necessary to distinguish praise from acknowledgement and criticism from the writer's alternative positions. Essentially, then, I wish to identify explicitly positive and negative judgements – statements that either offer or deny authors or editors credit for their work, rather than discourses which merely describe or debate what they say.

I begin with an overview of the evaluative focus of the reviews then discuss the ways in which writers manage its expression.

EVALUATION IN REVIEWS

While it is possible to find a review that contains neither praise nor criticism, this is essentially an evaluative genre where writers judge a text on its academic quality, clarity, integrity and value to the field. A search of the literature reveals that most of the research on compliments and criticisms has occurred within a framework based on politeness, has examined speech, and has focused on complimenting behaviour (e.g. Herbert, 1990; Holmes, 1988, 1995; Wolfson, 1989). This research suggests that speakers tend to rely on highly formulaic syntactic and lexical strategies when complimenting, but there is little work on how this may vary in particular genres and contexts. Our knowledge of how criticism is expressed is similarly very limited. Some research on complaints and expressions of disapproval exists (e.g. Beebe and Takahashi, 1989; D'Amico-Reisner, 1983; Olshtain and Weinbach, 1986), but this is also restricted to (often elicited) conversational routines, and has tended to focus on either cultural variation or the interactional norms of intimates.

Complimenting and criticism have also largely been seen in terms of politeness phenomena in written genres (Cherry, 1988; Hagge and Kostelnick, 1989). Hagge and Kostelnick, for instance, show that auditors criticisms of clients' business practices are frequently moderated by strategies such as euphemism and hedging to meet the complex interactional demands of professional settings. In academic texts Myers (1989) sees many of the regularities of expression in research articles (such as passives and pronoun use) as strategic politeness devices, while Johnson's (1992) study of compliments in students' peer reviews gives similar attention to how writers maintain rapport and mitigate criticism. In each of these studies compliments and criticisms are seen as enactments of strategic politeness, drawing on Brown and Levinson's (1987) influential model of face-maintenance, to which I referred in Chapter 1.

To recap briefly, a face model proposes that it is usually in everyone's best interests to satisfy the face needs of interlocutors. Routine social interactions are seen as fraught with potential face threats (FTAs), and criticisms are particularly risky as they undermine a hearer's positive face, the desire to be approved of and have one's goals seen as desirable. Compliments, on the other hand, directly attend to this aspect of face in that they convey support and interest, demonstrating solidarity between participants, but they also carry risks, for not everyone is entitled to compliment, and conveying praise implies an authority to appraise and make public one's judgements. While I have argued for the importance of more socially-based conventions in research articles, a face model may contribute to writer's strategic choices in book reviews. After all, not only is the writer here engaged in direct, visible and more or less detailed evaluation of a colleague's work, but the academic world is small, and it may be prudent not to antagonise those within it.

The presentation of a reviewer's viewpoint, therefore, not only involves an ideational position to that work, expressing cognitive judgements and scholarly perceptions, it also conveys affective, addressee-oriented meanings. How an evaluation is framed is therefore an important consideration as it carries a socio-pragmatic force beyond the propositional meaning of the utterance. Vicious criticism can seriously undermine an author's credibility and lavish praise can be unwelcome as superficial and undiscriminating. An evaluation thus bears interpersonal implications for both its author and the wider community. On the one hand, such evaluations are potentially damaging to the author of the volume as criticism can undermine his or her academic reputation. On the other hand, the reviewer poses a threat to the wider community by adopting a position of authority in relation to it, representing himself or herself as an expert qualified to speak, as it were, for the discipline. The genre is, in a sense, parasitic on the one it critiques; it offers no fresh evidence to the community yet appeals for colleague's attention, occupying precious pages of space in academic journals.

So, because these acts are closely related to the identity claims of participants, we might anticipate that praise and criticism are carefully managed strategies in book reviews, entailing careful framings that responds to their interpersonal effects while simultaneously addressing the demands of the genre.

In this study I first quantified the evaluations by reading the reviews and searching for both positive and negative cases of evaluation. I counted speech acts, analysing praise and criticism as semantic units which contributed to the ongoing discourse. This seemed to overcome the problem of the different values that may be attached to particular terms (*fantastic* vs *good*, for example), and the fact that utterances can vary widely in the amount of positive or negative evaluation they offer. In (1) for example, there are, respectively one, two and three semantically positive items, but I coded each sentence as one instance of praise because each refers to a single aspect of a book:

(1)   Kim's presentation of the contemporary philosophies of mind is <u>excellent</u>.

(Phil)

Anticipating China turns out to be an <u>excellent</u> and <u>invaluable</u> introduction to comparative philosophy.   (Phil)

This is an <u>excellent</u> and <u>timely</u> book that <u>should be in the library of every self-respecting Department of Biochemistry or Plant Science</u>.   (Bio)

It also seemed sensible to avoid grading strength of statements when given comments like this (!):

The writing is excellent if, like me, the reader appreciates the style of the Wall Street Journal.   (Mkt)

This procedure led to a general categorisation scheme which allowed me to quantify the comments in terms of their referential foci. I then examined the rhetorical and formal realisations in greater detail. The results are set out in the following sections.

DIMENSIONS OF PRAISE AND CRITICISM

Appraisal was an extensive aspect of the commentary in these reviews, comprising 1,743 statements with an average of 10.9 cases per paper, just over half of it being positive (57 per cent). These evaluations ranged over a number of issues and not only addressed the content and presentation of the reviewed book, but also its writer, its audience and its material quality. Table 3.1 summarises these foci.

Most of the evaluations, not surprisingly, addressed content issues, and about 68 per cent of all judgements fell into this category, almost equally between praise and criticism. It is interesting, however, that while over 80 per cent of the positive commentary on content addressed general aspects of the book (2), critical observations tended to be more specific, with 60 per cent referring to particular content issues (3):

(2)   Would that this excellent paperback had been available 20 years ago!   (ME)

Challenging Codes is certainly the best introduction to the study of ...   (Soc)

This is an excellent and accessible discussion.   (Mkt)

Simpson's book is an excellent guide.   (Phy)

Charvet's book is for the most part a thorough, lucid and well-argued book.

(Phil)

...we find Klein's work to be significant, not only for the detailed careful study she presents, but also for the myriad issues she raises for a still-young field. (AL)

(3)   ... the cardinal sin of giving a hard-coded polynomial approximation to gamma
...   (Phy)

This promise is not wholly fulfilled and the chapter disappointingly concludes
...   (Soc)

On p. 195 it is not made clear why SO_4^{2-} competitive inhibition of ....   (Bio)

But this claim turns out to be misleading.   (Phil)

The authors' treatment of psychometric issues is spotty and disorganised. (Mkt)

It does not give much of an explanation why neural networks are useful, and does not derive any of the equations.   (EE)

This tendency of writers to criticise specific issues and praise more global features was also apparent in the other categories. The most general evaluative features were those concerning (a) the worth of the book to the discipline or to a particular audience, and (b) attributes, such as the reputation and experience of the author. Both of these areas received considerably higher proportions of praise than criticism. In contrast, however, more specific features, such as comments on textual elements like diagrams, references and indexing, and aspects of the author's writing style, received almost equal praise and criticism.

Table 3.1   Categories of evaluation in book reviews (%)

Focus	Description	Praise	Criticism
Content			
(i) General	Overall discussion: eg. coverage, approach, interest, currency, quality	50.0	33.8
(ii) Specific	Argument: e.g. insight, coherence, explanatory or descriptive value	10.7	44.9
Style	Exposition: clarity, organisation, conciseness, difficulty, readability and editorial judgements	9.3	9.2
Readership	Value or relevance for a particular readership, purpose or discipline	15.3	3.2
Text	Extent, relevance and currency of references, the number, usefulness and quality of diagrams, Index items, tasks and exercises	6.2	5.9
Author	Writer's experience, reputation, qualifications or previous publications	6.7	0.1
Publishing	Price, quality and production standards of the book	1.8	3.1

Presumably the propensity for criticism to correlate with more specific features helps to contribute to the purpose of the genre. One writer suggests that this concerns the role of the book review as an instrument for creating a psychological climate for examination, investigation, correction, modification, creation and invention of ideas and theoretical constructs regarding current theoretical problems, professional practice and policy statements.   Orteza y Miranda (1996: 197)

Reviewers are exhorted to explore in their critiques the detail of the ideas they encounter, criticising specifics and picking up individual points in order to raise questions and contribute to the 'knowledge creating/knowledge examining domain of the journal'. On the other hand, the overwhelming preference for a global focus of positive comment appears to obey another imperative, perhaps the injunction of review editors, for writers to convey overall impressions within a restricted space. In this way reviewers can offer an evaluative structure most useful for readers.

The fact that positive comments largely addressed global issues while criticism was more specific tends to contribute to the dual purpose of book reviews: to provide an overview of the text for prospective readers while raising particular problematic issues for the field. Reviewers are therefore clearly oriented to the evaluative role of the genre, assessing a book's representation of existing knowledge or its contribution to this knowledge. Simultaneously, however, this pattern has important interpersonal consequences, as it acts to limit the scope of negative comment. The effect of global criticism is to condemn the entire work – a particularly threatening act – and this seems to have been avoided as far as possible in these reviews. Where it did occur, however, there was often some attempt to mitigate its full effects, either by diffusing the criticism in some way (4), or by restricting it to an individual opinion (5):

(4)   Books based on symposia are rarely balanced or comprehensive and this example is no exception.   (Bio)

       The book has flaws, particularly in the area of supporting evidence, but it is an important book.   (Mkt)

(5)   One is left with an uneasy sense of losing the wood among the trees, and feeling that one's sense of wonder, of engagement with exciting intellectual challenges, has been left unsatisfied, even devalued, by a slightly scholastic refusal to enter into the spirit of the thing.   (Phil)

       The reviewer believes that it is not an unfair assessment to say that the work suffers broadly from two faults, ...   (AL)

This is not to ignore the fact that some writers were robust in their criticisms. Reviews in philosophy and sociology in particular can be extremely blunt, but few were completely destructive and none found no redeeming features. Thus, while offering an evaluation as a contribution to scholarship, or perhaps as a means of presenting their own views while critiquing another's, writers rarely lost sight of a need to facilitate a continued sense of solidarity with their readers – restricting censure to specific arguments or infelicities of the author, rather than condemning the entire text.

In sum, authors were largely praised for global features of their work, particularly content generalisations and recommendations to potential readers, while criticism tended to be reserved mainly for specific content and textual features. This pattern, which was similar across disciplines, appears to serve both ideational and interpersonal purposes for writers as it not only conveys cognitive assessments of work, but helps to carry affective meanings. This dual purpose is also evident in the ways that writers organised and expressed their evaluations, and I turn to this after briefly examining the disciplinary patterns.

DISCIPLINARY DIFFERENCES IN EVALUATIONS

There were considerable disciplinary distinctions in the amount of overall evaluation and in the balance of praise and criticism. Table 3.2 shows that while the density of criticism was broadly similar across the fields, the engineering and science reviews contained far more praise than those in the soft fields, and thus more evaluation per 1,000 words. The percentage distribution of appraisal shows clearly how the disciplines separated along the hard–soft knowledge divide. Criticism exceeded praise in only the two social science disciplines, but substantially more of the evaluation by soft discipline writers tended to be critical. The final column suggests the extent of this division, showing how far one category exceeded the other, with reviewers in electronic engineering disposed to much greater generosity than those in other fields.

Table 3.2   Praise and criticism in reviews by discipline

Discipline	*Per 1,000 words*		*Per cent of total*		*Per cent difference*
	Praise	**Criticism**	**Praise**	**Criticism**	
Philosophy	3.3	4.3	42.9	57.1	33.0% + criticism
Sociology	4.5	5.1	47.2	52.8	11.8% + criticism
App. linguistics	3.9	3.3	53.9	46.1	17.1% + praise
Marketing	6.2	4.4	58.1	41.9	38.6% + praise
Elec. engineering	13.1	3.9	77.0	23.0	235.5% + praise
Mech. engineering	11.7	7.0	62.5	37.5	66.6% + praise
Physics	9.7	4.8	66.5	33.5	98.9% + praise
Biology	9.1	5.1	63.8	36.2	76.0% + praise
Totals	6.2	4.5	58.0	42.0	38.1% + praise

The figures in Table 3.2 are largely explained by the fact that reviews in the soft knowledge fields were more extensive in their evaluations and generally more critical in their judgements. Writers here sought to exploit the discursive space available to them to explore issues in some depth, anchoring the text in the concerns of the wider discipline and often expounding their own views at length. Reviews in science and engineering, on the other hand, were much shorter and assessments more compressed and more dense, averaging 15.6 per 1,000 words compared to 8.5 in the soft reviews. Praise tended to be more fulsome and criticism more acerbic in the soft knowledge papers. The hard knowledge reviews, on the other hand, were dominated by praise, which comprised over two-thirds of all evaluation in those disciplines and was almost twice as frequent per 1,000 words as in the soft domains.

Content issues were the main concern of most writers, and while this tended to be far more critical in the soft papers, specific content was the only category where criticism exceeded praise in any of the hard science disciplines. Table 3.3 summarises the data to give a broad idea of how writers in the hard and soft disciplines approached their texts, illustrating the greater concern of scientists and engineers with publishing, readership and textual aspects, and the soft discipline reviewers with critical aspects of content and style.

Table 3.3   Percentage distribution of evaluation by hard and soft fields.

Category		Hard fields			Soft fields		
		Praise	**Criticism**	**Total**	**Praise**	**Criticism**	**Total**
Content:	Overall	30.2	11.5	41.7	27.5	16.4	43.9
	Specific	5.8	12.4	18.2	6.6	24.1	30.7
Audience		11.2	1.8	13.0	6.7	0.9	7.6
Style		5.6	2.3	7.9	5.3	5.2	10.5
Text		7.4	3.3	10.7	1.3	1.8	3.1
Author		4.4	0.0	4.4	3.1	0.1	3.2
Publishing		2.0	2.1	4.1	0.3	0.6	0.9

Compressing the disciplines into two broad categories in this way obviously does some injury to the data as it introduces yet another layer of abstraction above gathering the individual reviews into disciplines. However, I am not making a major claim here, and I am certainly not suggesting that these categories embody monolithic and unvaried interactions in reviews, but while some important differences are obscured in this process, it does offer a surprisingly representative picture. No soft discipline, for example, devoted more attention to a book's readership, author, textual material or publishing details than any hard discipline, and no hard discipline devoted a higher proportion of evaluation to specific content. The overall content and style categories were less uniform, however.

Philosophers and sociologists were more critical of the general aspects of authors' expositions than other writers, and biologists tended to be more positive, but otherwise the distribution of comment was quite similar. Stylistic blemishes and poor writing in texts, on the other hand, often considerably exercised reviewers in marketing, sociology and applied linguistics:

(6)   I found levels of argumentativeness and melodrama that were not to my taste.
(Mkt)

This expository structure is somewhat awkward.   (Phil)

Hutton writes English only adequately.   (Soc)

Many readers will probably find unpalatable Bickerton's style of argumentation which rests all too often on sweeping dismissals of the views of others, or an incomplete consideration of relevant literature, plus a great deal of fanciful neuropsychology and magic.   (AL)

Philosophers, linguists and physicists, however, were equally likely to praise style as condemn it, commenting on the skill of the writer and aspects of the organisation of the volume:

(7)   This book is written in a particularly engaging conversational style.   (Phy)

The book is crisp and lucid.   (Phil)

The passionate tone, local detail and use of Gikuyu all help to recreate the experience of an East African village as it faces neocolonial crisis in development.
(AL)

Linguists joined engineers and scientists to denounce textual attributes of books, particularly how they incorporated and used visual material and references. Scientists, however, were far more likely to be concerned with publishing issues such as price and printing standards than other writers, perhaps reflecting the high proportion of textbooks reviewed, where cost, durability and the clarity of diagrams to represent information are particularly important.

Finally, I tried to find whether these broad disciplinary differences were reflected in contrasting vocabularies, identifying the most frequent evaluative terms in the different samples. Overall, and overwhelmingly, reviewers favoured *useful, important* and *interesting* as positive adjectives, clearly highlighting the content orientations of the texts. Clarity and accessibility were other frequently mentioned attributes in the soft fields, and while work which was *detailed* gratified philosophers and applied linguists, *significant* and *insightful* also appeared to be important terms for philosophers and marketing specialists. *Detailed* and *up-to-date* figured prominently in the hard science fields, while engineers were particularly concerned to see whether books were *comprehensive* and *practical.* Explicitly negative adjectives were less common and more varied. However, *difficult* was a recurring issue for writers in most fields, and *restricted, inconsistent* and *misleading* stood out as the most frequently-used forms in the soft disciplines.

Altogether, these very general differences in the extent to which writers' employed praise and criticism, the areas they tended to focus on, and their preferred terms of expression correspond to some of the disciplinary characteristics outlined in the previous chapter. One relevant factor here is the different ways these disciplines approach argument and knowledge. Because the problems of the social sciences and humanities are fairly loosely defined and inquiry tends to be treated as a reiterative process, the appraisal of a particular individual's work is a significant means of exploring ideas and getting to grips with important issues in the field. Thus in the soft fields, where controversy and debate are more important than demonstration and proof, greater attention was devoted to the quality of exposition and detailed critiques of particulars. These reviews were longer, more discursive, and more critical of both content and style of argument, and drew more heavily on a range of evaluative terms which displayed an orientation to the significance of the ideas expressed.

Another substantial point of difference is the relative importance of books as a means of conveying new knowledge in these disciplines. The rapid accretion of knowledge accounts for the comparative absence of a serious tradition of book publishing in the hard knowledge fields; many of the volumes discussed were either student texts or monographs/compilations of papers designed to review a particular area for non-specialists. My informants suggested that this kind of publishing is often regarded as self-contained products of scholarship, rather than contributions to the ongoing accumulation of a body of knowledge (see Chapter 6). The fact that such work is seen as lying outside the mainstream endeavour of producing new claims might explain the generally less critical stance taken towards it and the greater interest in writer and readership issues. It also helps to account for the fact that reviewers devoted more attention to diagrams, references and indexing – aspects of texts more useful to an audience of students or professionals seeking to update their knowledge of an unfamiliar area.

The different points of focus and expression outlined here do not, however, alter the general interactional patterns I discussed in the previous section. There appear to be a number of strategies for structuring and expressing praise and criticism employed by reviewers which cross-cut the preferences for particular argument forms of specific disciplines, and these will be discussed below.

STRUCTURAL PATTERNS OF PRAISE AND CRITICISM

The two most striking features of virtually all these 160 reviews was the amount of praise they contained and the frequency with which it functioned to open or conclude the papers. In conversational contexts, giving praise is often regarded with suspicion and may be experienced as either flattery or an assertion of superiority. Positive evaluations appear to be rare in spoken interactions among males (Herbert, 1990; Holmes, 1995) and in teacher-written feedback to students (e.g. Daiker, 1989). In this corpus, however, it comprised over half of all evaluations and functioned to express solidarity and positive assessment, and to mitigate criticism. In terms of distribution, some 58 per cent of the writers opened with a positive comment, either to begin the paper or immediately following a brief contextualising paragraph, and 64 per cent chose this strategy to close their reviews. On the other hand, less than 20 per cent of reviews ended with criticism and only 3 per cent began with it. The majority of reviewers therefore chose to structure their texts by sandwiching their commentary between praise for the work.

The decision to open with praise was an almost routine move in this corpus, yet did not predict the outcome of the review; it occurred in papers that were mainly critical or mainly favourable, and often functioned as a basis for the critique. It is interesting, however, that this strategy is similar to patterns of complimenting behaviour found at the openings of addressee-oriented speech events, such as phatic conversation (Holmes, 1995; Wolfson, 1989), letters of persuasion (Cherry, 1988), 'bad news' messages (Salerno, 1988) and written peer feedback (Johnson, 1992). While less ritually obligatory in the review genre, the decision to introduce positive comment early in the text may have similar interpersonal functions, operating to establish rapport with the audience and mitigate the criticism which is to follow.

The most frequent opening move was to offer global praise for the volume, relying heavily on a restricted range of adjectives, most commonly *interesting, comprehensive, significant* and *excellent*. Some examples are provided in (2) above. The next most favoured opening strategy appears to carry even more explicit interpersonal connotations, attributing credit directly to the author rather than to the volume itself:

(8) ... a total of 26 American and European scholars, many of whom are well known
    for their research in the field.   (Mkt)

    ... written by a world renowned expert in the particular subject area covered.
                                                                              (ME)

    ... is written by excellent specialists and contains information on ...   (Bio)

    This is a collection of essays by a leading philosopher of biology...   (Phil)

    Roger Brubaker has acquired a reputation in recent years as one of the most
    original scholars analysing the emergence of the 'New Europe'.   (Soc)

    Certainly it would be hard to find two men more qualified to speak about space
    and time.   (Phy)

While the reviewer is clearly seeking to endorse the volume under discussion by establishing the expertise or qualifications of its author or contributors, positive comment of this kind is a definite shift in the object of praise; from a cognitive judgement on the volume itself, to its producers. Praise here helps to demonstrate the solidarity of reviewers with the communities of which they are members and for whom they write, acknowledging the reputations of colleagues and their previous contributions to a shared endeavour. In addition, personal evaluations also appear to show the reviewer's recognition of the potential threat that the genre carries for the authors, and to redress this early in the text. This is suggested by the fact that author praise not only occurred in favourable reviews, but also in those that were otherwise largely negative, and that while reviewers frequently criticised an author's style or argument, they nowhere suggested that the writer was in any way intellectually or experientially unqualified to write the volume.

Closing comments also establish grounds for an interpersonal interpretation of praise in this genre. A similar pattern apparently prevails in teacher responses to high school essays (Harris, 1977) and peer response marking (Johnson, 1992). In book reviews a concluding positive comment not only serves to offer a stronger endorsement of the volume, but also reconfirms an attention to reader sensitivities, creating a socially appropriate solidarity framework for the entire text.

To the wider audience of community members, a closing complimentary remark helps to re-establish the reviewer's credentials as an honest and reasonable scholar. It positions him or her as a colleague who recognises the contribution of a balanced, impartial and discerning critique to the community's communal pursuit of knowledge. To the actual author of the monograph this strategy may help to repair the adverse effects of earlier criticism and acknowledge that the writer is aware of the author's positive face concerns. Clearly, publication always carries risks and there is nowhere that authors invest more of their credibility and reputation than within the pages of a book. Choosing to frame their criticisms within statements of praise might suggest that reviewers recognise this, and concede that such risks should be given some credit.

The most frequent closing strategy was to offer positive comment on the book's contribution or a commendation to readers. Together these comprised 60 per cent of all positive closures and formed a particularly popular ending in the hard knowledge reviews, where they often pointed to an appropriate audience for the volume:

(9)   This book is highly recommended as a textbook for final year undergraduate courses and for postgraduate students.   (EE)

It should prove useful to researchers in applied mathematics, and possibly also in engineering...   (ME)

The book is a fantastic contribution to the field and it is easy to predict that it will some day become a classic.   (Phy)

Well worth reading, warts and all!   (AL)

Soft knowledge papers tended to close with praise for the book as a whole, remarking on its general content rather than its possible value for readers. In contrast, closing criticism took more varied forms and was as likely to address publishing or stylistic issues as substantive comment.

The exception, of course, helps to illustrate the power of convention. I had to go outside my corpus, to linguistics, for the following closing paragraph, but it is worth including here, partly for its exceptionality but mainly for the way it draws a large amount of its effect from the writer's self-conscious flouting of the conventions I have just described:

(10)   It is almost *de rigueur* to conclude a review with the cliché that, despite any short-comings, the volume warrants a place on the shelves of any serious scholar in

the discipline. In this case, however, I feel unable to offer this advice, unless you wish to be exposed to tendentious argumentation from the outset, a strange combination of politically correct and neo-colonial prejudices, major leaps of logic, suspect facts, poorly informed judgements, and even some unwarranted slurs on yourself and your linguistic colleagues.   (Crowley, 1999: 103)

Generally, however, at this level of organisation we can see writers mitigating the overall or global impact of their reviews on their various audiences. By opening and closing their papers with praise, they are able to address both ideational and interpersonal issues, expressing cognitive judgements of the book itself and redressing the threat that such a critical genre necessarily carries for the reviewed author.

MITIGATION OF EVALUATIVE ACTS

Attention to interpersonal factors in these reviews was also evident at more local levels. Praise is generally fulsome, often even lavish, and while it is true that a considerable amount of negative comment was presented baldly, virtually all papers contained at least one mitigated criticism and redressive strategies were employed to attenuate the full effects of over 65 per cent of all the critical speech acts in the corpus. These mitigation strategies principally involved the use of praise–criticism pairs, hedging, personal responsibility, other attribution, metadiscoursal bracketing, and indirectness.

The full illocutionary force of specific criticisms was frequently (20 per cent of all criticisms) assuaged by the juxtaposition of polar comments in *praise–criticism pairs*. Francis Crick, Nobel laureate and one of the leading biologists of the last 30 years, sums up this strategy like this:

I learned that if you have something critical to say about a piece of scientific work, it is better to say it firmly but nicely and to preface it with praise of any good aspects of it. I only wish I had always stuck to this useful rule.

(Crick, 1990: 49)

Here then, praise is syntactically subordinated to a criticism, but their adjacency serves to create a more balanced comment, slightly softening the negativity of the evaluation:

(11) While I applaud Bickerton's willingness to question and turn conventional wisdom on its head, there are many problems with his views, not least of which is the fact that there is no empirical evidence to support his claims.   (AL)

Undoubtedly this book will be a valuable reference work, but it has also missed an opportunity.   (Bio)

This reviewer likes the style of the book; yet there is a paucity of state of the art algorithms.   (Phy)

There are some very good essays in this collection, but considered as a whole the book does have significant shortcomings.   (Phil)

> I found the book quite strong on low-level policing issues, but less convincing on the nature of drug trafficking, markets or police counter-measures.   (Soc)

> All basic information is given, although the style is rather terse and declarative.   (ME)

> The writing is excellent if, like me, the reader appreciates the style of the Wall Street Journal. However, the overall organization is difficult to follow, the index could have been better (e.g., where is Axelrod?), and the footnotes are distracting.   (Mkt)

Occasionally such pairings can be rather elaborate, further weakening the criticism by use of devices such as simile or metaphor which makes the criticism more abstract:

> Reading this book was like cutting into a loaf cake and discovering that delightful bits of chocolate had been baked into the dough. At the same time, it was disconcerting to find that each slice seemed to come from a different recipe.   (Mkt)

A second mitigation strategy was the use of *hedges*. Not surprisingly in such an evaluative genre, hedges were extensively employed to tone down criticisms and reflect a positive relationship with the reader and the author. While hedges have both an epistemic and affective function in knowledge-making genres (see Chapter 4 and Hyland, 1996b, 1998a), their principal purpose in these reviews was not to reflect degrees of probability, but to mitigate the interpersonal damage of critical comments. Hedges occurred in all but a handful of reviews and comprised 61 per cent of all mitigation strategies. The use of hedges as a proportion of criticism did not vary substantially between disciplines, although the hard knowledge papers, particularly physics and engineering, relied on a more limited range of items. The modal verbs, especially *would, might, may* and *could*, and the epistemic verb *seem*, predominated in virtually all disciplines:

(12) In all probability, the sub-routines would require further development; ... (ME)

Discussion of specific trade agreements and export flows may be dated.   (Mkt)

... it could plausibly be retorted that what seems attractive about it are just ...
(Phil)

... one might consider the single focus approach misguided.   (AL)

This seems a somewhat curious proposition given the thesis ...   (Soc)

Hedges overwhelmingly occurred in evaluations of content, where one might expect the interpersonal effects to be potentially most harmful, but they were also occasionally to be found in other categories of comment, particularly those concerning style and readership:

(13) It is unlikely to appeal to practicing engineers.   (ME)

... – but may pose comprehension difficulties for intermediate learners.   (AL)

... much of the text is not particularly easy to read.   (Mkt)

Generally however hedges sought to reduce the full impact of critical comment of the overall value of the book or particular facets of its arguments.

(14) ... is <u>perhaps a little</u> unbalanced for a general book. (Bio)

<u>This would appear to</u> undermine the main point of Lakshmanan's book, ...
(AL)

Also, <u>in common with many other texts</u> that are based on specific software systems, the contents <u>may</u> date rather quickly as software and hardware specifications improve. (ME)

A third strategy to soften the illocutionary force of criticisms, comprising 26 per cent of all mitigation, was to label such criticism as reflecting a *personal opinion.* Interactionists such as Rosenblatt (1985) and Probst (1989) stress the importance of reader response as part of a communication dyad in a process of meaning-making, as it is the reader who completes the meaning potential of a text. We also noted in chapter 1, however, that this response can be influenced by reader-oriented strategies which address the *acceptability conditions* of an argument, with the writer adopting a rhetorical stance which attends to the affective expectations of readers. Writers can thus choose to associate themselves with the power relations inherent in judging another's work, or employ conventions which construct a more egalitarian identity. By foregrounding their commentary as a personal response, reviewers can make a subtle adjustment to the interactional context and set up a different relationship with their readers. This allows them to adopt a less threatening authorial voice, repositioning themselves and their authority by reacting as an ordinary reader rather than as an 'expert'.

Myers (1989) observes that specifying oneself as the source of a viewpoint can act to qualify its force by acknowledging that others may hold an alternative, and equally valid, view. While the review is necessarily, and obviously, a partisan genre, carrying the biases and predispositions of its writer, the personal expression of criticism reminds the reader of this, and acts to mitigate negative comment by placing it in this context. Personal attribution, then, conveys the limitation of the criticism, representing it as the writer's individual opinion rather than an objective characteristic of the volume:

(15) This section suffers, in my opinion, from the circularity of including ... (Bio)

I have to say that I think that it does not meet fully this very ambitious claim.
(ME)

I found this quite daunting and, if I am right about the intended audience, unnecessary. (EE)

For this reader the leap required was too great. (Soc)

Personally, I would have liked to see more attention paid to the ambiguities, ...
(AL)

To my mind, this position exhibits a curious instability, in that the first of its ...
(Phil)

Anyone involved in radiation health physics is aware of this debate and I would have liked other views better represented. (Phy)

Perhaps paradoxically, writers also sought to mitigate the effect of their criticisms by withholding rather than accepting personal responsibility. This fourth strategy therefore *attributes critical comment to an abstract reader or general audience.* Although much less common in the corpus than taking responsibility, this seems to be a familiar strategy in a variety of written academic and professional genres. The writer's move here is to make the criticism more diffuse by shifting its source elsewhere. This obscures the link between the reviewer and the FTA and allows the writer to insinuate membership of a community dedicated to particular standards of scholarship and a shared pursuit of knowledge:

(16) Not everyone will accept the aims of teacher education as formulated by Perraton.   (AL)

Readers might quibble with the order of these two chapters, because...   (Mkt)

... some readers may regret the absence of other advanced topics.   (EE)

His definition (p. 332) of the finite-element method is much broader than most would accept ...   (Phy)

... also leave the reader with some feelings of discomfort.   (Bio)

Thus the reviewer is able, simultaneously, to express the criticism, to encourage readers to accept it by assuming common ground with them, and to avoid the potential risk of personal responsibility.

The use of personal attribution was also frequently used to introduce praise, where it more firmly aligned the writer with his or her judgements. Instead of weakening the speech act, as with criticism, designating oneself as the source of praise served to mark certainty and so emphasise the force of an evaluation, enabling the reviewer to take greater personal responsibility for it:

(17) I was pleasantly surprised to find within each of these subsections that ... (Bio)

I was impressed by this book and would recommend it as an excellent introduction ...   (ME)

It is a pleasure to see a textbook for graduate students which is as comprehensive as Chuang's offering.   (EE)

I think I can promise that there is something here for each of you.   (Phy)

I believe this principle is highly illuminating for subsequent comparative studies.   (Phil)

This strategy leaves readers in no doubt about the writer's commitment to an idea, and so both strengthens the opinion offered and encourages its acceptance, restricting the negotiating space available to readers (Hyland, 1998c).

Because personal judgements are an integral feature of this genre, explicitly standing behind an expression of praise can be seen as a reinforcement of that praise. Unless stated otherwise, one assumes that the entire review will reflect the writer's opinion and so a personal attribution provides what is essentially superfluous information. This generates what Grice (1975) calls implicatures – that is, the reader presumes that the writer is adding this information for a reason; in this case to exaggerate the force of the speech act. This clear expression of unqualified assertion consequently makes personal attribution a somewhat risky strategy, exposing the writer to censure for extravagance and to criticism from those who hold other opinions. So, although personally marked praise did occur in these reviews, there were far fewer cases than personally marked criticism.

The decision of writers to soften criticism by rhetorically announcing their presence in the text was also evident in their use of a fifth mitigating strategy: that of *metadiscourse*. Metadiscourse refers to those aspects of the text which explicitly refer to the organisation of the discourse or the writer's stance towards its content or the reader (see Chapter 6). In these reviews, writers frequently chose to signal praise, and especially criticism, explicitly with metadiscourse. This has the effect of bracketing negative comment from what was, by implication, the general positive flow of the review. The introduction of another voice into the text via explicit discursive comment therefore also has the important effect of distancing the reviewer from the comment. This new voice, intruding into the interaction, is perhaps one with whom the reviewer may not entirely agree, or one with whom he or she may obliquely disagree.

Thus, because metadiscourse draws attention to the intentions and activities of the writer, it serves in these texts to refocus the reader on the act of evaluating, rather than the evaluation itself. As can be seen, the general effect is often to introduce criticisms almost as an aside:

(18) One or two drops of vinegar need to be added to the salad oil.   (AL)

     A few weaknesses can also be noted.   (AL)

     There were momentary disappointments.   (ME)

     From an engineer's point of view, the text has some disadvantages.   (ME)

     There are a few minor errors.   (Phy)

     It is as well to get the gripes out of the way first.   (Mkt)

     One small criticism would be that ...   (Mkt)

A final mitigation strategy in these reviews was to offer *limited praise* as a means of conveying criticisms indirectly. This weakens the negative force of the proposition by saying less than the writer means and leaves the reader to make the appropriate connections. Such strategies exploit Gricean implicatures (see Chapter 1), the inferences that readers make on the basis of what the writer says, together with their knowledge of similar texts and the institutional context of the discourse. The fragments below give some flavour of this, and while it is difficult to appreciate their actual import outside a fuller context, they all appeared in otherwise largely cool reviews and a large part of their force was due to their relative isolation in the discourse:

(19) There is a great number of photographs.   (ME)

     It is good value for money.   (Bio)

I would recommend this as an interesting book to borrow from the library shelf.
(EE)

Its title is therefore an accurate indication of its technical content.   (EE)

The physical appearance of the book is attractive.   (Phy)

The graphics in Singh's text are adequate.   (Phy)

I found the book reasonably well written.   (Phy)

This is in many respects a good book.   (Phil)

The criticisms here, then, are largely implied by the fact that the utterances seem to provide less (or less vital) information than might reasonably be anticipated. Following Grice, we generally attribute to writers an intention to communicate clearly information that will be useful and relevant to us. In the review genre this includes the writer setting the volume in a disciplinary context and addressing its most salient benefits and faults. Thus, employing our intertextual understandings and drawing on one part of Grice's Maxim of Quantity, we suppose that the writer will tell us as much as we need to know along these lines – that is, if the writer believes the book is worthy of substantive praise, then he or she would tell us so.

Thus we generally anticipate that published books will be *well written* and *attractive*, just as we hope they will be *well organised*, *accurate* and *well researched*, as these are essential ingredients of worthwhile academic texts, undeserving of comment. Consequently, such remarks approach what Johnson and Roen (1992: 50) refer to as pro forma compliments, 'those that writers use simply to avoid being only negative, to say something positive without providing an undeserved or insincere positive evaluation'. This sets up a contrast, however, with more deserved and sincere praise. When we encounter statements such as those above, we are led to reconstruct the intention behind the words to interpret their meaning. The criticisms are not directly stated; we infer them only from the contrast set up with our expectations.

Similarly, in the following examples the writer appears to be drawing on more specific community knowledge to comment negatively on the work:

(20) He begins with an introductory chapter of which an Oxford ordinary language philosopher would have been proud.   (Phil)

What he has to say fits neatly into the mainstream.   (Soc)

In this sense the work remains firmly in the criminological tradition, alongside the Home Office sponsored research.   (Soc)

The claim made here is that this is the first practical book, and indeed it does describe systems that really have been built and used, although how many have been seen outside a research laboratory is not clear.   (EE)

Mitigation, here, appears to be addressed less to the author than to the wider audience, invoking shared understandings to make a rather oblique criticism. The writer is not so much relying on rhetorical or world knowledge to convey criticism, but injecting evaluative ambiguities for the reader to identify and share – a strategy of collusion which simultaneously makes the criticism less explicit and identifies the writer as a member of a community who understands these kinds of things. Thus criticism is diffused with solidarity, assuming shared disciplinary knowledge which presumably also includes the author while marginalising the contribution of the book. Being an Oxford ordinary language philosopher, in the mainstream, or in the Home Office tradition are clearly the kinds of things best avoided if you wish your book to be favourably reviewed.

So, unlike research articles, outright criticism is not avoided in book reviews, indeed it is an integral feature of the genre, substantiating its claim to be a scholarly form of writing to be taken seriously by fellow academics as a knowledge-examining domain. Writers cannot avoid attributing the views they criticise to a particular author, nor can they skate over or ignore weak arguments or unsubstantiated claims, but they can address them with varying degrees of sensitivity to the threats that such criticisms contain. Thus, while casting aspersion on a writer's work exceeds the constraints on allowable criticism in research papers, reviews are rarely as destructive as they might be, and are often mitigated in various ways. Indeed, as can be seen in many of the above examples, the strategies I have identified are often used in combinations; hedges may occur in opposing pairs for example, or personal attributions with metadiscoursal framing. This repeated alliance of rhetorical features serves to produce a patterning which reinforces the effect of individual devices, presenting a concord which helps contribute to the overall interpersonal tenor of the genre.

In sum, the affective goals of these texts are as central to the genre as issues of substantive content. The strategies I have outlined appear to be as much of a generic feature as evaluation itself, helping to soften the threat of criticism to the author of the book and to establish the disciplinary ethos of the writer of the review.

CONCLUSIONS

Once again we can see here the social interactions that contribute to the construction of an academic genre. Reviews reveal not only how writers express ideational judgements of importance, value and correctness, but how they handle the complex interpersonal relationships that this expression necessitates. My analysis shows that writers are not responding to creative whim or individual purpose when they engage in this discourse. On the contrary, the regularities we have observed across these texts are strategies within which they shape their social purposes to the formal constraints of the genre and the preferred practices of their disciplines. Each review is an instance of an established but evolving genre which draws on participants' previous experience of that genre. These cumulative experiences guide writers and inform its expression and its schematic structure; they also reveal something of the insiders' perception of how best to negotiate with their peers.

In sum, while the review is a potentially threatening genre, for both the author of the text reviewed and the community more generally, it works because of the extent to which writer and reader approach the text with 'mutual co-awareness' of the other (Nystrand 1987: 48). Its meaning is the result of a collaborative orientation to certain norms of engagement, which are oriented to by the communities to which they belong. Reviewers and their reviews are shaped by the expectations and practices of their disciplines, and part of a reviewer's competence lies in the appropriate expression of criticism, attending to disciplinary practices which embody values of collegial respect and scholastic fairness. In these ways the book review not only draws on readers' familiarity with the research networks and disciplinary knowledge of the field, but also on an interpretive framework which includes an understanding of appropriate social interactions.

Once more, our attention is directed from the texts themselves to the communities in which they are written and to discourses as members' practices. It leads us to consider texts as interactions and to the ways writers inscribe and interpret these in specific academic genres. In the next chapter I turn to different kinds of interaction in academic writing, examining the ways that writers seek to persuade colleagues of their insider competence and their right to be heard in knowledge-making.

NOTE

1. The reviews were taken from the 1997 editions of 28 different journal titles and totalled just over 165,000 words. The corpus is listed in Appendix 1, section 1.2.

Chapter 4

Speaking as an insider: promotion and credibility in abstracts

This chapter examines a genre critical to disciplinary knowledge-making and therefore to the work of academics: that of research article abstracts. After the title, the abstract is generally the readers' first encounter with a text, and is often the point at which they decide whether to continue reading and give the accompanying article further attention, or to ignore it. The research and the writer are therefore under close scrutiny in abstracts and, because of this, writers have carefully, and increasingly, tended to foreground their main claims and present themselves as competent community members. To gain readers' attention and persuade them to read on, writers need to demonstrate that they not only have something new and worthwhile to say, but that they also have the professional credibility to address their topic as an insider.

As I have argued, this kind of persuasion is not simply accomplished with words, but with words that demonstrate legitimacy. This means that abstracts, like articles, letters, reviews and other genres, must recognise and replicate the field's organisational structures, beliefs and authorised institutional practices; they must appeal to readers from within the boundaries of a disciplinary discourse. Abstracts are worthy of study because they are significant carriers of a discipline's epistemological and social assumptions, and therefore a rich source of interactional features that allow us to see how individuals work to position themselves within their communities.

This involves a certain 'marketisation' – a promotion of oneself and one's paper through discursive means which might be considered analogous to the promotion of goods (e.g. Fairclough, 1995). There is a considerable degree of interdiscursivity present in abstracts as writers seek to package their articles in a manner that highlights their relevance and credibility, thereby borrowing from the discursive practices of a more central, promotional culture. Such a borrowing, of course, is not simply a means of presenting ideational material; it also projects a specific professional identity and a way of conducting social relations with colleagues.

This chapter examines the generic patterns and certain formal qualities of over 800 article abstracts to determine how writers use this genre to typically situate themselves and their work in their disciplines, how they display credibility and 'membership'. Once again I shall be searching for similarities and differences between a number of academic fields, and shall, in addition, briefly consider a few of the changes that have occurred in abstracts since 1980.

ABOUT ABSTRACTS

Abstracts have been considered in the literature as an independent discourse, but one which functions as a 'representation' (Bazerman, 1984: 58), a 'distillation' (Swales, 1990: 179), a 'crystallisation' (Salager-Mayer, 1990: 367) or a 'summary' (Kaplan et al., 1994: 405) of an associated text. Often the purpose of an abstract is regarded as 'a description or factual summary of the much longer report, and is meant to give the reader an exact and concise knowledge of the full article' (Bhatia, 1993: 78). This emphasis on the summarising function of abstracts is common (e.g. Graetz, 1985; Ventola, 1997). It is clear in the work of Salager-Mayer (1990), for example, who argues that abstracts should reproduce the structuring of the full paper, reflecting the moves which 'are fundamental and obligatory in the process of scientific inquiry and patterns of thought' (ibid.: 370). Similarly, Kaplan et al. regard the 'jargon, acronyms, repetitions, adjectival modifications, subordinate clauses, and nominalizations' (1994: 422) that they find in a large sample of conference abstracts as 'counter-intuitive' deviations from the need to provide a brief synopsis of the full text.

While the abstract might point towards an associated text, and may indeed offer a representation of it, its purpose, rhetorical construction and persuasive intent are all distinct from the article itself. The research article is, in essence, a codification of disciplinary knowledge, where writers seek to persuade their communities to accept their claims and certify them as recognised and legitimate knowledge. Abstracts, on the other hand, have both a more modest and more urgent purpose: to persuade readers that the article is worth reading. It is therefore a selective representation rather than an attempt to give the reader exact knowledge of an article's content. It does more than simply provide the 'gist of the article in a precise and maximally efficient way' (Ventola, 1997: 333). The abstract selectively sets out the stall, highlighting important information and framing the article that it precedes, but it does so in such a way as to encourage further examination and draw the reader into the more detailed exposition.

The importance of abstracts in influencing the readers' decisions about whether the accompanying article is worth reading has been demonstrated in a number of studies. Academics are overburdened with a growing amount of scholarly papers which make impossible demands on their ability to digest and synthesise what is relevant and worth attention. The time needed to scan and process this massive research output means that to keep up with the hyper-production of knowledge in their fields they increasingly. rely on scanning-reading strategies (Lock, 1988). These strategies are guided by personal schemata dominated by a search for novelty and relevance to their own active research programmes and they rely heavily on information contained in abstracts (Bazerman, 1988: 240; Berkenkotter and Huckin, 1995: 30). After searching the table of contents of a journal for keywords, academics typically read the title and abstract to decide whether to go further. This, then, is the point at which a piece of research may stand or fall – at which the reader must be 'hooked'.

To describe precisely how writers accomplish this, there have been a number of attempts to identify the features that distinguish abstracts as a recognisable genre. Graetz (1985: 125), for example, argues that:

> The abstract is characterized by the use of past tense, third person, passive, and the non-use of negatives. It avoids subordinate clauses, uses phrases instead of clauses, words instead of phrases. It avoids abbreviation, jargon, symbols and other language shortcuts which might lead to confusion. (...) In short it eliminates the redundancy which the skilled reader counts on finding in written language and which usually facilitates comprehension.

Swales (1990: 180) considers this assertion 'a little bold' and Kaplan et al. (1994) discovered considerable variation of tense and voice choices, a fair number of abbreviations and acronyms, and a heavy use of subordinate clauses in their conference abstracts. It is, in fact, easy enough to find counter-examples, and while abstracts are characterised by compaction, propositional density, and syntactic complexity, the requirement for brevity is clearly tempered by rhetorical considerations.

Salager-Mayer (1992), for instance, shows that while the past is the most frequently used tense in medical abstracts, the present is commonly employed to emphasize the generalisability of specific findings, and the present perfect to show disagreement with prior research. Similarly, Rounds (1982) found lexical choices to reflect writers' rhetorical concerns by revealing the extent of hedging and propositional mitigation in abstracts, toning down claims to avoid potential audience rejection. This persuasive element is also suggested in the cognitive structuring of abstracts which seems to respond to a potential interrogation of the article itself. A number of writers, for example, point to an introduction – method – results – discussion pattern reflecting in 'microstructure' the stages of the entire text (e.g. Graetz, 1985; Kaplan et al., 1994; Salager-Mayer, 1990, 1992; Samraj, 1998; Ventola, 1997).

My purpose in this chapter is not to suggest a definitive description of the move (i.e. generic stages) structure or features of this genre, but to offer an account of abstract writing that reflects its central place in the ways that writers interactionally negotiate the significance of their research. Therefore, I shall detail some of the linguistic and rhetorical practices by which academics demonstrate their professional credibility and the value of their work to the discipline – the practices, in other words, accepted by their communities as legitimate displays of membership.

TEXTS, INFORMANTS AND METHODS

Once again, the discussion is based on both textual and interview data, although here I offer a largely qualitative and interpretive analysis. The written corpus comprised 800 abstracts from the 1997 issues of ten journals in each of eight disciplines[1] comprising 127, 000 words. The interview data were collected from the same expert informants I discussed in the Preface. My method was to carry out a move analysis of the abstracts and to search for features which might be used to advance the writer's purpose by strengthening the value of claims or by denoting disciplinary membership (what Berkenkotter and Huckin call 'insider status'). I then discussed these with the subject specialists.

I discuss my approach to texts in detail in Chapter 7, but because my analysis of these texts involved longer stretches of discourse than concordancing typically allows, it may be worth setting out the procedure more fully here. First, I went through the entire corpus examining each abstract several times to get a feel for the overall organisation of the abstracts and to identify recurring rhetorical patterns. The literature on abstract moves discussed above was useful in establishing a classificatory framework. I then marked the moves with coloured highlighter pens, an effective if rather labour-intensive and low-tech method. To check for inter-rater reliability, the specialist informants were also asked to categorise move functions in several of the abstracts from their disciplines, and a colleague independently carried out an analysis of 10 per cent of the abstracts randomly taken from the corpus. A cross-check with my categorisations showed an agreement in 84 per cent of cases.

I then used text analysis software to locate 'membershipping' features. Brenton's (1996) study of abstracts submitted to the Conference on College Composition and Communication was helpful in compiling a list of features that can discursively signal community status. He identified a range of traits such as jargon, acronyms, often repeated words or expressions, and occasional citation practices which contributed to the success of accepted papers by reflecting and shaping a valued disciplinary ethos. I therefore scanned the texts for these features to determine the methods by which writers demonstrated their right to have their work taken seriously by readers. I also searched for phrases and lexical items that could be used to offer persuasive weight to the texts, particularly those which advocated claims by asserting their value or novelty. I then contrasted their frequencies between disciplines and compared them with a smaller corpus of 240 abstracts from the same disciplines published in 1980. Finally, I discussed the findings with the consultants and interviewed them about their own abstract reading and writing practices.

A MOVE-STRUCTURE CLASSIFICATION OF ABSTRACTS

I first divided the abstracts into a series of communicative categories, or moves, representing the realisation of a specific overall communicative purpose (Swales, 1990, offers a detailed discussion). As I noted above, previous analyses of abstracts have identified a rhetorical macrostructure broadly corresponding to the organisation of the paper itself: Introduction–Methods–Results–Conclusion (e.g. Bhatia, 1993; Brenton, 1996). These four elements are occasionally mentioned in editorial guidelines and provide an explicit intertextual link to the accompanying article. While fitting this schema of positivist inquiry onto humanities abstracts is not without difficulties, it offers a fairly robust, if rather general, classification for cross-disciplinary comparison if we admit a certain flexibility. I have also distinguished the writer's purpose from the introduction, where it is often located, as it seems to perform a very different role to the introduction's typical purpose of providing a justificatory context for the research. The schema is outlined in Table 4.1.

Table 4.1 A classification of rhetorical moves in article abstracts

Move	Function
Introduction	Establishes context of the paper and motivates the research or discussion.
Purpose	Indicates purpose, thesis or hypothesis, outlines the intention behind the paper.
Method	Provides information on design, procedures, assumptions, approach, data, etc.
Product	States main findings or results, the argument, or what was accomplished.
Conclusion	Interprets or extends results beyond scope of paper, draws inferences, points to applications or wider implications.

This arrangement of generic stages or moves can be seen in the following abstract from *Plant Molecular Biology* (the symbol // marks move boundaries):

(1) Acetaldehyde is one of the intermediate products of ethanolic fermentation, which can be reduced to ethanol by alcohol dehydrogenase (ADH). Alternatively, acetaldehyde can be oxidized to acetate by aldehyde dehydrogenase (ALDH) and subsequently converted to acetyl–CoA by acetyl–CoA synthetase (ACS). // To study the expression of ALDHs in plants we isolated and characterized a cDNA coding for a putative mitochondrial ALDH (TobAldh2A) in Nicotiana tabacum. // TobALDH2A shows 54–60 per cent identity at the amino acid level with other ALDHs and shows 76 per cent identity with maize Rf2, a gene involved in restoration of male fertility in cms-T maize. TobALDH2A transcripts and protein were present at high levels in the male and female reproductive tissues. Expression in vegetative tissues was much lower and no induction by anaerobic incubation was observed. //This suggests

that TobALDH expression is not part of the anaerobic response, but may have another function. The use of specific inhibitors of ALDH and the pyruvate dehydrogenase (PDH) complex indicates that ALDH activity is important for pollen tube growth, and thus may have a function in biosynthesis or energy production.//   (Bio)

A brief introduction sets the scene for the reader, providing essential background to the paper and, equally importantly, indicating the significance of the topic to the community and the writer's grasp of the issues involved. A purpose statement is then given, introduced by the infinitive 'to study' and embedded in a general description of the method. The writer then presents the product of the research, in this case the results of an experimental study together with a bottom-line generalisation based on these findings, suggesting an outcome that readers may find surprising. The conclusion explicitly announces the wider significance of the research to the discipline and implicitly suggests a line of further research.

However, while the formal characteristics of this abstract correspond to descriptions often proposed in the literature, this model is actually quite rare in my corpus, even in the science sample. In fact less than 5 per cent of the papers contained all five steps in this sequence. Roughly half of the papers contained no method section, about 55 per cent omitted an explicit introduction, and only 22 per cent offered a conclusion. Thus, despite the admonishments of some researchers (e.g. Salager-Mayer, 1990), writers obviously chose to represent their work in ways that fail to conform to a universal 'ideal' of information structuring. Clearly, then, more than summarising is taking place.

MOVE-STRUCTURE AND RHETORICAL PERSUASION

The most striking feature of the data is that virtually all papers included a Product statement (94 per cent) which foregrounded the main argument or findings. This underlines the assertion by Berkenkotter and Huckin (1995: 34) that the abstract is essentially a promotional genre. Writers are anxious to underline their most central claims as a means of gaining reader interest and acceptance; a point clearly made by a number of my informants:

> *Without results you can't do justice to the paper. They are the key to the study and they need to be there so that people know what to expect. What they can get out of the paper, whether it will be useful to them or not.*   (Bio interview)

> *It is essential. If I didn't say anything else I would put my main claims in the abstract. I think readers expect it and I always look for them when I'm reading.*   (Soc interview)

> *The main points, what we've found and what we think it means. These are the most important things to go into the abstract. A summary of what the paper is really about.*
>   (ME interview)

The most frequent move structures in the corpus were the sequences Purpose–Method–Product (P–M–Pr), accounting for about 25 per cent of all cases, and Introduction–Purpose–Product (I–P–Pr), comprising around 15 per cent of the sample. These patterns are illustrated below as (2) and (3) respectively:

(2)   This paper is intended to evaluate the linearity that can be provided by general-purpose MESFET's. // By a simple physics-based analysis and a practical amplifier design, // it will be shown how educated device and bias-point selection can approximate intermodulation distortion (IMD) performance of some normal channel-doping profiles, for which previous theories would not be able to predict good IMD performance, to the one expected from MESFET devices with specially tailored doping profiles.   (EE)

(3)   The process of modernization in China is speedy and turbulent, requiring an effective solution to various social problems. The situation of handicapped people in China poses an increasingly serious social problem but publications on this subject are rare. // This article outlines the author's proposals for how to remedy the problem, // giving an initial outline and an analysis of the current state of handicapped people in China.   (Soc)

In (2) a clear Purpose is offered in the first sentence, followed by a sketch of the Method to be used, 'a simple physics-based analysis and a practical amplifier design'. A Product statement follows, presenting the principle findings of the study, introduced by verb *show*, together with a promotion of these results, favourably comparing them with previous approaches. The sociology text (3), on the other hand, contains a relatively lengthy Introduction and no Method statement. The Introduction provides readers with a context for the study and persuades them of a significant problem to be addressed, in fact two problems, a social issue, 'the situation of handicapped people in China', and a disciplinary issue, an important gap in the literature. The writer indicates that his Purpose is to 'remedy the problem', and finally states the Product. Essentially a product is an outcome, or what the paper achieves. In the soft disciplines this is often an argument, where writers discuss or address a topic rather than report research findings. In (3) the writer represents the Product as a discussion which will analyse the situation of the handicapped in China.

While P–M–Pr and I–P–Pr were the dominant sequences using these four moves – the most 'prototypical' in the Swalesian sense – there was some generic variation, principally with Purpose following Method in the first pattern and preceding the Introduction in the second. Some longer abstracts, mainly in the sciences, also recycled moves throughout the abstract, often in order to highlight a series of results by presenting them as outcomes of different purposes or methods. There were also a high number of two-move abstracts, most often where writers presented their purpose and product only, presupposing the background to be recoverable by an informed audience. The choice of presentation verb often distinguished the two moves, items such as *discuss, describe, explore* and *address* marking intentions, and *show, demonstrate, find* and *establish* signalling results.

I do not intend painstakingly to itemise the possible diversity of abstracts here; I am less interested in offering a detailed classification of these data than in using them to see how academics socially negotiate their purposes in different institutional contexts – how the moves become 'strategic elements in a rhetorical game' (Mauranen, 1993: 251). It is clear, however, that writers are acutely aware of the linguistic resources that the functional structures of abstracts offer them and exploit these possibilities rhetorically in many ways. This shows, to say the least, that move sequences appear to be less predictable than previously supposed, and that consequently current descriptions of move sequences may be overly restrictive.

DISCIPLINARY DIFFERENCES IN ABSTRACT STRUCTURES

More importantly, the analysis points to considerable disciplinary variations in move structuring in the corpus, which once again suggests that credibility, significance and persuasion are community-specific matters.

Table 4 shows a general preference for the P–M–Pr pattern among the physicists and engineers (60 per cent of all cases), and the I–P–Pr model among the humanities/social science writers (75 per cent of cases). Biologists once again fell between the two groups. These differences indicate that writers in the soft knowledge domains saw a greater need to situate their discourse with an Introduction, while writers in the hard knowledge fields tended to omit this move in favour of a description of the Method. So, while over 60 per cent of abstracts in the soft disciplines contained Introductions, this figure was only 30 per cent for the hard disciplines. The percentages were almost exactly reversed for Methods.

Table 4.2 Most frequent move sequences in abstracts by discipline (% rounded)

Discipline	I-P-M-Pr	[C]	P-M-Pr	[C]	I-P-Pr	[C]	P-Pr	[C]	I-Pr	Others
Phil	1	[0]	3	[1]	27	[8]	14	[1]	37	8
Soc	15	[4]	22	[5]	26	[9]	9	[3]	0	7
AL	14	[4]	19	[7]	20	[3]	16	[3]	4	10
Mkt	15	[6]	17	[4]	20	[8]	9	[1]	0	20
EE	7	[0]	37	[7]	9	[4]	17	[6]	3	10
ME	13	[3]	38	[7]	10	[0]	11	[3]	3	12
Phy	8	[1]	39	[6]	4	[1]	18	[4]	1	18
Bio	10	[11]	20	[7]	9	[7]	8	[9]	5	14
Overall (%)	10	[4]	25	[5]	15	[5]	13	[4]	7	11

These preferences are clearly related to the disciplinary variations discussed in Chapter 2. There I noted that an important dimension of disciplinary knowledge-making is the extent to which fields agree on a common set of outstanding problems and appropriate procedures for pursuing them. Toulmin (1972) suggests that communities can be approximately arranged on a continuum from 'compact' to 'diffuse' in the ways that they identify and study problems. The former are more closely associated with the sciences which form close-knit 'urban' (Becher, 1989) fields where a small, discrete number of problems have relatively large numbers of people working on them. Researchable problems are therefore fairly well defined and there is a general expectation that readers will be familiar with the issues in which any piece of research is embedded. As my informants pointed out:

> *There are certain things one expects one's readers to know. It would be insulting to spell everything out to them.* (ME interview)

> *I want to use my 150 or 200 words to tell them what I've done and how I've done it, not why. Most people who read my work will know the why. They will probably be working in the same area and have the background anyway.* (EE interview)

> *This abstract concerns quite a specialised line of research. The number of labs capable of making the kind of investment needed to do this is probably very small and they are probably mainly writing for each other. You couldn't hope to get everyone else up to speed in a three line introduction, there's just too much background.* (Phy interview)

Writers in the hard sciences are therefore often able to draw on a reservoir of understandings, presupposing much of the background required to contextualise their studies. They can anticipate that readers will be able to access these understandings to determine the value of the research, the productivity of the procedures, the theoretical rationale of the study, and its significance to the incremental development of knowledge. So, by opening the abstract with a Purpose move, or occasionally a Method statement, a writer can explicitly signal these assumptions, pointing not only to the shared knowledge required to unpack the text, but also to shared membership of a community. These examples show how this is often achieved:

(4) A Co–Cr–Ta/Ni–Fe double-layer tape was fabricated on 10 gm-thick polyimide film by facing targets sputtering. The Co–Cr–Ta/Ni–Fe double-layer tape showed higher read/write performance than the Co–Cr–Ta single-layer tape in not only the short but also the long wavelength region. (Phy)

Here, we report the localization and characterization of BHKp23, a member of the p24 family of transmembrane proteins, in mammalian cells. (Bio)

The objective of this work is to search the optimal shapes and locations of ribs in order to increase the stiffness of structures using the topology optimization technique. (ME)

The soft disciplines, on the other hand, are characterised by the relative absence of well-defined sets of problems and a definite direction in which to follow them. Community members participate in less clearly identifiable areas of study and proceed along less heavily trodden paths of research. As a result, writers have to work much harder to acquaint readers with the background to their research and to construct its significance rhetorically. The presence of sometimes lengthy introductions in these abstracts therefore demonstrates attempts both to accommodate and engage explicitly with readers. In Swales's (1990: 140) terms, they have to 'Create a Research Space' for the work.

> *I tend to spend a lot of time providing the background, making sure people understand the context I'm working in, the questions I'm addressing. You have to position yourself in an identifiable area and then talk up the issue.*   (Soc interview)

> *There are just so many live topics in my field. No-one can keep abreast of them all so it's necessary to establish, or at least reestablish anyway, the importance of the subject.*
(Mkt interview)

So, because research in the humanities and social sciences tends to be more diverse and have more permeable boundaries, statements which functioned to provide a general context were more common:

(5)   Despite widespread confusion over its meaning, the notion of a conceptual scheme is pervasive in Anglo-American philosophy, particularly amongst those who call themselves 'conceptual relativists'.   (Phil)

The decline in traditional nuclear family households, and the marked increase in the proportion of people living alone, or alone with dependent children have led some to claim that individualism has replaced the importance of family life.
(Soc)

Relative to younger adults, older adults appear to exhibit greater use of schema-based, as opposed to detailed, processing strategies.   (Mkt)

Disciplinary peers look for a reason to read the paper, and generally expect to find it in an explicit Introduction to justify the time the reader will have to devote to understanding it.

This greater contextualisation also reflects another obvious difference here: that the purposes of the papers themselves are often quite different. While the science and engineering articles reported the fact of acts of research and their outcomes, writers in the softer fields frequently sought to discuss or define an issue rather than establish empirical truths (cf. Myers, 1992b). Consequently, Purpose statements were more likely to introduce the reader to the area to be covered, and perhaps the interpretation that would be made, rather than signal an explicit research claim.

(6)   In this article we (a) argue that mainstream composition studies is at present too narrow in its scope and limited in its perspective and (b) offer some thoughts, from our unique interdisciplinary position, that we feel could help mainstream composition professionals improve this situation.   (AL)

This paper is a critical engagement with some of the writings of Judith Butler who is perhaps best known for popularising the idea of gender as performative.
(Soc)

In this article we review recent economic, demographic and cultural trends in Spain and discuss changes in consumer buying behaviour and in the macromarketing environment.   (Mkt)

Biology, as I noted earlier, was once again an exception to these broad patterns, departing from the hard science conventions by containing fewer P–M–Pr and P–Pr sequences and far more concluding moves. As I discussed in Chapter 2, molecular biology is in many senses a more interpretive and inferential discipline than many of its scientific cousins, allowing considerably more discursive scope to writers. Francis Crick (1990: 5), with typical incisiveness, has drawn this comparison very clearly:

> It is the resulting complexity that makes biological organisms so hard to unscramble. Biology is thus very different from physics. The basic laws of physics can usually be expressed in exact mathematical form, and they are probably the same throughout the universe. The 'laws' of biology, by contrast, are often only broad generalizations, since they describe rather elaborate chemical mechanisms that natural selection has evolved over billions of years.

Data and evolutionary premises can only suggest possible lines of research and interpretations, and these may not always be reliable guides. This means that arguments in biology are often more geared to devising, testing and persuading one's colleagues of the veracity of speculations and theories. The rhetorical practices that lead from these approaches to research therefore often resemble those more typical of disciplines at the softer end of the knowledge spectrum.

Accommodating one's work to fellow community members, however, not only means taking into account the knowledge they are likely to have of the topic, but also involves providing information that they anticipate will be given. In the science and engineering disciplines in particular, there was a fairly strong expectation that the abstract would indicate how the study was conducted. Method was therefore the most frequently occurring section after the Product and Purpose moves and sometimes dominated the hard knowledge abstracts. In cases where what was done was seen as more important than what was found, it replaced the Product move altogether. But more often, Method was handled briefly and occasionally merged with the Purpose move:

(7)   The effects of milling a–Fe2O3 in a range of NaCl solutions (0.1M, 0.5M, 1.0M and 2.0M) as investigated by x-ray diffraction and Mossbauer effect spectroscopy are reported.   (Phy)

This paper discusses the design and implementation of a novel two-element active transmit–receive array using dual linear polarization and sequential rotation.   (EE)

To determine if low diversity was caused by a lack of polymorphism at vegetative incompatibility (vic) loci, we made crosses between isolates in the three common vc types and estimated the number of vic genes segregating.   (Bio)

Using survey responses ($n = 401$) of a sample of households in one market area in Austria, we test hypotheses grounded in accessibility theory: a concept or object may be 'available' from memory but may be 'accessible' only under certain conditions.   (Mkt)

This merging of Purpose and Method moves into a single sentence appears to be a rational response to the space constraints of the abstract, but it also performs a useful rhetorical function. Presenting them together in this way, the writer can insinuate the appropriacy of the technique by strategically linking the approach in a unproblematic and reasonable way to accomplishing the research objective.

Method sections were also evident in the more empirical social science studies, and particularly in the marketing abstracts (61 per cent). Such studies are predominantly focused on relatively tangible, real-world phenomena and often seek to yield measurable results with material advantages for government bodies or the commercial sector. Method moves were, of course, rare in the philosophy abstracts, where procedures generally involve the elaboration of concepts and argument through analogy, detailed exemplification, hypothetical cases, peer engagement and so on rather than modes of inquiry that can be objectively characterised and labelled:

> *What I try and do is say something about the issue, put it into the reader's immediate consciousness so they have something to hang the argument on, then I set out my main points. Give something of the flavour of the way I'm thinking and where the argument will lead.*
>
> (Phil interview)

Setting the scene for readers is then a far more significant rhetorical act in philosophy and Introductions occurred in about 80 per cent of papers, often with only a Product move or as part of a three-part I–P–Pr sequence.

Finally, Conclusions seemed to be an optional extra in all disciplines, appearing in only 21 per cent of the abstracts, principally in biology and marketing. This move typically takes the reader from the text into the world by commenting on the implications of the research or its applications. Conclusions therefore explicitly emphasise the value of the paper, either to the discipline or to the wider community:

(8)   Implications for marketing management are drawn by proposing controversial developments to be considered.   (Mkt)

These results reinforce the utility of combining genetic and biochemical analyses to studies of biosynthetic pathways and strengthen the argument that brassinosteroids play an essential role in Arabidopsis development.   (Bio)

I conclude with the hope that the issue will help address the current fragmentation in the literature on the relationship between language and identity and encourage further debate and research on a thought-provoking and important topic.   (AL)

The IQ literature needs to be reconceptualized.   (AL)

Such simulated inductors have important applications in microwave active filters.   (EE)

To some extent a writer's choice of moves is constrained by the editorial directives set out in the journal's submission guidelines, but these are generally very vague and give little guidance on creating a discursive context beyond the need to be 'informative', 'succinct' and to 'summarise the main points'. Only a handful of journals stipulate what is to be included and most, as these examples illustrate, specify little more than a maximum length:

> Include a brief abstract (not more than 100 words) summarising the findings.
>
> (American Journal of Sociology)

The abstract may not exceed 200 words.   (Journal of Cell Biology)

Next should appear an abstract of not more than 80 words, in the same language as the paper.   (Mechanical and Machine Theory)

Each article should include an abstract of between 150–200 words which succinctly presents the content of the article.   (System)

More centrally, these decisions are based on a kind of virtual dialogue between the individual practitioner and his or her community of peers, a decision to use the same agreed upon discipline-specific standards and practices of method choice, reasoning and argument that have evolved within a research tradition The variety of patterns within each discipline suggest that how writers use such practices is not *determined* by editorial prescription or genre constraints. Rather, it represents a choice of how best to convince others of their work, given the particular circumstances of their research, their individual goals and considerations of discipline membership.

CLAIMING SIGNIFICANCE IN ABSTRACTS

We have seen that writers construct their abstracts using the functional moves which best position both their research and themselves. However, in addition to framing their research with an appropriate rhetorical structure, they also claimed significance and disciplinary competence by employing a variety of discursive markings.

One way that writers claimed significance was by opening their abstracts with a promotional statement. Although the science and engineering abstracts rarely included an Introduction, when this move did occur it was often less with the purpose of naively establishing a territory to be covered, than of strengthening the importance of the topic. Writers frequently invested their Introductions with persuasive intent, offering the research as a valuable contribution to pressing real-world issues:

(9)   Solid state diffusion is of great theoretical and practical importance. The tracer-technique can be applied to help solve many theoretical and practical problems.
                    (Phy)

In many applications electronic sensors are used to improve performance and reliability of measurement systems. Such sensors should provide a correct transfer from the physical signal to be measured to the electronic output signal. One important step to achieve this, is to calibrate each sensor by applying different reference input signals and adjusting the sensor transfer accordingly.   (EE)

Vibration analysis of rotating machinery can give an indication of possible faults, thus allowing maintenance before further damage occurs. Automating this analysis allows machinery to be run unattended for longer periods of time.
                    (ME)

Thus, while we might expect competent practitioners to be aware of these points, and therefore their potential appeal to be greater the less specialised

the domain, their inclusion in the Introduction serves to reinforce the significance of the topic in the minds of readers.

Similarly, while Introductions in the humanities/social science texts often
served to fill-in potential gaps in readers' topic awareness, they more frequently claimed topic centrality (Swales, 1990: 141). The principal means of
establishing importance was to identify a problem convincingly enough to
encourage further reading into the article to learn more, about either the
problem itself or its 'solution'. My sociologist informant emphasised the
importance of this:

> *I always try and problematise the topic of my research, to create an issue that is worth studying*
> *and worth reading. You have to carve an issue out of any number of areas and a framing it*
> *as a problem makes it more important as a piece of research.*   (Soc interview)

Unlike the science and engineering abstracts which principally addressed
real-world issues, these problems often sought to establish a disciplinary relevance and dealt with problems internal to the research community itself:

(10)   An important problem in inductive probability theory is the design of exchange-
       able analogical methods, i.e., of exchangeable inductive methods that take into
       account certain considerations of analogy by similarity for predictive inferences.
                                                                            (Phil)

       The problem of separating the effects of household heterogeneity from state
       dependence in brand choice models is important from a theoretical as well as a
       managerial perspective.   (Mkt)

       Two central unresolved problems in labour process theory are the disjuncture
       between structure and agency and the problem of what constitutes 'good' work.
                                                                            (Soc)

Because this strategy also has important membershipping consequences,
allowing writers to stake a position as credible researchers, I shall return to it
in more detail in the next section.

Turning to particular rhetorical strategies, we find that writers used a variety of devices to emphasise the value of their papers. A key-word-in-context
(KWIC) search on some 50 commonly occurring 'promotional' items in the
corpus revealed some interesting disciplinary patterns in the ways writers presented their research. The most frequent rhetorical appeals, in order of
occurrence, were to what can be glossed as 'benefit', 'novelty', 'importance'
and 'interest'. The hard knowledge abstracts principally employed appeals to
novelty and benefit, comprising over 75 per cent of all cases in each of these
categories, while writers in marketing, applied linguistics and sociology
largely drew on the notion of importance to promote their work (60 per cent
of all cases). Statements overtly claiming the interest value of the research
were surprisingly rare in all fields.

Engineers employed the most appeals of all disciplines, with both mechanical and electronic engineering abstracts containing about twice as many as
any other discipline and almost five times as many as philosophy. These two
fields underlined their practical, applied orientation by emphasising the util-

ity of the reported research, mainly to the industrial world which relies on it. This was also the major strategy employed in the marketing abstracts, another field closely associated with non-academic interests, but the engineering papers contained over 55 per cent of all cases:

(11)   The new model gives significantly improved predictions for both liquid holdup and pressure drop during gas–liquid, stratified-wavy flow in horizontal pipelines.
                                                                                              (ME)

Further economical analysis indicated that the concept could effectively help in reducing the electric energy consumption and improving the energy demand pattern.   (ME)

We report on the linear and enhanced transconductance by Multi-step doped channel camel-gate field-effect transistors (CAMFETS) as compared with conventional CAMFETS.   (EE)

This paper answers these questions by developing an integer nonlinear programming model and solving it using a very efficient dynamic programming approach.   (EE)

The two science fields, on the other hand, tended to stress the novelty of their research as a means of claiming significance. For these fields constant innovation and progress is a central part of their disciplinary cultures and reasons for being. Practitioners expect advancement and scientific readers tend to look mainly for new results in order to further develop their own research (Bazerman, 1988: ch. 8). Consequently, the need to stress novelty was paramount, although this was sometimes also combined with a statement of its value:

(12)   Four new species, *X. elegans* sp. nov., *X. giganteus* sp. nov., *X. punctatus* sp. nov. and *X. pusillus* sp. nov. are described from wood submerged in freshwater collected in various countries.   (Bio)

The assays presented herein illustrate two novel approaches to monitor the intracellular dynamics of nuclear proteins.   (Bio)

A new design for a minimum inductance, distributed current, longitudinal (z) gradient coil, fabricated on the surface of an elliptic cylinder is proposed. (Phy)

A novel method for the measurement of self-diffusion coefficients employing oscillating gradients is presented. The method used has advantages over conventional techniques and will allow measurements to be made at very short diffusion times (< 1 ms) and should prove particularly useful for short T2 materials.   (Phy)

Finally, the Conclusion was also widely used to advance claims for significance and it is perhaps surprising that this move is not used more often. The reasons why writers chose not to make greater use of the promotional opportunities offered by a Concluding move are no doubt complex, but one reason may be that writers consider brute promotion alone too crude a strategy to carry a sophisticated audience into the article itself. As two informants remarked:

I'm not sure if it's counter-productive to bang people over the head with what you are doing. If they are working in my area they will be able to judge whether what I'm doing is important or not. (Phy interview)

Its important to give a clear picture of how you approached the problem by explaining the method in some detail. They can then decide if you are on track or not. (ME interview)

Readers make judgements about whether to read further based on their knowledge of the topic and how it is being handled, and part of this involves making an evaluation of the writer. A researcher who appears to demonstrate sufficient background knowledge in other parts of the abstract may therefore be regarded as someone able to offer a contribution to the problem at hand. By omitting a conclusion, then, a writer might signal by its absence that the significance or value of the research can be recovered by intelligent readers – the presupposition of shared knowledge emphasising their joint membership of a single community.

CLAIMING INSIDER CREDIBILITY

Clearly readers consider more than the strength of an abstract's promotional appeal when deciding whether to read an article, and an important consideration is the writer's apparent ability to deliver on the topic. Readers make judgements about the credibility of the writer as an informed colleague, a bona fide member of the discourse community who is able to speak with authority on the subject. It might be observed in passing that academic genres are no different from other domains in this respect, the voice of sanctioned authority is a familiar figure of our age, from the expert witness in courtrooms to the trustworthy specialist in detergent commercials. There are numerous ways in which writers are able to project an insider ethos and thus signal their right to be heard as competent members of the field. In this section I shall point to the ways such intimations of insider status create an effective persuasive context.

The first concerns the role of topic choice. Bruner (1994) observes that topics are resources of joint attention which co-ordinate activities and mark co-participation in communities of practice. The selection of a particular area, method or approach can therefore be critical, not only in securing colleagues' interest, but also in displaying one's credentials as a group member. This is especially the case in the soft knowledge disciplines where theories often fail to provide a coherent programme to guide research (Chalmers, 1978). Lines of inquiry are less linear and topic selection apparently less constrained by clear disciplinary problems. This helps to explain why identifying a credible problem was the main way that writers in the soft disciplines justified their work to readers, with over four times as many 'soft field' abstracts making use of this strategy.

The ability to identify a discipline-relevant issue is thus not only a means of motivating readers but a clear indication of disciplinary competence. It implies a familiarity with the discipline's literature and awareness of the topics which it currently considers urgent, interesting, or worth addressing. It is, in other words, an element of the rhetorical promotion of oneself and one's paper which draws on an order of discourse from another, more entrepreneurial domain of interaction (e.g. Fairclough, 1995).

Representing the topic as important to the community was thus occasionally achieved, particularly by philosophers, sociologists and applied linguists, by indicating that it had formed the subject of earlier work. However, while persuasion is frequently accomplished by linking past and present research in the RA itself, formal, dated citations were rare in the abstracts. Less than 10 per cent of the hard discipline abstracts contained references to other writers, and only applied linguists cited work with dates to any degree. A more common, and perhaps more effective strategy if one is concerned to display one's disciplinary savvy and insider knowledge, simply for writers to drop names or summarise current knowledge in a few lines, thus hinting at even greater depths of understanding:

(13) Frege and many following him, such as Dummett, Geach, Stenius and Hare, have envisaged a role for illocutionary force indicators in a logically perspicuous notation.   (Phil)

The literature includes many studies on consumer attitudes toward marketing and/or business practices, and consumerism.   (Mkt)

It is widely acknowledged in the literature that reports on beliefs of the type ...
                                                                               (AL)

Recent work on social movements has drawn attention to the interactions of movements and power-holding elites.   (Soc)

To move one step further in claiming significance and in demonstrating one's community membership is to indicate a gap in this literature (Swales, 1990). Here writers represent a problem as something which is unknown or unresolved by the community. The following cases, for example, do not directly address the focus under study – i.e. 'race', 'hedging' or 'cross-cultural communication' – but the state of argument and knowledge current in the field:

(14) Despite its commonplace acceptance by sociologists, the constructionist notion of 'race' has not been the subject of adequate empirical research.   (Soc)

Recent studies of hedging in academic writing have argued for the inclusion of hedging in EAP syllabi but have not, unfortunately, worked from a common understanding of the concept.   (AL)

Much has been written about the differences in the perception, motivation and behaviour of people from different cultures, in particular about the American and Japanese interface. However, very little scientific confirmation and measurements exist.   (Mkt)

The ability to identify such omissions is a critical step in claiming insider status in all disciplines, but is particularly crucial in the soft fields where the greater diffusion of research areas and approaches often requires validation of the topic itself.

Another, and related, insinuation of insider credibility is a writer's use of explicit appeals to the community's situated cultural understandings. Instead of demonstrating the relevance of their research by invoking the literature, writers frequently drew on, or exploited, the implicit domain knowledge of the discipline. They occasionally emphasised that they were doing this by marking the connection explicitly, through references to familiar approaches, 'well known' behaviour or 'traditional' assumptions:

(15) Many philosophers would approach this question from the point of view of an expressive theory of linguistic communication, ...   (Phil)

It is well known that in bi-anisotropic media, e.g., chiral media, gyrotropic media, the polarization vector of linearly polarized waves undergoes rotation.
                                                                             (Phy)

Ideological assumptions of equality and economic individualism have permeated the traditional analysis of social mobility.   (Soc)

This strategy is found in all disciplines, but a variation heavily used in the soft fields was to appeal to the community directly rather than its domain knowledge. Here writers deliberately promoted their membership of the community by invoking it specifically, aligning themselves with readers as peers:

(16) What do we now mean by the term 'applied linguistics'? Can we provide a coherent characterisation that says it's more than simply all and anything that isn't 'autonomous'/'core'? Should we even try?   (AL)

Sociologists today are faced with a fundamental dilemma: whether to conceive of the social world as consisting primarily in substances or processes, in static 'things' or in dynamic, unfolding relations.   (Soc)

Insider credibility is therefore promoted in these abstracts through various displays of intimacy with implicit cultural knowledge. The acronyms, jargon, citations and other features which Kaplan et al. regarded as 'counter-intuitive' can, in this sense, be seen as discursive markings of disciplinary identity which serve to position the writer within 'the apparently naturalised boundaries' of the discipline (Brenton, 1996: 356). Acronyms, for instance, draw heavily on insider knowledge for their elaboration into full forms, and thus function to signal discipline-specific understandings and suggest the writer's familiarity with them. This was principally a feature of the highly codified hard knowledge abstracts, where 45 per cent of the papers included acronyms compared with only 18 per cent in the soft disciplines. There were, however, considerable variations. The biology corpus contained a disproportionate 37 per cent of all cases, and while there were only a only a handful in sociology and philosophy. The ubiquity of EFL, TESOL, ESP, SLA and L2 – examples of relatively stable and widely used conceptualisations – ensured that applied linguistics accounted for a fifth of all acronyms in the corpus.

These and other signals of privileged discourse therefore play an important role in membershipping writers as community-situated participants and thereby contributing to their goal of opening a channel with the reader and encouraging greater interest in the following research paper. By the use of particular move structures and by highlighting specific activities or positions, writers can demonstrate their insider status to promote themselves and their research, constructing a persona that can interact with readers from a location within the boundaries of their disciplines.

EVOLVING PATTERNS: 1980-1997

This discussion has so far provided a static description, a snapshot characterising the way things are rather than a moving image of how they have become. While all genres are responses to what are perceived as recurrent situations, such stability is not eternally enduring. Social and material conditions, and writers' understandings of them, change over time and genres gradually change with them. Genres, even the apparently conservative scientific paper, are sites of both constancy and movement. Bazerman (1988) and Atkinson (1996) have provided extensive discussion of the evolution of the research article genre, tracking how textual features have changed in response to changes in the social and epistemological directions of scientific disciplines. In recent times such changes have resulted in articles in various fields showing greater concern with theoretical than empirical issues, increasingly downplaying methods, reducing authorial presence, and expanding discussions.

While these socio-historical studies have little to say about abstracts, Berkenkotter and Huckin (1995: 34) note that they have become a standard feature of articles in the last 30 years. My own corpus shows the increasing importance of abstracts to academics in all the fields studied. Based on a comparison with 30 articles in each discipline taken from journals published in 1980, I found that more journals carried abstracts in 1997 and that these abstracts were longer and more informative. Overall the average length rose from 120.5 to 158.4 words, an increase of 32 per cent, with the greatest increase occurring in the engineering and science fields and in marketing, while there was a marked tendency in most disciplines towards more complex, multi-move patterns and longer Product moves.

Table 4.3 shows a considerable expansion in the use of Introduction and, in particular, Conclusion moves, with the sciences, philosophy and marketing showing huge increases.

As I discussed above, these sections of the abstract are essentially suasive, seeking to construct a context within which the work has significance and value. Such contextualisation has perhaps become more critical with the need to situate activity in fields that are rapidly expanding or becoming increasingly subdivided into ever more specialised units. Some disciplines, such as communication studies in the USA, have also experienced a certain 'hardening' in their preferred methods and modes of working, necessitating a reorientation of readers. Marketing, in particular, has witnessed incredible growth as a discipline in the last two decades, becoming a major participant

Table 4.3   Percentage of abstracts containing particular moves (rounded %)

Discipline	Introduction 1980	Introduction 1997	Purpose 1980	Purpose 1997	Method 1980	Method 1997	Product 1980	Product 1997	Conclusion 1980	Conclusion 1997
Phil	46	78	50	57	4	7	90	90	0	9
Soc	43	58	83	84	50	41	97	99	3	18
AL	40	46	70	87	47	42	96	96	1	19
Mkt	27	62	73	91	47	46	96	95	13	34
EE	40	33	87	87	73	66	97	94	3	24
ME	40	30	83	94	53	66	98	92	0	13
Phy	13	32	77	77	52	62	97	96	7	19
Bio	13	32	57	71	59	63	97	100	20	40
Overall (%)	33	47	72	81	48	49	96	95	7	22

Note: 1980, n = 30 texts; 1997, n = 100 texts

on the academic stage. Similarly, the sheer growth in the volume of knowledge and its increasing costs in the sciences compel researchers to concentrate their funds into specific projects and to carve out their own niches of expertise. Both epistemological and social forces therefore work towards differentiation and growth, and these discoursal and generic changes perhaps reflect the growing complexity of issues that confront these disciplines.

The growing tendency to provide a disciplinary relevant background and to problematise research, however, may also represent an increasingly competitive market situation where more academics are seeking to publish their research. The pressures on academics to publish are well known and the personal stakes – in terms of reputation and rewards, in the form of promotion, tenure and future research funding – are now much higher. As two senior researchers admitted:

> *Its definitely harder to get work published now. It's true there are more journals than before, but universities have become numbers mad. Publications count, they're vital to your career and everyone needs to get them.*   (AL interview)

> *The number of papers submitted to the journal has definitely increased. Sometimes its quite difficult to get readers for all of them so delays get longer.*   (Bio interview)

This interpretation is supported by the fact that there was also, over this period, a considerable increase in the use of the promotional features discussed above. References to novelty in the sciences and to importance in the soft disciplines, which have begun to form a central part of the persuasive apparatus of abstracts today, were far less prominent in 1980. While the sample is small and relatively recent, there is some reason to believe that 20 years ago abstracts were simpler in their move structures and less overt in the use of the claims they contained for the originality, significance or utility of the product. Readers were less often given clear guidance as to the value they should place on the topic or on the research and were frequently granted more freedom to reconstruct the importance of the paper for themselves.

Features designed to project a disciplinary ethos and establish the writer's insider status, however, appeared to be equally in evidence as they are today. Claiming credibility for oneself as a strategy to enhance the persuasiveness of one's research seems to have been an important feature of academic rhetoric since the early representation of experiments of the Royal Society in the late eighteenth century. Then the appropriate rhetorical stance was 'organized around the recognition of individualist, honorable, and modest veracity as the special province of men of genteel birth or posture' (Atkinson, 1996: 364). At that time the word of a gentleman was his bond and guaranteed the accuracy of the reported observations; today, as in 1980, writers have to construct this reliability explicitly by alerting readers to a collegial relationship. In the 1980 abstracts we find similar appeals to community-specific shared knowledge that writers used today, demonstrating one's insider status through acronyms, specialist terms, reference to an assumed awareness of a generalised literature, or by evocation of a common membership of a community.

The disciplinary distinctions discussed earlier were also conspicuous in the earlier sample, with the hard and soft field writers marking themselves as credible community members in different ways. The sociologists and philosophers, for example, typically sought to balance individuation and collectivism through frequent references to the community or its background understandings. Applied linguists, marketing writers and philosophers tended to draw heavily on the literature of their disciplines, either referring to it as assumed knowledge or citing particular schools or authors. The scientists and engineers, on the other hand, principally negotiated credibility via a repertoire of coded terms and shorthand references to procedures impenetrable to all but the initiated.

So, while perhaps a rather neglected social artefact of disciplinary life, the abstract offers a fascinating insight into the discursive practices of different academic communities. Moreover, like other forms of writing that emerge from the process of publication and peer review, abstracts also reveal, through these generic practices, something of the beliefs and understandings that inform them and which enable them to reach out from their individual sources to the community within which, and for which, they were written. Embedded within them are writers' perceptions of appropriate norms of engagement, their epistemological beliefs of how knowledge is understood, and the best ways to package this knowledge and persuasively represent it to their colleagues. Like other genres, the abstract provides writers with a relatively stable generic template to accomplish their professional and personal goals and, also like other genres, it can perform this function because it is constantly evolving to suit new purposes and social conditions.

In sum, by creating their abstracts to contain elements of promotion and membership, these writers were able to project a specific disciplinary context and to situate themselves within it. In doing so they were able to legitimate their work by identifying it as significant and worth reading further, and by defining themselves as competent professionals capable of making a significant contribution to its discussion. Finally, I hope to have again shown some of the ways that particular discursive practices articulate the social relationships and understandings that underpin and facilitate the creation and dissemination of knowledge. Once again, we see that disciplinary discourse is both a symbol system used by community members to negotiate their goals, and a privileged form of communication which serves to include some and exclude others, helping to institutionalise a particular structure of social relationships within the community.

NOTE

1. Five of the philosophy journals and two of the sociology journals that made up the corpus for this book do not contain abstracts. Additional abstracts were therefore taken from the remaining journals.

Chapter 5

Priority and prudence:
the scientific letter

A dominant feature of disciplines towards the hard end of the epistemological spectrum is that new knowledge is typically seen as generated from what is known. Each new finding illuminates a little more of our ignorance and inexorably contributes to the eventual solution of the issue under study. Because knowledge is regarded as incremental and progressive in this way, there is a strong sense of making progress and, indeed, a routine expectation of constant momentum. In the fast-paced world of modern science, then, increasing specialisation and rapid knowledge growth have become the norm, and with this has come intense competition. Many fields of science are characterised by fierce rivalry as the rewards of reputation, including the funding to continue one's research, are often tied to establishing one's priority by reaching publication before others. One consequence of this is that genres have quickly emerged and changed in response to the social and intellectual activity they are part of.

The letter genre is an excellent example of the generic and discoursal consequences of such social changes, and in this chapter I shall examine a feature of the interactions at the heart of its construction. Essentially these interactions involve establishing a plausible representation of consensual knowledge against which an appropriate claim for novelty can be presented. I shall show that this involves a careful balance of hedging and boosting, a command of the expression of rhetorical doubt and certainty. First, however, it might be helpful to outline briefly what the genre is and the role it plays in scientific communities.

THE LETTER GENRE

The scientific letter, 'squib' or 'quick report' is a feature of very fast-moving scientific specialisms such as physics, chemistry and microbiology. Here concern with innovation and speed of dissemination has led to the publication of separate letters journals which facilitate the rapid circulation of new and urgent findings by restricting the length and streamlining the review process. Typically less than four pages long, letters are often published within five to eight weeks of initial submission, emphasising the anxiety of writers to establish priority for their research claims in a social environment that rewards first announcement. As Garvey (1979: 2) points out, 'being the first to make an important scientific contribution is the only way to obtain recognition (for one's) success'.

These letters journals have largely evolved from letters-to-the-editor columns reporting work in progress in parent journals, and have rapidly become the primary forum for the dissemination of innovative work in the natural sciences. Publications such as *Physical Review Letters, Chemistry Letters* and *Biotechnology Letters* are now among the leading journals in their fields, accounting for a phenomenal output of work, often published monthly or even weekly, and generally containing over 40 papers in each issue. The popularity of this forum is such that it has not only replaced the research article as the main medium for announcing new breakthroughs, but has rapidly come to rival that genre in academic and institutional respectability. Publication of letters has become one of the major criteria for the promotion of young scientists in the USA, and submissions to such journals as *Physical Review Letters* is increasing by about 10 per cent per year (Passell, 1988).

Letters differ from their more established cousin, the research article, in both scope and purpose. Letters journals emphasise the succinct reporting of new results and ideas that are of potential interest to the wider community. *Europhysics Letters,* for example, instructs authors to 'satisfy the specialist, yet remain understandable to researchers in other fields'. Journals which publish research articles, on the other hand, are targeted to highly specialised audiences and aim to certify claims rather than to disseminate new and relatively untested ideas. As a result, letters tend to focus on what is currently fashionable and exciting in science while research articles have taken on a more archival function, containing detailed elaborations and proofs. As a previous editor of *Physics Review Letters* has observed:

> Letters journals swing back and forth from one field to another while the archival journals plod resolutely along, collecting and cataloging the accumulating wisdom of the scientific community.   (Passell, 1988: 37)

The increasing competitiveness of scientific communication has led to a certain blurring of features between these genres. Both now carry informative titles and promotional abstracts, foreground important claims, minimise methodology and background statements, and pack information into visuals. Letters, however, are pre-eminently declarations of findings.

In keeping with their function of announcing innovation, letters foreground novel claims and newsworthy information (Berkenkotter and Huckin, 1995: 39). They are 'characterized by a sense of urgency and importance, and they have a style and structure which allows authors to display key ideas prominently' (Blakeslee, 1994: 91). Titles and abstracts are written to announce major findings and interpretations and to foreground what is innovative in the work, while methods are typically cursory. Background is generally scanty and the literature largely assumed, while introductions are used to foreground importance and originality.

Overall, letters lack the closely argued detail and elaboration typically associated with scientific writing. The tight space constraints mean that writers are unable to demonstrate their claims decisively or to provide complete scientific arguments for what they say. A higher rate of inaccuracy is generally tolerated as a corollary of exploring unfamiliar territory and, together, these features also tend to allow writers a certain license. The character of the letter genre invites a promotional response. While the genre has gained too much respectability to offer innovatory freedom without grounded responsibility, it does open a rhetorical space for advancing both one's self and work that is generally more constrained in other research genres.

This emphasis on claim-staking and minimal exposition poses a considerable challenge to writers. Presenting an argument succinctly enough to meet the space constraints of the genre yet effectively enough to reconstruct a disciplinary consensus requires a certain rhetorical balance. On the one hand, boldness and confidence are needed to satisfy readers that the ideas are plausible and convincing. On the other, a degree of tentativeness is required to acknowledge the brevity and inadequacy of the support offered for them. This expression of conviction and caution, of certainty and doubt, is often referred to as hedging and boosting (Holmes, 1983, 1990; Hyland, 1998c), it is at the heart of the interactions of academic writing – and is a major component of the rhetorical expression of the relationship between writer and reader. In the next section I shall briefly outline the general discoursal role of these features and describe their part in negotiating interactions in this genre.

WHAT ARE HEDGES AND BOOSTERS?

Hedges and boosters are communicative strategies for increasing or reducing the force of statements. In academic discourse their importance lies in their contribution to an appropriate rhetorical and interactive tenor, conveying both epistemic and affective meanings – that is, they not only carry the writer's degree of confidence in the truth of a proposition, but also an attitude to the audience. As we have seen, knowledge claims must be carefully handled to overcome the possibility of negation by the reader. Writers need to invest a convincing degree of assurance in their propositions, yet must avoid overstating their case and risk inviting the rejection of their arguments.

Boosters (e.g. *clearly, obviously, of course*) allow writers to express their certainty in what they say and to mark involvement and solidarity with their audience, stressing shared information, group membership and direct engagement with readers. In the following typical case, the writer employs a series of boosters to underline the conviction he wishes to attach to his argument:

(1)   The <u>essential</u> role of interference between coherent wave functions is <u>further strengthened</u> by inspection of the results between $t = 0$ and $t = 60$ ns, a time

interval not considered in the numerical model. This <u>clearly indicates</u> that attractive interactions alone cannot explain the nonlinear signal: coherence is a <u>crucial</u> additional ingredient.   (Phy)

Hedges, like *possible, might* and *perhaps*, on the other hand, represent explicit qualification of the writer's commitment. This may be to show uncertainty and indicate that information is presented as opinion rather than accredited fact, or it may be to convey deference, modesty or respect for colleagues' views. Like boosters, these are also often found in clusters, but here they work to reinforce the uncertainty of the writer's propositions, or at least the degree of certainty that it may be prudent to attribute to them:

(2)   This <u>suggests</u> that a competition exists between nucleation at the hopper edges and within the hopper, which <u>might account</u> for the narrow temperature range over which these features are observed. Filling <u>appears to</u> develop more from the pit of the hopper than the interior edges.   (Phy)

Hedges and boosters therefore draw attention to the fact that statements don't just communicate ideas, they also indicate the writer's attitude to them and to readers. These examples show writers weighting (a) the expression of their commitment depending on how they judge the epistemic status of their statements, as facts or interpretations, and (b) the effect they anticipate this commitment might have on readers' responses. Skelton (1988, 1997), for example, points out that the claims we make about the truth status of our propositions are almost invariably accompanied by a comment on their status, and this distinction between 'what we say' and 'what we say about what we say' is at the root of choice and subtlety in language use. Myers (1989) was perhaps the first to stress the interactive potential of these devices and their relationship to the academic writer's communicative purpose in negotiating claims with readers.

Different epistemic devices clearly express different degrees of writer commitment and I have noted that *clearly*, for example, conveys greater certainty in the asserted proposition than *might*. However, while it is relatively straightforward to identify particular items as either intensifying or attenuating commitment in given instances, it is far more difficult to accurately locate them on a cline of certainty. The problem arises because of the essential indeterminacy of how language is used in interactional contexts and, in particular, in the polypragmatic character of epistemic devices themselves.

Indeterminacy is a widely recognised feature of modal semantics (e.g. Coates, 1983; Hoye, 1997; Palmer, 1990) and attributing a particular force, or even a specific function, to particular forms is a hazardous enterprise. Modal meanings are rarely discrete and there are often areas of overlap in the senses they are used to convey, so that 'it is not possible in principle to decide between two possible categorizations' (Palmer, 1990: 21). The literature distinguishes two kinds of possibility, referring to the writer's convictions (epistemic modality) or to the role of external circumstances (deontic modality), roughly corresponding to *possible that* (3a) and *possible for* (3b):

(3a)   A <u>possible</u> explanation for the former is a change in cell envelope permeability related to the effects of INH on mycolic acid biosynthesis.   (Bio)

This <u>may</u> be an indication that the InGaN buffer layer relaxes the strain more efficiently by confining the dislocations.   (Phy)

(3b)   However, with the PCR procedure described in this work, it is <u>possible</u> to detect at least types A, B, E and F using a single set of primers.   (Bio)

In general, CP violation <u>may</u> be present both in the production and decay of top quarks.   (Phy)

Only the former might actually be said to convey the writer's evaluation of factivity. The issue is further complicated by the affective dimension involved in lexical selection, as a writer may be strongly committed to a proposition, for example, but hedge it out of a sensitivity to the views of readers and to strategically encourage a positive response to a claim.

In other words, the value of any term is always vulnerable to pragmatic constraints which can prevent a one-to-one mapping of form and force. The problem is equally acute when we try to determine stable and precise strengths for particular items. Wright (1999), for instance, reports findings that readers of medicine containers labels often accord common frequency terms, such as *seldom* and *sometimes*, very different meanings to those intended by healthcare professionals. Similarly, an apparently benign word like *quite* is often inconsistently interpreted by readers and is rarely employed to specify an unchanging degree of commitment (Hyland, 1996b). In both cases meanings tend to vary in ways that are not easily predicted from either linguistic or psycholinguistic theories, and generally operate at a subliminal rather than a conscious level.

In a pragmatic analysis then, we are not concerned with what a form *could* mean, or the denotative or semantic value it carries, but with its import in a particular instance. We have to view the relative intensity of an item in terms of use in the context of a given genre and domain of discourse, the co-text in which it is imbedded, and the clues that these provide concerning the writer's purpose in the unfolding text. Indeed, this very indeterminacy is likely to be part of the writer's intention in selecting a particular form on any occasion of use. It is therefore misleading to try to specify the variable force of these forms beyond describing them as hedges or boosters. Meanings do not reside in the items themselves but are assigned to utterances that contain them.

These devices are, for these very reasons, important features of academic discourse and a principal way that writers can use language flexibly to adopt positions, express points of view and signal allegiances (Hyland, 1996a, 1996b, 1998a, 1998b; Salager-Mayer, 1994). They also represent a major contribution to the social negotiation of knowledge and writers' efforts to persuade readers of the correctness of their claims, helping them to gain community acceptance for their work.

To discover the importance of these features in this genre I examined 90 letters from 10 specialist letters journals in biology, physics and chemistry, and spoke to a number of researchers who regularly contribute to these journals. The study was based on a list of 180 lexical expressions of hedging and boosting (Appendix 2) that I compiled from the research literature on modality (e.g. Coates, 1983; Holmes, 1988; Perkins, 1983), reference grammars (e.g. Quirk et al., 1972) and earlier studies of my own (Hyland, 1996a, 1998a, 1999b; Hyland and Milton, 1997). This was supplemented with the work on indefinite frequency expressions (e.g. Kennedy, 1987), which can be used to adjust the strength of claims (Halliday, 1994), and the most frequent epistemic items in the letters themselves. All cases were then examined by the author and a colleague, working independently to ensure that doubt or certainty was expressed.

FORMS AND FREQUENCIES OF HEDGES AND BOOSTERS

The search on these items demonstrate the huge importance of hedging and boosting to the negotiation of a writer–reader relationship in letters. Writers used about one device every 54 words, which is a figure roughly equivalent to the use of past tense forms or to passive voice in general academic prose (Biber, 1988: 255).[1] Table 5.1 shows that while an average paper in biology or physics was likely to contain more items overall, there was actually little variation in density across the three fields, ranging between 17 and 20 items per 1,000 words. It can also be seen that hedges constituted about two-thirds of the total devices in each discipline.

Table 5.1 Hedges and boosters in scientific letters

	Per paper		Per 1,000 words		Number	
	Hedges	**Boosters**	**Hedges**	**Boosters**	**Hedges**	**Boosters**
Biology	18.6	11.4	10.8	6.6	559	342
Chemistry	15.4	8.0	13.7	7.1	462	241
Physics	22.1	12.0	11.7	6.3	664	360
Totals	18.7	10.5	11.8	6.6	1685	943

Table 5.2 shows the most frequently occurring items used to modify statements, revealing the significance of a relatively small number of devices. The most common boosters account for almost 70 per cent of the total and the most frequent hedges for almost half. The lists are dominated by modal verbs (*would, may, might, will, could*) and epistemic lexical verbs, either those referring to mental states (*assume, seem, know, find, determine*) or involving the discursive presentation of evidence (*suggest, indicate, show, demonstrate*). These epistemic lexical verbs are also the most frequent forms writers use to express their degree of commitment in science research articles (Hyland, 1996a,

1999b) and their frequency indicates the importance that academic writers attach to overtly signalling both the degree of conjecture involved in a claim and the evidential reliability of its source.

Table 5.2   Most frequent hedges and boosters in the corpus

Hedges		Boosters	
would	96	show (that)	154
may	88	find (that)	94
suggest	88	determine	92
indicate	88	will	68
about	86	it is clear/clearly	56
assume	71	the fact that	53
possible (ly)	67	demonstrate (that)	45
could	61	confirm	40
might	57	know/known that	31
seem	31	particularly	20

One major difference between the two genres, however, is the far greater use of boosters in letters. A 70,000 word sample taken from 14 articles in biology and physics[2] reveals a similar frequency of hedges (12.1 per 1,000 words) but only two-thirds of the boosters (4.5 per 1,000 words). Clearly, scientific writers consider this to be a more appropriate, and perhaps less risky, strategy to use when writing in the letter genre. It is also interesting that many of these devices occurred in introductions and conclusions, precisely those rhetorical sections that, according to Bazerman (1988: 243), physicists read first when scanning a paper to gain a general idea of what the writer was trying to do and to judge the value of a paper for their own research purposes. So, while hedges are strongly represented in these papers, the use of boosters also plays a distinctive role in promoting the worth and importance of what the writer has to say.

CIRCUMSPECTION AND UNCERTAINTY: HEDGING IN KNOWLEDGE-MAKING

Hedges and boosters are interpersonal aspects of language use, complex textual signals by which writers personally intervene into their discourse to evaluate material and negotiate the status of their knowledge claims. Clearly these choices are to some extent influenced by individual factors, such as self-confidence and experience, and we often regard them as largely unreflective and automatic aspects of writing. Once again, however, all acts of communication carry the imprint of their contexts. ·

As we have seen in other genres, the choices individuals make are socially shaped, partly by their private goals and experiences, partly by the possibilities made available by the discourse conventions of their disciplines, and partly by the constraints and opportunities provided by the genre in which they are writing. We might expect, then, that letters will reflect the values and practices typical of scientific discourse. Making an appropriate level of claim is a critical aspect of research reporting in all disciplines, but the physical sciences are often portrayed as a model of scholarly objectivity, at least partly because of the care writers take when weighing evidence and drawing conclusions from their data. This is clear in the comments of my respondents:

> *In chemistry you just can't take a chance on being categorical about what you think. You need to be deliberate. Always cautious.*   (Chem interview)

> *With biological systems you are always not quite sure. Most of the time you could be right, but there is always a chance it might be something different.*   (Bio interview)

> *There are always doubts even though findings might point a certain way. As a journal editor I've often had to insist on authors reducing their claims if the evidence doesn't support it.*
>   (Phy interview)

Circumspection and discretion are clearly important constraints in calculating what weight to put behind a knowledge claim. This is because all statements are evaluated and interpreted through a prism of disciplinary assumptions. Readers bring certain expectations of exactitude to a text and writers attempt to meet these. By limiting their commitment with hedges, writers offer an assessment of their work for colleagues, attesting to the degree of precision or reliability that they want it to carry (Hyland, 1996b, 1998a; Nash, 1990; Salager-Meyer, 1994). In this way they seek to head off the possible negative consequences of overstatement and so anticipate rejection of their claims:

(4)   The strong lines left unassigned around rQ, mentioned at the beginning of this section, <u>could possibly</u> belong to $^1Q^0$, shifted by <u>some</u> perturbation. <u>We have however no further support</u> for this interpretation.   (Chem)

Although <u>it is plausible</u> that these long wavelength eigen modes <u>may not</u> play an important role in the turbulent dynamics because of their small growth rate, their existence still <u>casts a doubt</u> on the above construction.   (Phy)

Furthermore, for <u>most</u> of the micro-organisms studied in this paper, <u>it seemed to be possible</u> to discern a relationship between the source of the strains and their cell-wall pattern.   (Bio)

Thus, hedges imply that a statement is based on plausible reasoning rather than certain knowledge. This is obviously a prudent rhetorical move when writing in a genre that does not allow a full elaboration of procedures and precious little time between obtaining experimental results and publishing an interpretation of them.

In addition to distinguishing certainty from opinion, hedges also allow writers to open a discursive space where readers can dispute their interpretations. As we have seen, engagement in disciplinary forums relies on certain assumptions of appropriate interaction, and all arguments have to incorporate an awareness of interpersonal factors. In Chapter 3 I discussed how hedges are used by writers to soften interpersonal criticism in reviews. In letters, peer interactions involve different risks. Writers may fail to gain acceptance for their work, not because of logical frailties or methodological weaknesses, but because their claims have negative effects on the self-image of their readers. Individual reputations are built on pioneering new ground and claiming originality for novel work, but this solicits acceptance and seeks to supersede or overturn the claims of colleagues. Claim-making is a risky practice because it often contradicts existing literature or challenges the assumptions underlying the research of one's readers.

Arguments must therefore accommodate readers' expectations that they will be allowed to participate in a dialogue, and that their own views will somehow be acknowledged in the discourse. Categorical assertions, however, leave little room for this kind of feedback and their bluntness excludes the possibility of permissible alternative readings.

An appropriate disciplinary tenor therefore requires that writers frame their statements in ways that establish rapport with their audience and express a degree of deference to the understandings of the community. A judicious use of hedges is a principal means of accomplishing this, heading off negative responses to statements by emphasising their provisionality. In sum, mitigating certainty allows writers to take a stance towards their claims while protecting them from potentially critical responses from readers. My informants put it like this:

> We don't encourage people to go out and nail their colours to the mast, as this is how you get your ideas heard. You have to relate what you have to say to your colleagues. (Bio interview)

> You're only going to get a reputation by moving away from the data, but almost every interpretation is going to tread on someone's toes. To make any headway, just present it as a possibility. (Chem interview)

> You need to be careful, particularly in this format where you have to get your results over in a few pages. You want people to listen, but scientists are not always as disinterested as they say they are. (Bio interview)

Such reader-oriented hedges are often signalled through the explicit mention of a personal source (Hyland, 1996b, 1998a). Reference to the investigator's personal involvement moves the discourse away from an objective, empiricist stance towards a more contingent, interpersonal one. It alludes to an interpretive context in which facts do not speak for themselves but are decoded through human intervention. By this strategy then the writer can create a small shift in the interpretive frame. By drawing attention to the involvement of the investigator, a hedging verb with a personal subject makes the claim dependent on an individual, and thus fallible, human judgement. It departs from the universality of scientific objectivity to draw attention to a social form of accounting which marks the statement as an <u>alternative view</u> rather than a definitive statement with scientific accreditation:

(5)   <u>We believe</u> that this strain state is <u>mainly</u> controlled by the interface bonding between ZnO and GaN.   (Phy)

<u>To our knowledge</u>, no negative power absorption has yet been demonstrated in experiment.   (Phy)

From the similarity in the temperature and the analogy with the GaAs case, <u>we suppose</u> that the species 1n0 plays a key role in the H-induced removal of the In203 component of the surface oxide layer on an InP substrate.   (Chem)

<u>We suspect</u> that the level of binding energy between the component monosaccharides of the lactan gum increases with increased mannose content in gum. <u>We also inferred</u> that the level of steady shear viscosity of lactan gum increases in proportion to the level of binding energy between the component monosaccharides of the lactan gum.   (Bio)

These writers appear to be signalling that their claims are personal opinions, leaving agreement open to readers' judgements.

Most hedges in these letters, however, were expressed impersonally. Impersonalisation strategies such as the use of passives, nominalisation and objective theme selections have been well-documented in the literature and represent the rhetorical face of science (e.g. Gosden, 1993; Halliday, 1988; Swales, 1990). Together these features help to reinforce the predominant view of science as an impersonal, inductive enterprise. They minimise the role of socially contingent factors in research and contribute to the ideological representation that 'truth' is discovered, not constructed.

When examining hedging, we find considerable use of discourse-oriented verbs like *indicate*, suggest and *imply*. These devices carry less subjective connotations than cognition verbs such as *think, believe* and *suspect*, and are also more easily combined with inanimate subjects, allowing agency to be attributed to 'abstract rhetors', a common practice in this corpus:

(6)   <u>These results, both experimental and theoretical, suggest</u> that under acid conditions the reacting species in water droplets containing bisulfite is <u>probably</u> So_2.   (Chem)

<u>The experiments indicate</u> that the uranium ions in both UCU4Pd and UCU3.5Pdl.5 fluctuate independently ...   (Phy)

<u>These data suggest</u> that differences in cell-wall protein profiles of the strains <u>might</u> be related to their adaptation to different 'ecological niches' and cheese technology.   (Bio)

<u>The Eqs. (24)–(26) imply</u> that $A - C = A_2 - C_2$ which only has one sensible solution, $A = C$.   (Phy)

Interestingly, this practice is also common in the preference for discourse-focused boosters, such as *show* and *demonstrate*, rather than cognitive verb alternates:

(7)   <u>The results demonstrate</u> a striking effect of INH and establish a basis for further investigation of growth cycle-related phenomena in mycobacteria by flow cytometry.   (Bio)

<u>A comparison of the P0 values extrapolated from the experimental results at</u>

> 1300 nm with these ones extrapolated from the results at 1064 nm proves that
> the influence of fluorescence is small. (Chem)

> Experimental observations show clearly that while the former state is repulsive,
> the latter '2rl electronic state, is strongly bound. (Chem)

As with citation choices (Chapter 2), scientists seek to disguise both their interpretative responsibilities and rhetorical identities behind a screen of linguistic objectivity. A prudent writer thus avoids using features which reveal either a personal involvement in the rendition of findings or a commitment to that reading. Lab experiments are submitted as accurate depictions of the real world, their agentless textual representations claiming an appearance of objectivity and neutrality. Thus the decision to foreground the 'extrapolated P0 values' above, for example, presents a view where a research entity takes responsibility for the asserted proposition and acts to minimise the researcher's interpretative role.

This practice of giving prominence to procedures or data, rather than themselves, when drawing inferences was recognised by my informants in their own work:

> *We rely very much on statistical appraisal of results to be able to say something is happening or not, but the big difficulty is making a causative link. Generally I think we'd prefer to say the relationship lies in the data than our heads.* (Bio interview)

> *Of course, I make decisions about the findings I have, but it is more convincing to tie them closely to the results.* (Phy interview)

> *These are conventional ways of talking about inferences. They show that our interpretations are based on what we see and do in the lab.* (Chem Interview)

Clearly there are different reasons why writers may seek to distance themselves from their interpretations of data (Hyland, 1998a), but the net effect is the suppression of the author's voice and the creation of a discourse where the research appears to speak for itself.

It should be borne in mind, however, that hedging is essentially an interpersonal strategy, involving an intervention by the writer in a text. Because of this it tends to occur far more frequently in the social sciences and humanities (Hyland, 1999b). Once again, this is perhaps a rhetorical consequence of an epistemology which emphasises the invisibility of the interpreting agent. In the rapid, space-constrained and competitive research environment of the letter genre, writers are perhaps even more impelled to represent their results as relatively unmediated phenomena. This kind of impersonality in the choice of hedges is, then, part of the formalised and abstract way of coding knowledge in the sciences; one element of the shorthand which draws on a great deal of background knowledge of procedures, concepts and problems in constructing meanings for peers (see Chapter 2).

This 'shorthand' method of drawing on specialised knowledge is apparent in the extremely high use in letters of what I have elsewhere called 'attribute hedges' (Hyland, 1996a, 1998a). These are devices like *about, approximately, partially, generally, quite* and so on which differ from other hedges in that they refer, at least ostensibly, to the relationship between propositional elements rather than between propositions and writers. Such devices limit the scope of the accompanying statement, rather than cast doubt on its certainty:

(8)   Muramidase activity was <u>generally</u> higher in axenic than non-sterile cultures.
                                                                                            (Bio)

This structure involves <u>somewhat</u> greater perturbation of the SO_2 moiety than in the corresponding reaction of $HOSO_2$.   (Chem)

However, it was <u>largely</u> eliminated by exposure of the cells to INH (Fig. 1c, d).
                                                                                            (Bio)

<u>Typically</u>, the hoppered faces appeared on films that were grown with a filament and substrate brightness temperature of 2120 and 1050° C, respectively.   (Phy)

Other growth features present at the bottom of the hopper resemble triangular tiles that combine to give the appearance of <u>a more or less</u> planar composite feature.   (Phy)

In these examples writers are not using hedges to dilute their certainty or withhold commitment to their propositions. Instead, they are seeking to present a situation in terms of how far it varies from the ways the discourse community conventionally sees the world, either restricting the temporal or qualitative range of the claim or its generalisability. Attribute hedges, therefore, indicate the extent to which results fit a standard disciplinary schema of what the world is thought to be like. They signal a departure from commonly assumed prototypicality (e.g. Ungerer and Schmid, 1996) and directly invoke a relationship with the reader by suggesting shared disciplinary understandings.

Attribute hedges do not only suggest a certain amount of community agreement on what might reasonably be expected from the lab, they also draw on shared standards of permissible imprecision (Channell, 1990; Dubois, 1987). Writers are generally expected to present data accurately enough for the purposes they serve (Grice, 1975), but attribute hedges appear to diminish such accuracy. Because of their apparent imprecision, they often act to place different values on parts of the discourse. Basically, attribute hedges allow writers to rely on the reader's recognition that the information presented at this point is non-significant, they invoke shared understandings which provide the writer with a warrant to subordinate the data rhetorically in order to highlight more central, and more precise, quantities elsewhere:

(9)   … whose calculated value is <u>about</u> 20 per cent lower than the present value and the experimental one.   (Chem)

The concentration of TDG following neutralization by chemical hydrolysis of sulfur mustard was <u>estimated to be approximately</u> 80–200 mM.   (Bio)

Moreover, in view of their very small natural widths (<u>no more than a few</u> 10^{-4} eV), the f resonances can be expected to show up even more prominently in future PIFS experiments with further improved resolution.   (Phy)

Distinguishing a precise motivation for a particular instance of hedging is complicated by the fact that hedges can simultaneously convey a range of different meanings. Moreover, not only can the same forms be employed to express uncertainty or to facilitate open discussion, but writers themselves rarely clearly separate these purposes. Interviewees often expressed uncertainty when asked to comment on textual examples and confessed to a mix of affective and epistemic intentions in cases in their own work. The truth is that writers are frequently exploiting the polypragmatic nature of these forms to achieve several interactive goals at once and are themselves unclear about the primacy of any one of them. However, any instance of hedging can be seen to *count as* a contribution to the writer–reader relationship, for by qualifying one's confidence in the truth of referential information, one is also demonstrating audience-sensitivity. Negotiating the successful outcome of knowledge claims requires an orientation to both examined phenomena and professional colleagues, a stance that observes community expectations of both evaluation and deference.

PRIORITY AND SOLIDARITY: BOOSTERS IN SIGNIFICANCE NEGOTIATION

At first glance, boosters seem to contradict the kind of conciliatory and defensive tactics I have been discussing. They emphasise the force of propositions and display strong commitment to statements, thereby asserting the writer's conviction and restricting the negotiating space available to the reader. While an apparently risky tactic, writers of scientific letters nevertheless need to get the attention of their audience quickly, and convince them of the importance of their work when they have it. Boosters can help writers to accomplish both goals; allowing writers to present their work with assurance while strategically engaging with colleagues. Boosters both push claims and effect interpersonal solidarity and membership of a disciplinary in-group. In other words, the caution and self-effacement suggested by hedges needs to be balanced by a degree of assertion and self-involvement accomplished through boosters.

As I noted above, boosters are a major rhetorical feature of letters, with almost 50 per cent more cases than in a similar sized corpus of research articles. This frequency is a function of the strategic necessity to establish the novelty of one's ideas in relation to existing community understandings (Kaufer and Guisler, 1989). It underlines the central knowledge-making role that letters play in the discipline, and the persuasive goals of those who write them. Boosters were often used to comment on propositional validity in this corpus and here worked in one of two ways. They either served to stress the force of warrants, suggesting the strength of the relationship between data and claims with verbs such as *establish*, *find* and *show* (often with abstract rhetors as discussed earlier), or they expressed the certainty of expected outcomes, usually with *predict* and *will*:

(10) <u>This unambiguously shows</u> that the picture of antiferromagnetically coupled pairs is not adequate to describe the thermodynamics of local moments in the metallic phase.   (Phy)

> The results demonstrate a striking effect of INH and establish a basis for further investigation of growth cycle-related phenomena in mycobacteria by flow cytometry.   (Bio)

> There are thus compelling reasons to believe that the reactive species involved in the formation of acid rain, from bisulfite and hydrogen peroxide in acid solution, is SO_2.   (Chem)

> The extent of cathodic activity occurring immediately proximate to the polymer–metal interface will be the most significant factor determining rates of coating disbandment.   (Chem)

More generally, boosters assisted writers in accentuating both the reliability of their work and its wider significance, and we saw how this was accomplished in abstracts in the previous chapter. Boosting is by no means a new phenomenon. There is reliable and scholarly evidence that Ptolemy, Galileo, Newton and Mendel all exaggerated the importance of their experimental results[3] (Richards, 1987: 219). Boosting is particularly important in letters, however, as one addresses a diverse audience which may include both an esoteric group of non-specialists whose interests lie outside the immediate topic of the paper, as well as a highly informed exoteric readership engaged in the same research area (Myers, 1989). One has to impress upon the former – which often includes the journal referees – that weighty issues are at stake, and upon the latter that the ideas are both sound and consequential. Boosters help to accomplish these persuasive ends.

This is one reason for the fact that boosters were heavily packed into the introduction and conclusion sections of the letters. Their function here appeared to highlight the significance or novelty of the work in parts of the text most often skimmed by busy scientists quickly searching for findings relevant to their own research. Although sections are not usually explicitly labelled in this genre, the introductions are clear enough and typically contained a brief, and often aggressive, pitch for the importance of the work and a statement of the most significant findings. This is most often achieved in letters by juxtaposing the approach or results of the present study with an existing significant problem (cf. Swales and Najar, 1987; Swales, 1990). The following is a typical introduction; Spartan, yet entire:

(11) There is sufficient evidence to conclude that naturally occurring mixtures of aflatoxins are carcinogenic to animals and humans (Smith et al. 1995), in addition to being toxic. Therefore, it is important to consider all potential sources that may add to the total aflatoxin load on animal and human populations. Aflatoxins are produced by the filamentous fungi *Aspergillus flavus* (Link) and *A. parasiticus* (Speare). The detection of aflatoxins in water from a cold water storage tank is described here, and this represents the first such published report.
                                                                                     (Bio)

Boosters often appeared in introductions as a means of promoting the novelty and value of the research, emphasising that it addressed an important problem in a helpful way, or that substantial new findings were to be reported:

(12) As CW and room temperature operation are <u>highly desirable,</u> <u>it is important</u> that we have methods for studying local heating and self-focusing in different laser designs and under different pumping conditions. In this letter, we describe <u>a novel method</u> for characterizing the temperature distribution along the lateral mode direction by using temporally and spatially resolved spectra.   (Phy)

Disclosed herein is the experimental <u>evidence</u> that the titled carbanion cyclization proceeds with complete retention of configuration at the Li-bearing sp^3-carbon.   (Chem)

The present authors have <u>established</u> a solid medium growth system that replicates the morphological transitions observed by McCarthy (Ibrahim 1996). The results <u>demonstrate</u> a <u>striking</u> effect of INH and <u>establish</u> a basis for further investigation of growth cycle-related phenomena in mycobacteria by flow cytometry.   (Bio)

The ways that academics address readers in conclusions has received little attention in the literature, but my informants indicated that they all read this section in letters if they progressed past the abstract and graphical data. In this corpus, the conclusions typically reiterated the strongest claim made in the letter, summarising the main results in a way that gave prominence to their originality or wider value. Once again, boosters were often mobilised to ensure that readers were left in no doubt of the writer's estimation of the full significance of the research:

(13) In summary <u>we have demonstrated</u> that the carbanion cyclization of α-(homoallyloxy) alkyllithium proceeds with complete retention of configuration at the Li-bearing carbonian center. (…) <u>Of particular interest</u> from a mechanistic point of view is that the …   (Chem)

In conclusion the present study <u>established that</u> chiral bis(12-crown-4) derivatives are <u>very useful</u> to design practical Na^+-selective electrodes.   (Chem)

The <u>most striking</u> result regarding the C_{60}-nickel interaction is that the LEED pattern of the 1 ML $C_{60}/Ni(III)$ system does not change upon high fluence laser irradiation – up to $1.0 J/cm^2$ using ns laser pulses.   (Phy)

These results also <u>demonstrated</u> the <u>absolute necessity</u> to consider the polarity of the reaction medium, because of its ability to modify the water partition between the solid phase (enzyme preparation) and the liquid phase (substrate and product).   (Bio)

The experiments described here <u>confirm</u> the different role of each strain of yeast in the bacterial control. The present study <u>provides the first evidence</u> that wines produced by … This system of microbiological stabilization of wine allows the reduction of SO_2, with <u>considerable advantages</u> for the health of the consumer.   (Bio)

While the primary role of boosters here is not overtly interpersonal, they are clearly interactive, seeking to convince the reader through the writer's belief in the logical force of the argument. An authoritative stance serves to put the writer firmly behind the words, and two comments from informants exemplify this view:

Sometimes you have to get behind your ideas or they may miss the mark, pass the reader by. You need to get their importance noticed.   (Bio interview)

I prefer to be a bit more circumspect myself, but you see this in these papers, in letters, so I suppose its becoming more accepted. It's a very competitive forum.   (Phy interview)

In addition to promoting the significance of work, pressing its 'news value' (Berkenkotter and Huckin, 1995: 27) or the strength of results, boosters also served important interpersonal functions in these letters. Although this function has received little attention in academic writing, boosters are seen to play an important role in creating solidarity in conversation (Holmes, 1984, 1995) and in constructing an authoritative persona in counselling interviews (He, 1993). In science articles Myers (1989) regards intensifying features as positive-politeness devices, enabling writers to assume shared ground with their readers and to stress common group membership.

Thus one way writers can negotiate the status of their claims is to use devices that help to establish their own definition of the situation, strategically presenting information as consensually given:

(14)   The lux-marked assay (...) shows that the phenyltins are slightly more toxic towards *Ps. Fluorescens* than the equivalent butyltins; this is obviously of relevance for terrestrial contamination.   (Bio)

It would, of course, be interesting and desirable to examine both experimentally and computationally the predictions of the simple electronic orbital model for related systems. Naturally, by arguments similar to those used for Rh^+ and Co^+, one could predict stable 'magic' octahedrally solvated cluster ions for ...   (Chem)

It is well-known that protease formation is impaired by catabolite repression caused by glucose.   (Bio)

In this case, one directly obtains from Eq. (5) a well-known formula for the spectral density of current fluctuations represented through the cosinus transformation of corresponding cross-correlation functions.   (Phy)

In these examples, then, we find writers identifying their work with the field and with others engaged in similar research. More commonly, however, writers displayed a preference for boosters in impersonal framings, thereby selecting an interactional strategy which offered the best chance of securing the agreement of scientific colleagues. I noted above the predominance of discourse-oriented verbs to achieve this effect, and this is often reinforced by the use of an embedded clause with an anticipatory or dummy *it* replacing a human agent as subject:

(15)   It is evident that for spatially homogeneous systems without current flux, the cross-correlation functions of conduction current fluctuations ...   (Phy)

However it is clear that the general structure of the equations will be a ...   (Phy)

It is apparent that the 12-membered ring is considerably distorted, giving the smaller than expected pore size.   (Chem)

It is proposed that the four minor bands with activity are due to minor protease digestion of the major protein during extraction.   (Bio)

By emphasising writer invisibility, they appear to allow the facts to more transparently speak for themselves.

In sum, boosters, like hedges, are a response to the potential negatability of claims, and are an indication of the writer's acknowledgement of disciplinary norms of appropriate argument. They work to balance objective information, subjective evaluation and interpersonal negotiation, and this can be a powerfully persuasive factor in gaining acceptance for claims.

PUTTING IT TOGETHER: HEDGES AND BOOSTERS IN LETTERS

I have discussed hedges and boosters separately to illustrate their distinctive discoursal functions and, in fact, in many cases they tend to group with like devices in 'modally harmonic' combinations (Lyons, 1977: 807). Because these clusters express generally equivalent degrees of certainty and force, collocational restrictions act to express a kind of epistemic concord running through a clause or sentence, increasing or reducing the force of what is said. An idea of the effect of such combinations can be seen in these examples:

(16) Hydrogen bridges between the ethynyl hydrogen atom to bromine or iodine might exist if statistical disorder is assumed; however, this is not very likely because the resulting =–CH ... X distances are much shorter than, the sums of the van der Waals radii.   (Chem)

It is uncertain why the toxicity of DBT was increased in soil extract. Possibly it is related to the assumed higher aqueous solubilities of the di- compared to tri-organotins.   (Bio)

The results demonstrate a striking effect of INH and establish a basis for further investigation of growth cycle-related phenomena in mycobacteria by flow cytometry.   (Bio)

It is clear that the plane $q = 0$ is exceptional; in this plane the coupled equations are in fact linear which is why y_{str} takes integer values. Viewed as part of a three-coupling constant (v) space, $y_{str} = 2$ can only exist on a plane and $y_{str} = 3$ only on a line.   (Phy)

Often however, we find a more strategic deployment, where hedges and boosters work together to vary the strength of statements. By contrasting caution and assertion, this works to give a clear indication of precisely the commitment the writer wishes to grant to different parts of the argument. Hedges are typically employed when writers move away from what can be safely assumed or experimentally demonstrated, while boosters are introduced where they consider it more important to stress their conviction or the significance of the work. In other words, presenting a convincing argument demands an appropriate blend of assurance and circumspection, towards both one's data and what one's colleagues are likely to accept, and the combination of these features can be quite effective.

It is clear in (17), for example, which propositions the writers consider to be established (or which can be presented as such), and which ones they regard as more contentious. The combination of hedges and boosters here serve to distinguish the validity of different parts of an argument, highlighting importance and certainty or cautiously presenting what may be less readily accepted:

(17)   Although the example is only liquid crystal, the method <u>can be reasonably generalized</u> to other systems. Because <u>what is important</u> is the matching between adsorption and cohesion, which can be adjusted by introducing solvent or modifying the tip. In this way <u>we think</u> the method <u>may</u> open a new door for the formation of nanometer aggregates in a controlled way.   (Chem)

The two <u>most striking</u> results of this study were the enhancement of labeling and resolution of fluorescence into discrete peaks affected by INH exposure. <u>A possible explanation</u> for the former is a change in cell envelope permeability related to the effects of INH on mycolic acid biosynthesis (Takayama et al. 1972). It was <u>particularly interesting</u> that fixation with ethanol or formaldehyde without INH treatment did not lead to enhanced levels of labeling. This <u>suggests</u> that the permeability barrier to SYTO16 remains intact even after fixation. This is <u>consistent with</u> an <u>important role</u> for mycolic acids, since they should not be extracted by these fixatives (Inderlied et al. 1993). It is also <u>noteworthy that</u> <u>some</u> cells showed the higher levels of labeling without INH treatment (Figs 1b and 2e). This <u>suggests</u> significant variation in cell envelope properties during the growth cycle.   (Bio)

So, while scientists seek to construct a context in which claims appear to arise from the research itself, there are good reasons for understanding these preferences for mitigation and assertion as rational attempts to make the best use of linguistic resources – not merely as obedience to arbitrary conventions, but as a means to interact effectively with colleagues and secure agreement for one's arguments. We see once again that academic writing is a manifestation of both the epistemological and social goals of disciplinary communities. We see knowledge emerging from human interactions as a cultural product shaped by the criteria of justification within disciplines and constituted by rhetoric. Writers must socially mediate their arguments, shaping their evidence, observations, data and flashes of insight into the patterns of inquiry and knowledge accepted by their peers. Simultaneously, they must also negotiate a harmonious relationship with their readers. In the scientific letter, where cutting edge research is presented and new knowledge negotiated, hedges and boosters clearly play a critical role in accomplishing these goals.

I have argued here that the ways writers present their claims is clearly related to what they believe their readers will find most acceptable in a particular context. In scientific letters such choices partly respect the disciplinary knowledge-making practices typically associated with the sciences, such as impersonality, and the caution attendant upon inductive reasoning. They also, on the other hand, reflect the demands of an increasingly competitive social environment, a climate of rivalry yet one where the first announcement of significant claims must be appropriately framed to accommodate possible reader objections. Put simply, in the hybrid genre of the letter, scientists must rhetorically construct novel claims in new ways, responding to a new quasi-promotional format while observing traditional norms of caution and tentativeness.

NOTES

1. Biber's analysis was based on 80 academic samples of 2,000 words each in the Lancaster–Olsen–Bergen corpus.
2. This is extracted from a larger study of hedging and boosting in research articles discussed in Hyland (1999b).
3. It seems that the word of the gentleman-scientist mentioned earlier was not such a trustworthy indicator of reliability.

Chapter 6

Constructing an expert identity: interactions in textbooks

In the last few chapters we have examined some of the ways in which academics construct, negotiate and make persuasive their ideas through published texts. By focusing on research articles, book reviews and scientific letters I have tried to situate writers' interactions in some of the principal sites of disciplinary knowledge-making. Because of this, they have all been essentially peer-oriented genres, discourses constructed to address and influence an audience of fellow professionals directly. Most students, on the other hand, are far more likely to encounter another genre altogether: the undergraduate textbook.

University textbooks are something of a neglected genre; little is known about their rhetorical structure, their relationship to other genres, or the ways in which they vary across disciplines. They tend to have a peripheral status and are frequently seen as commercial projects unrelated to research. Indeed, textbook writers are often viewed as not participating in a disciplinary discourse at all, but a pedagogic one – a practice somehow vaguely grubby and mercantile rather than scholarly. All genres, however, emerge from within the practices of a social community and inevitably contain at least some features of its culture and communicative conventions. Textbooks, in fact, play an important role in professional practice, standing as representations of disciplinary orthodoxy while providing a medium for writers to disseminate a vision of their discipline to both experts and novices.

This chapter – the last involving text analyses – looks at this important genre. It examines the ways that textbook authors speak to students, and indirectly to their peers, in constructing a plausible depiction of their disciplines. To do this I shall focus on metadiscourse: the devices writers use to explicitly organise their texts, engage readers and signal their attitudes to both their material and their audience. I begin, however, with an overview of the genre.

THE TEXTBOOK GENRE

Textbooks are indispensable to academic life, facilitating the professional's role as a teacher and constituting one of the primary means by which the concepts and analytical methods of a discipline are acquired. They play a major role in the learners' experience and understanding of a subject by providing a coherently ordered epistemological map of the disciplinary landscape and, through their textual practices, can help to convey the values and ideological assumptions of a particular academic culture. This link to the discipline is crucial for novices seeking to extend their competence into new areas of knowledge and to cope with the specific demands of a new interpretive community. Thus students, particularly in the sciences, often see textbooks as concrete embodiments of the knowledge of their disciplines.

This view of textbooks as repositories of codified knowledge and classroom lore is widely held (Hewings, 1990; Myers, 1992b), and reflects Kuhn's influential belief that, in the sciences at least, textbooks are conservative exemplars of current disciplinary paradigms. They are seen as places where we find the tamed and accepted theories of a discipline, where 'normal science' is defined and acknowledged fact is represented. Brown (1993: 65) refers to this as canonising discourse:

> At any point in time, the canon is fixed in that it represents as conventional wisdom that any competent member of the discipline would except as uncontroversial. In this way the canon presents a view of the discipline that epitomizes and underscores the discipline's own sense of identity and intellectual tradition.

The canon then, is a dominant perspective that helps to construct a coherent conception of what the discipline is and what it stands for, an ideological representation of stability and authority. Bakhtin (1981: 427) refers to this as 'undialogized' discourse: privileged in its absolute definition of reality.

This purpose, and a student target audience, seems to set textbooks apart from the more prestigious genres through which academics exchange research findings, dispute theories and accumulate professional credit. Thus, while the research article is a highly valued genre central to the disciplinary construction of new knowledge, the textbook simply represents an attempt to reduce the multivocity of past texts to a single voice of authority. Connors (1986: 190) represents the dichotomy like this:

> In most developed intellectual disciplines, the function of texts has always been essentially conservative: textbooks, which change with glacial slowness, provide stability amid the shifting winds of theoretical argument. They serve as sources for the proven truths needed for students' basic training while advanced scholarship extends the theoretical envelope, usually in journal articles.

The distinction between articles and textbooks in the achievement of increasing social participation in a disciplinary community is important. This is because textbooks do not only represent the knowledge and methods of a discipline but, for many students, also provide a model of literacy practices, how the discipline states what it knows. As we have seen, understanding the written genres in one's field is essential to successful membership. Together with an understanding of subject knowledge, students entering university must acquire the specialised literacy of their community (Ballard and

Clanchy, 1991; Candlin and Hyland, 1999), but the interactions involved in setting out an accredited canon are clearly not those of presenting claims and disputing interpretations.

The practices of constructing a disciplinary image and mediating unfamiliar material seem to involve rhetorical characteristics not always shared by other genres (e.g. Love, 1991, 1993; Myers, 1992; Swales, 1993). It is thus unclear whether they can simultaneously convey scholarship to neophytes and develop the 'peculiar ways of knowing, selecting, evaluating, reporting, concluding and arguing that define the discourse of the community' (Bartholomae, 1986: 4). In fact, the need to make content accessible seems to take precedence over providing undergraduates with the interactive resources of the discipline (Hyland, 1999b). This is likely to complicate students' progress from an undergraduate culture of 'knowledge-telling' to a disciplinary one of 'knowledge-transforming' (Bereiter and Scardamalia, 1987) through participation in research genres. Kuhn's (1963: 353) point that familiarity with textbooks straitjackets students into disciplinary paradigms, might also apply to limitations on their writing practices.

This view of textbook writing as simply the compilation of uncontested facts for impressionable undergraduates also means that they are often rejected as scholarship. Writers gain little institutional credit for producing textbooks, and researchers often view them as a marginal activity. As Myers (1992: 3) observes, 'reading physics textbooks does not make you a physicist, and if you are a physicist, writing physics textbooks will not get you promoted'. Part of this ambivalence towards textbooks results from the fact that they are seen as the established basics aimed at an unsophisticated audience. Underlying this view is, of course, a clear pedagogic model. The expert is distinguished from the novice and the process of learning is seen as a one-way transfer of knowledge as the student is initiated, through the text, into a new world of cultural and social competence. Partly through textbooks, the learner acquires an understanding of the field as a coherent canon, a uni-linear progression to current knowledge rather than a rational reconstruction of contested perspectives.[1]

Regarding textbooks as a purely pedagogic discourse, however, neglects other important relationships in the text and simplifies what is a rhetorically more complex picture. Although publishers invest heavily in design and promotion to raise the commercial profile of textbooks with learners, particularly in science and business disciplines, it is a rare student who, unbidden, goes out and buys a textbook. On the contrary, purchasing decisions are more often made by instructors than students (Alred and Thelen, 1993). As Swales (1995: 6) points out: 'It is we professionals who evaluate manuscripts, write reviews, peruse catalogues, visit book exhibits, recommend adoptions, and orchestrate the use of textbooks in classes.'

While textbooks construct a fiction of the discipline for novices and outsiders, they also address a professional audience concerned about the impact of a text on their courses and the image a particular choice might create with colleagues. Certainly in soft disciplines, textbooks help to construct how others perceive our professional, and our engagement with them is prolonged and consequential. Textbook decisions are not lightly made.

Textbooks therefore seem to represent a complex professional discourse that involves the writer in, at least, two dimensions of social interaction: one pedagogic and constructed to engage with student consumers, and another addressed to colleagues as evaluators. This elaborate negotiation involving both the student and professional audience is, as Alred and Thelen (1993: 469) observe, 'often shrouded, however, because textbook authors speak to their readers – instructors and students alike – through the shared fiction of the classroom'. So, while textbooks may appear to be a curriculum genre, it is only with the peer audience that credibility is gained and copies sold. They therefore represent an important example of insider discourse, where writers display their expert authority and their disciplinary visions to multiple audiences.

These multiple purposes and audiences link textbooks to their disciplines in interesting ways, once again suggesting how disciplinary discourses reflect the social practices and epistemological assumptions of particular groups.

We have repeatedly seen in this book how individuals write as members of communities and how they tend to draw on the social and cultural under-standings of these communities in their discourses. An important aspect of these cultural contexts is what Fairclough (1992) calls 'orders of discourse', or the resources available for representing reality in any given community. While fluid and often contested, these orders of discourse point to the fact that discourses are aspects of a social world which comprises other discourses, and that the options available to members for creating and packaging coherent talk both employ and take meaning from these discourses. They accomplish this by drawing on specific other texts, what Fairclough (1992) calls 'intertextuality', and on particular orders of discourse, or 'inter-discursivity'.

Intertextuality, discussed briefly in Chapter 2, refers to the 'reactualiza-tion' of statements from other sources, the property that texts possess of comprising 'snatches of other texts, which may be explicitly demarcated or merged in, and which the text may assimilate, contradict, ironically echo, and so forth' (Fairclough, 1992: 84). Interdiscursivity, on the other hand, con-cerns the use of elements in a text which carry institutional and social meanings from other discourses. Candlin and Maley (1997: 203) put the dis-tinction clearly:

> Such evolving discourses are thus intertextual in that they manifest plurality of text sources. However, in so far as any characteristic text evokes a particular dis-coursal value, in that it is associated with some institutional and social meaning, such evolving discourses are at the same time interdiscursive.

Any discursive practice is then defined by its relation with other discourses and practices and, because of its multiple purposes and audiences, the text-book genre is an excellent example of these interdependencies.

On the one hand, their pedagogic and didactic usefulness demands that textbooks draw on other works in the field, representing the issues, ideas, current beliefs and major findings of the discipline by borrowing from their original sources and incorporating them into the instructional discourse. In this way other texts are manifestly present in textbooks; material is cited, quoted or otherwise adopted for a new audience and explicated by commentary, tasks, examples or analyses. The words of Webber and Delbruck, Friedman and Ryle, and Planck and Krashen are recast and responded to, appearing as bullet points, sidebars, flowcharts, paraphrases, summaries, or otherwise worked into a new discourse and recoverable from it. Textbooks thus contain within themselves evidence of other texts which are then available for manipulation, contestation and change, allowing the writer to accept the ideas of others or to dispute and reinterpret them.

On the other hand, textbooks are largely creatures of their communities. They are interdiscursive configurations of the conventions, values, practices, activity types and so on that together constitute a particular order of discourse. Textbook authors, whether knowingly or unconsciously, draw on the genres and beliefs of current and previous disciplinary vocabularies in constructing their material, representing their field of reality in terms of understandings and sets of relations that are familiar to co-professionals. While such orders of discourse are not unitary and fixed, there are often a limited number to choose from and one may be dominant in a discipline. So although writers have the option of choice, certain configurations act as extralinguistic motives for selecting or rejecting certain discursive patterns in constructing a discourse. Such choices contribute to the attribution of membership by disciplinary peers and the recognition of authorial control, but they also allow the creation of new configurations and the mixing of different discourse practices. Textbooks, for instance, vary considerably, both inter- and intradisciplinarily, in the elements of promotion, information-giving and knowledge-construction that constitute them.

Even a superficial appraisal of course texts reveals their considerable generic heterogeneity. Most obviously, there are often wide disciplinary differences in the form and presentation of textbooks. In business studies, for example, they often resemble coffee-table books and display marketing norms in their use of coloured diagrams and glossy photographs, while the experimental procedures, taxonomies and electron micrographs common in biology textbooks help to represent and construct a knowable, objective world. Texts recommended to students in applied linguistics and philosophy, on the other hand, differ little in appearance from the scholarly paperbacks on the instructor's shelves, and address many of the same issues.

More centrally, textbooks seem to play different roles in different disciplines. In hard knowledge fields the discipline appears to be defined in its texts in the Kuhnian perspective that I have set out above, embodying its truths and current platforms of professional activity. So, in the sciences (e.g. Love, 1991, 1993; Myers, 1992) and economics (Hewings, 1990; Tadros, 1994), certitude, abstract nominalisations, thematic structure and style seem to reinforce existing paradigms. In philosophy and composition, on the other hand, textbooks are often regarded as important vehicles for advancing scholarship and presenting original research (e.g. Gebhardt, 1993). The regular publication of new editions of popular textbooks in fields such as communication theory and marketing not only serves to update fast-changing information, but also the dissemination of new work. Indeed, several of my soft field respondents claimed that textbooks were regularly a means of disseminating new work or demonstrating the value of existing theory in an applied context.

This chapter seeks to explore some of the ways that authors manage the complex social interactions of textbook writing in their fields, treading a line between representing new material for learners, and constructing an acceptable representation of the discipline for colleagues. Authors of textbooks balance authority and modesty, and simultaneously seek to gain scholastic influence among learners and professional credibility among peers, and I shall attempt to trace these interactions through an analysis of metadiscourse (discussed briefly as a mitigation strategy in Chapter 3). Because it constitutes aspects of texts which are context-sensitive yet largely independent of propositional content, this allows us to examine differences in how writers conceive of their audiences. First, however, some background on metadiscourse.

AUDIENCE AND METADISCOURSE

Metadiscourse has always been a rather fuzzy term, often characterised as simply 'discourse about discourse' or 'talk about talk'. However, because it is based on a view of writing as a social and communicative engagement, it offers a very powerful way of looking at how writers project themselves into their work to manage their communicative intentions. I shall use the term 'metadiscourse' to discuss those aspects of the text which explicitly refer to the organisation of the discourse or the writer's stance towards either its content or the reader.

While the concept is not always used in the same way (cf. Swales, 1990: 188), discussions of metadiscourse have been heavily influenced by Halliday's (1973) distinction between the ideational elements of a text and its textual and expressive meanings. Thus the term is used to refer to non-propositional aspects of discourse which help to organise prose as a coherent text and convey a writer's personality, credibility, reader sensitivity and relationship to the message. Metadiscourse is the author's linguistic and rhetorical manifestation in the text in order to 'bracket the discourse organisation and the expressive implications of what is being said' (Schiffrin, 1980: 231). While some analysts have narrowed the focus of metadiscourse to features of textual organisation (Mauranen, 1993; Valero-Garces, 1996) or explicit illocutionary predicates (Beauvais, 1989), a wider view draws attention to how writers reveal both themselves and their communicative purposes.

Metadiscourse is a major feature of communication in a range of genres and settings. Studies have, for instance, suggested its importance for estab-

lishing positive politeness and an addressee-friendly attitude in casual conversations (Schiffrin, 1980) and school texts (Crismore, 1989). It has been
shown to be a useful means of expressing greater guidance and orientation
for the reader in science popularisations (Crismore and Farnsworth, 1990),
postgraduate theses (Swales, 1990) and company annual reports (Hyland,
1998b), and also appears to be a critical feature of good ESL and native-
speaker student writing (Crismore et al., 1993; Cheng and Steffensen, 1996;
Intraprawat and Steffensen, 1995). In academic writing it has been seen as an
important pragmatic resource for influencing readers' responses to claims in
research articles (Hyland, 1998c; Mauranen, 1993; Morino, 1997) and in
Darwin's *Origin of the Species* (Crismore and Farnsworth, 1989). In sum,
metadiscourse is an essential element of interaction because of its role in
facilitating communication, supporting a writer's position and building a
relationship with an audience.

There is, however, a tendency in some work to focus on surface forms and
the effects created by writers. This helps to explain why, for example, the variation in metadiscourse use noted across linguistic cultures (Crismore et al.,
1993; Mauranen, 1993; Valero-Garces, 1996) has not been similarly investigated in different disciplinary cultures. Metadiscourse, however, is not an
independent stylistic device which authors can vary at will; it is integral to the
contexts in which it occurs and is intimately linked to the norms and expectations of particular cultural and professional communities. As I have argued
throughout, writing is a culturally-situated social activity, and metadiscourse is
another example of how writing reflects a rhetorical sensitivity to interpersonal and intertextual relationships. In other words, the meanings of
metadiscourse are only realised within a particular context, both invoking
and reinforcing that context with regard to audience, purpose and situation.

Clearly a text communicates effectively only when the writer has correctly
assessed the reader's resources for interpreting it. In textbooks, this will not
only involve providing sufficient cues to assist comprehension and taking an
appropriately insider stance towards the material, but also necessitate negotiating a particular relationship with the reader to display professional status
and expertise. In addition, because writers are also talking from within their
discipline, and to fellow professionals, the effectiveness of these metadiscourse choices will also lie in their cultural value to a community. In sum,
they are likely to indicate the writer's assessment of the cognitive demands
that the text makes on the reader, and to acknowledge the preferred interpersonal conventions of the community.

A MODEL OF METADISCOURSE

Metadiscourse can be realised though a range of linguistic devices from
exclamation marks and underlining, which might indicate an author's surprise or emphasis, to whole clauses and sentences (e.g. '*You can see from the
above table that* ...'). However, distinctions between meta- and propositional

discourse cannot be made from linguistic form alone as they almost always depend on the relationship of items to other parts of the text. The analysis, therefore, is once again functional rather than linguistic and recognises that many items can be either propositional or metafunctional depending on their context. There is also a certain amount of insider opacity in metadiscourse use. Thus, metaphors can help to focus attention, allusion is often used to forge a common bond with readers, and adjective choice can convey subtle shades of affect. This analysis, however, focuses on explicit textual devices and, in particular, on a list of almost 300 commonly used items (Appendix 3).

Several classification schemes have been proposed (e.g. Crismore and Farnsworth, 1989; Nash, 1992; Vande Kopple, 1985), but in this study I adopt a modified version of Crismore et al.'s (1993) taxonomy. This distinguishes textual and interpersonal dimensions and recognises more specific functions within them. This seemed a potentially useful approach as it effectively characterises the need of writers to address conditions of both adequacy and acceptability which are at the heart of academic interactions. My version of this schema is summarised in Table 6.1 and discussed below.

Table 6.1   Functions of metadiscourse in academic texts

Category	Function	Examples
Textual metadiscourse		
Logical connectives	Express semantic relation between main clauses	in addition / but / thus / and
Frame markers	Explicitly refer to discourse acts or text stages	finally / to repeat / here we try to
Endophoric markers	Refer to information in other parts of the text	noted above / see Fig / in section 2
Evidentials	Refer to source of information from other texts	according to X / (1990) / Z states
Code glosses	Help readers grasp meanings of ideational material	namely / e.g. / such as / i.e.
Interpersonal metadiscourse		
Hedges	Withhold writer's full commitment to statements	might / perhaps / possible /about
Boosters	Emphasise force or writer's certainty in message	in fact / definitely / It is clear
Attitude markers	Express writer's attitude to propositional content	Unfortunately / I agree / X claims
Relational markers	Explicitly refer to or build relationship with reader	frankly / note that / you can see
Person markers	Explicit reference to author(s)	I / we / my / mine / our

Textual metadiscourse is used to organise propositional information in ways that a perceived audience is likely to find coherent and convincing. Its use depends on the knowledge relationships between participants and the writer's assessment of a reader's possible processing difficulties, intertextual requirements and need for interpretative guidance. There are five broad functions:

- *Logical connectives* are mainly conjunctions and adverbial phrases which help readers to interpret pragmatic connections between ideas by signalling additive, resultive and contrastive relations in the writer's thinking. The texts were carefully screened to ensure that items performed a metadiscoursal role, helping the reader to interpret links between ideas, rather than simply contributing to syntactic coordination.
- *Frame markers* signal text boundaries or elements of schematic text structure. I include here items used to sequence (such as *first, then, 1, 2, a, b*), to label text stages (*to conclude, in sum*), to announce discourse goals (*I argue here, my purpose is*) and to indicate topic shifts (*well, now*). Items in this category therefore provide framing information about elements of the discourse.
- *Endophoric markers* are expressions which refer to other parts of the text (*see below, as noted above*). These make additional ideational material salient and therefore available to the reader in aiding the recovery of the writer's meanings.
- *Evidentials* are 'metalinguistic representations of an idea from another source' (Thomas and Hawes, 1994: 129), guiding the reader's interpretation and establishing an authorial command of the literature. While we saw in Chapter 2 that reporting often predicts appraisal, it is important from a metadiscoursal viewpoint to distinguish citation from evaluation. Evidentials distinguish *who* is responsible for a position and are distinguished here from the writer's *stance* towards the view, which is coded as an interpersonal feature.
- *Code glosses* supply additional information, by explaining or expanding what has been said, to ensure the reader is able to recover the writer's intended meaning. They reflect the writer's predictions about the reader's knowledge-base and are introduced by phrases like *this is called* and *in other words*, or are included in parentheses.

Interpersonal metadiscourse, on the other hand, allows writers to express a perspective towards their propositions and their readers. Here metadiscourse relates to the level of personality, or tenor, of the discourse. It concerns evidentiality, relation and affect (Hyland, 1999a), and influences such matters as the author's intimacy and remoteness, expression of attitude, commitment to claims and extent of reader involvement. Again, I identify five subgroups.

- *Hedges* and *boosters* indicate the degree of commitment, certainty and collegial deference a writer wishes to convey, signalled by items such as *possible, might* and *clearly*. As we have seen in Chapter 5, the balance of these epistemic categories plays an important role in conveying the extent of author commitment to text content, and observing interactional norms of rhetorical respect.

- *Attitude markers*, on the other hand, indicate the writer's affective, rather than epistemic, attitude to textual information, expressing surprise, importance, obligation, agreement, and so on.
- *Relational markers* are devices that explicitly address readers, either to focus their attention or include them as discourse participants. Because affective devices can also have relational implications, attitude and relational markers are often difficult to distinguish in practice. Cases of affect, however, are typically writer-oriented and are signalled by attitude verbs, necessity modals and sentence adverbs. Relational markers focus more on reader participation and include second person pronouns, imperatives, question forms, and asides that interrupt the ongoing discourse.
- *Person markers* refers to the degree of explicit author presence in the text measured by the frequency of first person pronouns and possessive adjectives.

It should be borne in mind that while this schema offers a pragmatically grounded description of the data, it can do no more than partially represent a fuzzy reality. There will inevitably be some overlap between categories as writers often seek to achieve several concurrent purposes, working to establish credible propositional connections while conveying an appropriate interactional stance. This polypragmatic aspect of language blurs an 'all-or-nothing' interpretation of how particular devices are used. Contrastive connectives like *but* and *however*, for example, principally link textual material, but can also act interpersonally by a shifting an evaluative coding from a positive to a negative judgement (Hood and Forey, 1999) or by mitigating the introduction of a counter claim (Barton, 1995). Similarly, code glosses not only reveal the writer's assessments of shared subject matter, but also imply an authoritative position *vis-à-vis* the reader. Interacting effectively means anticipating the needs of readers, both to follow an exposition and to participate in a dialogue; it should be no surprise that many devices are used to perform both functions at once.

A classification scheme can therefore only approximate the complexity of natural language use. While it may give no firm evidence about author intentions, it is a useful means of revealing the meanings available in the text and perhaps some of the assumptions writers hold about the issues they address and their audiences. Once again, this involves going beyond the taxonomy to identify factors of the rhetorical context that may influence such differences.

AN OVERVIEW OF TEXTBOOK METADISCOURSE

The 56 textbook chapters (481,000 words) contained 32,543 examples of metadiscourse, an average of 580 per chapter or about one every 15 words.[2]

Table 6.2 shows that writers used far more textual than interpersonal forms in textbooks and that connectives, hedges and relational markers were the most frequent devices overall.

Table 6.2 Metadiscourse in academic textbooks per 1,000 words

Category	Bio	Phy	ME	EE	Mkt	AL	Soc	Phil	%
Connectives	25.9	22.6	21.1	19.0	29.6	21.9	26.1	33.1	37.0
Code glosses	5.3	5.8	5.4	5.6	5.1	7.6	5.3	4.0	8.0
Endophoric mkrs	6.5	7.9	8.5	9.2	1.6	3.7	0.8	0.3	6.7
Frame mkrs	3.1	3.5	3.2	3.5	3.5	4.6	2.6	3.3	4.9
Evidentials	1.9	0.8	0.1	0.1	0.7	4.3	4.9	0.8	2.7
Textual	*42.7*	*40.6*	*38.3*	*37.4*	*40.5*	*42.1*	*39.7*	*41.5*	*59.4*
Hedges	8.7	5.5	4.4	4.8	10.3	8.5	10.6	12.3	12.2
Relational mkrs	2.4	6.0	6.2	4.7	3.4	8.4	5.5	19.7	11.3
Boosters	5.4	3.8	4.9	5.1	5.1	5.3	4.6	8.3	7.9
Attitude mkrs	3.8	2.7	4.2	3.3	6.4	4.2	5.1	5.9	6.6
Person mkrs	0.7	1.2	0.7	0.8	1.1	1.8	0.7	5.7	2.5
Interpersonal	*22.1*	*19.2*	*20.4*	*18.7*	*26.3*	*28.2*	*26.5*	*51.9*	*40.6*
Totals	**64.8**	**59.8**	**58.7**	**56.1**	**66.8**	**70.3**	**66.2**	**93.4**	**100**

The overwhelming preponderance of textual forms (60 per cent) reflects the common interpretation of metadiscourse as a strategy for guiding the reading process and perhaps emphasises the instructional role of the genre. Writers in all disciplines appear to take considerable care to set out material and clarify propositional connections and meanings for learners. Epistemic markers (hedges and boosters) comprised almost a fifth of the devices overall and exactly half of all interpersonal forms, clearly suggesting that textbook discourse is not simply an unreflecting repetition of uncontested disciplinary facts. Writers obviously have something to say on the epistemological status of what they report. Overall, it seems that textbook authors are concerned to express their arguments explicitly, yet with due circumspection where necessary.

The comparative data shows a number of differences and similarities between the disciplines. Most obviously, there are broad similarities in the density of textual metadiscourse across the fields. The figures for interpersonal forms, however, show considerable differences, accounting for the overall higher use of metadiscourse in the soft knowledge disciplines (Figure 6.1). The philosophy corpus in particular was striking for its heavy use of interpersonal metadiscourse, containing twice as many devices as any other discipline, mainly because of considerable use of relational and person markers, principally personal pronouns. The percentage figures show that the

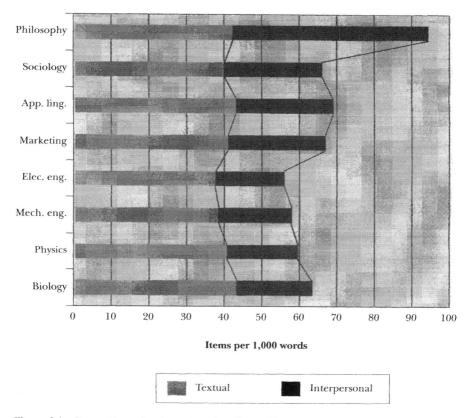

Philosophy
Sociology
App. ling.
Marketing
Elec. eng.
Mech. eng.
Physics
Biology

0   10   20   30   40   50   60   70   80   90   100

Items per 1,000 words

Textual   Interpersonal

Figure 6.1   Proportion of major categories of metadiscourse

proportion of textual metadiscourse clustered closely around 67 per cent in the hard fields and exactly 60 per cent in each of marketing, applied linguistics and sociology, with only philosophy containing more interpersonal forms (55 per cent). Broadly, then, disciplinary differences seem to reflect the kinds of patterns we have seen in other genres, with the science and engineering texts displaying generally less concern with elaborating an explicit interpersonal context for the negotiation of meanings.

Looking within these major categories we can also see variations in how writers used metadiscourse (Table 6.3). Proportionately, connectives tended to dominate textual forms, particularly in the soft disciplines, with a greater density of endophoric markers and code glosses in the hard sciences, and proportionately more evidential markers in sociology and applied linguistics. There was less divergence among interpersonal devices, although engineering and physics contained a smaller proportion of hedges and engineering had a higher density of boosters.

It is clear that the use of metadiscourse is important in each of these academic fields, although to different degrees and in different ways. Such

Table 6.3   Proportion of textual metadiscourse across disciplines (%)

	Bio	Phy	ME	EE	Mkt	AL	Soc	Phil
Connectives	40.6	38	36	33.8	44.2	31.2	39.5	35.4
Code gloss	8.3	9.7	9.3	9.9	7.7	10.8	8	4.3
Endophoric mkrs	10.1	13.1	14.4	16.4	2.4	5.2	1.3	0.3
Frame mkrs	4.9	5.8	5.4	6.2	5.2	6.6	3.9	3.5
Evidentials	3	1.3	0.1	0.2	1	6.2	7.4	0.9
Textual	*66.9*	*67.9*	*65.2*	*66.5*	*60.5*	*60*	*60.1*	*44.4*
Hedges	13.8	9.2	7.5	8.6	15.5	12.1	16	13.2
Relational mkrs	3.8	10	10.6	8.3	5.2	11.9	8.2	21.1
Boosters	8.5	6.3	8.3	9.1	7.6	7.6	7	8.9
Attitude mkrs	5.9	4.6	7.2	6	9.6	6	7.7	6.3
Personal mkrs	1.1	2	1.2	1.5	1.6	2.4	1	6.1
Interpersonal	*33.1*	*32.1*	*34.8*	*33.5*	*39.5*	*40*	*39.9*	*55.6*
Overall total	**100**	**100**	**100**	**100**	**100**	**100**	**100**	**100**

differences suggest strategic purposes in their use and, given my argument in this book so far, we might expect that distinctions in how writers address readers in these ways can tell us something about the disciplines in which they participate. I shall begin by looking at textual forms.

MAKING CONNECTIONS: PATTERNS OF TEXTUAL INTERACTIONS

The dominance of textual metadiscourse in almost all these disciplines underlines writers' regard for keeping readers informed about where they are and where they are going. As such they represent careful decisions about what the audience can be expected to know and what needs to be spelt out. As we have seen repeatedly, academic writing is not simply a passive expression of a world-view, it involves a deployment of rhetorical strategies that express a theory of experience in conventionally coherent ways. Textual metadiscourse contributes to this by providing an overt framework which clarifies the schematic structure of the discourse, revealing connections to related ideas, both within and outside the text.

Where texts are intended for a specialist audience, as in research papers, we find fewer textual devices (Hyland, 1998c). In such cases, writers often rely on their readers' understandings of lexical relations to see the implicit cohesion of the text, encoding connections in an underlying semantic structure which draws on a web of social and cognitive expectations about what the text is doing (Myers, 1991). Naive readers lack this domain knowledge, however, which means that textbook authors are unable to invoke understandings of craft skills, interpretive practices and rhetorical structuring. Because novices lack experience of the forms which give coherence and life to those understandings, the author must attempt to construct this experience, seeking to make the shared meanings of the discipline explicit, indicating clear lines of thought through surface logicality.

Compare how these two typical extracts use textual metadiscourse, for example:

(1)   Steryl glucosides are characteristic lipids of plant membranes. The biosynthesis of these lipids is catalyzed by the membrane-bound UDP-glucose sterol glucosyltransferase. The purified enzyme (Warnecke and Heinz, 1994) has been used for the cloning of a corresponding CDNA from oat (*Avena sativa* L.). Amino acid sequences derived from the amino terminus of the purified protein and from peptides of a trypsin digestion were used to construct oligonucleotide primers for polymerase chain reaction experiments.   (Bio)

(2)   Although the nature of the fatty acid can be highly variable, the key point is that the chemical linkage to glycerol is an ester link. By contrast, archaeal lipids consist of ether-linked molecules (see Figure 20.1). In ester-linked lipids, the fatty acids are straight chain (linear) molecules, whereas in ether-linked lipids, branched chained hydrocarbons are present. In Archaea, long chain branched hydrocarbons, either of the phytanyl or biphytanyl type, are bonded by ether linkage to glycerol molecules (see Figure 20.1).   (Bio)

While both broadly address the constituents and products of lipids, the first extract (from an article), contains only an evidential marker and a code gloss, labelling the plant. Aside from some lexical repetition, one needs specific knowledge to infer the connections between entities and sentences, and to recover the significance of the activity described. The textbook extract in (2), however, contains a range of metadiscoursal devices, including endophoric markers, code glosses, an attitude indicator highlighting importance, and a bevy of logical connectives. The textbook author is here making considerable rhetorical effort to not only establish relations between terms in the field, but clearly to link the reader's familiar vocabulary with the new specialised terms of the discipline.

The pedagogic purpose of textbook authors is not only clear in the elaboration of propositional relations through heavy use of logical connectives, but also in the extensive use in most disciplines of frame markers and code glosses. Frame markers operate to point readers rhetorically in the direction the writer wishes to travel, guiding them through the information. These were mainly used explicitly to sequence information or mark topic shifts (3a), but in the more discursive soft fields they also worked to orientate readers to material by providing metatextual reference to the writer's goals or stages of the text (3b), ensuring that the reader would not miss the main points:

(3a) Finally, one must consider the effects of the measurement methods used to obtain data for repeatability and accuracy.   (ME)

> Now, let us analyze the motion of a mass in free-fall subject to an upward air resistive force whose magnitude is $R = 1$.   (Phy)

(3b) In the next section I will focus explicitly on linguistic politeness, using terms of address for exemplification.   (AL)

This chapter explains some of the approaches used in segmenting consumer and organizational markets and discusses six-step approach for market segmentation and selecting a target market.   (Mkt)

Let's conclude this part of our discussion by considering yet another possibility – a mechanical man.   (Phil)

Code glosses were also an important feature in reducing the cognitive load of propositional material for novices. By providing a definition (4a) or adding information (4b), these devices served to instruct rather than simply clarify, helping not only to convey meanings that are assumed problematic for learners, but to ensure that they grasped matters in the way the writer intended:

(4a) Saxicolours (growing on rocks) lichens are probably instrumental in initiating soil...   (Bio)

The steps in a program in the CPU are called instructions; the steps in a program for a channel are called commands.   (EE)

(4b) In other words, it is a restatement of the problem, which still remains.   (Phil)

Cross-cultural variation is a primary barrier – that is, understanding cognitively and affectively what levels of formality are appropriate or inappropriate.   (AL)

Another way of putting this would be to say that traditional societies assign definite and permanent identities to their members.   (Soc)

These features represent a substantial intervention by the writer in these texts and are a critical dimension of their overall persuasive force. The heavy use of code glosses, connectives and frame markers specify very clearly how the reader should decipher the discourse and work to close down alternative readings. Very little space is provided for either misunderstanding or the possibility of discretionary or aberrant interpretations. The writer speaks here as an authority, an expert knower possessing superior knowledge in an interaction which simultaneously constitutes the reader as less expert. Textual metadiscourse then, both cooccurs with, and helps to construct, participant identities of professional and novice status through the writer's assumptions about reader competence. In this regard, at least, interactions within the textbook reveal the genre as reflecting a perception of learning which approximates to the 'apprenticeship' metaphor of disciplinary induction, in which experts initiate novices into a particular world of disciplinary knowledge.

There are, however, differences between these texts which suggest that something more is going on. Precisely *how* writers present their subjects and negotiate their personal status with readers appears to vary between disciplines, perhaps indicating that authors are not merely setting out ideas for novices, but are also simultaneously seeking to do so in ways that perhaps draw, to some extent at least, on its preferred literacy practices.

This seems to be the case with the use of endophorics, 85 per cent of which occurred in the chapters from science and engineering textbooks. Endophorics direct the reader to explanatory or related material elsewhere in the text, often facilitating comprehension and supporting arguments by referring to earlier chapters or stages, or by anticipating something yet to come:

(5) In the Oedipal phase (see chapter 3, 'Socialization and the Life-Cycle'), a boy feels threatened by the discipline and autonomy which his father demands of him.   (Soc)

We will come back to a more detailed discussion of communicative language teaching in a later section in this chapter.   (AL)

These are the line managers who are responsible for one (or more) of the thirteen marketing functions listed on page 399.   (Mkt)

Applied linguistics, however, was the only discipline to use this strategy with any regularity, and the social science writers used it hardly at all, presenting a relatively self-contained discursive style that rarely sought to affiliate particular points to a wider knowledge schema by signposting links.

The density of endophorics in the science and engineering corpus, on the other hand, demonstrates their significance in hard knowledge argumentation, where the referent is overwhelmingly a nearby table or graph. About 90 per cent of endophoric cases in these four fields directed the reader to another mode of knowledge representation, inducting learners into the ways that science typically employs a variety of semiotic systems to make meanings:

(6) ... and power grounds are finally all tied to the single designated point on the systems earth grounded conductor (see, for example, Fig. 16–9).   (EE)

Figure 3.8.4 shows the unidirectional repeatability, while Figure 3.8.5 shows a possible definition of bidirectional repeatability.   (ME)

Table 10.6 is an approximate summary of what probably occurs during the firing of a whiteware body.   (Phy)

Endophorics in these chapters represent the constant to-ing and fro-ing between written and diagrammatic texts common in other hard field genres. As Lemke (1998: 87) observes, scientific concepts are not only verbal but are typically 'semiotic hybrids, simultaneously and essentially verbal, mathematical, visual-graphical, and action-operational'. Kress and Van Leeuwen (1996) argue that visual images are accorded prominence in scientific texts because they are independent vehicles for meaning which do not simply accompany academic texts, but actively construe meanings. Consequently they interact with the text and the reader in complex ways, providing a scientific rendering of knowledge which moves learners from their personal first-hand experience of the world towards the world of abstract scientific knowledge.

The sciences, then, reconfigure available linguistic resources for making meanings through the rhetorical combination of images and text, and the constant switching of the reader between them via metadiscourse markers to highlight particular features of prominence. To discourse in the hard fields is to be comfortable with these combinations of modes and with the ways that verbal texts interact and integrate with quantitative graphs, abstract diagrams and information tables. Lemke (1998: 105) points out moreover that visuals in scientific discourse are not usually redundant with verbal main text information but add important and necessary data that complement it. The metadiscoursal linking of textual material to diagrammatic forms is therefore an important method by which scientists communicate. In these textbooks it can be seen as both a means of clearly presenting propositional information and of familiarising learners with the ways their disciplines create and recover meanings. Endophoric metadiscourse helps to induct learners into a new literacy by requiring them to interpret and orient to this way of representing reality, acquainting them with how meanings are reconfigured and recontextualised in scientific discourses.

In contrast, the greater use of evidential markers in the softer fields, particularly in applied linguistics and sociology, displays to learners a very different argument structure, one that reaches outside the current text in support of claims (see Chapter 2). While a command of the disciplinary literature can clearly be a means of demonstrating authorial expertise to novices and insider credentials to peers, it also contributes to the learning of particular attitudes towards argument and ways of presenting research. Literacy in these more discursive fields involves an understanding of explicit intertextuality, and an awareness that claims are inseparable from their originators:

(7)   Rosalind Coward argues that women often have a role in their own oppression.
(Soc)

According to the observations of Harry Gracey, kindergarten can be as demanding as a boot camp in teaching the lessons of regimentation and obedience to authority.   (Soc)

But such an inference, says Hume, 'is uncertain, because the subject lies entirely beyond the reach of human experience'.   (Phil)

Searle (1979: 23) points out that there are a limited number of things that we do with language ...   (AL)

Participants in hard field discourses, however, typically expect very different kinds of argument. In these textbooks attribution is minimal and evidence is largely presented in terms of general experimental work or unassigned activity in the field. These examples are typical:

(8)   Surface structures of the pathogenic <u>Neisseria have been the subject of intense microbiological investigations for some time</u>.   (Bio)

<u>A great amount of research has been carried out in the past years</u> to improve the toughness of ceramic materials.   (Phy)

<u>Experimental evidence derived from various fungi reveals that</u> spore dormancy may be controlled by a variety of factors, perhaps working in combination. (Bio)

> Experiments indicate that such behavior does indeed occur for impact velocities in excess of the critical impact velocity, and ... (ME)

The use of these forms reflects the wider discursive practices of the disciplines in which they occur, representing important conventions of field-specific argumentation. We can see, therefore, that while textbooks are largely regarded as a means of conveying appropriate disciplinary 'content', they also contribute towards the acquisition of a specialist discourse among learners.

This should not really be surprising. We have repeatedly seen that disciplinarity lies in situated interaction, in ways of construing an accepted reality through discoursal distinctiveness, as much as it lies in specific objects of study. Textbook authors cannot avoid speaking from within these same domains of literate experience. It is this which helps to contribute to our sense that we, whether lay or professional readers, are reading a text in a particular field. Moreover, approximating the discourses of the discipline is also a crucial dimension of reconstituting learners, giving them a sense of participating in a particular community and leading them towards eventually becoming independent producers of such discourses. Three of my informants made this explicit:

> *When I set a textbook for a course I'm not only telling students what knowledge I want them to have of the discipline, I'm providing a model of good writing. How to set out arguments, refer to other studies, link ideas, and so on.* (AL interview)

> *The content is important of course, the science has to be right, but also how scientists do research and how we talk about it.* (Bio interview)

> *Philosophy is mainly about argument, not facts. I'm not interested in teaching facts, but in reasoning, interpreting, arguing clearly. The readings have to give good examples of that.*
> (Phil interview)

The pedagogic discourse, in other words, makes available to learners various institutionally sanctioned values and practices. Pedagogic texts are not, of course, research texts, and may not provide perfect models for graduate students wishing to participate in the research genres of their fields (Hyland, 1999b; Myers, 1992b). They do, however, represent a step towards this, and in laying out (what he or she perceives to be) the principles of the discipline the writer is acting as a guide in this process. The texts establish clear role relationships, with the writer acting as a primary-knower in assisting novice readers towards a range of values, ideologies and practices that will enable them to interpret and employ academic knowledge in institutionally approved ways.

CONSTRUCTING A WRITER PERSONA: INTERPERSONAL METADISCOURSE

Interpersonal metadiscourse concerns more explicitly interactional and evaluative aspects of authorial presence, expressing the writer's individually defined, but disciplinary circumscribed, *persona*. Here the writer intervenes to convey attitudes to propositional material and vary his or her level of intimacy and involvement with the reader. Consequently this kind of metadiscourse has been shown to be a marked feature of overtly argumentative and persuasive genres such as research articles (Hyland, 1998c, 1999a; Mauranen, 1993) and CEO's annual reports (Hyland, 1998b). It may be surprising then, to find that it makes up 40 per cent of the metadiscourse in a genre whose apparently uncontentious purpose is simply to arrange currently accepted knowledge into a coherent form for naive readers. In this section I shall suggest that both the presence and distribution of these forms in textbooks reveals more subtle interactions.

The most noticeable feature of interpersonal metadiscourse in these chapters is that it was more heavily employed by writers in the social sciences and humanities, with philosophy texts containing almost twice as many interpersonal forms as any other discipline. This dispersal is predicted in the analyses of other genres in this book, which show that the need to project authorial authority and engage with readers explicitly are characteristic features of the more discursive argument forms of the soft disciplines. In the more analytical and structuralist hard fields, where explanations derive to a greater extent from model building, precise measurement and the scrutiny of controlled variables, the firmer criteria of acceptability creates a very different set of rhetorical responses and participant interactions, with less need for personal standing and reader involvement.

These epistemological issues seem to resonate in the use of hedges and boosters in the corpus, where they also reflect the patterns of disciplinary use found in research genres, discussed in the previous chapter. We saw there that the manipulation of certainty can be a critical rhetorical and interpersonal resource in academic discourses, and several studies have described how these features are affected by the transformation of statements from new claims in research articles to accredited facts in textbooks. Latour and Woolgar (1979) and Myers (1992), for example, observe that textbooks contain a higher proportion of unmodified assertions than research articles because the writer does not have to persuade an expert audience of a new claim. Comparison of my textbook findings with an earlier study of research articles (Hyland, 1998d) suggests that these observations are valid.

When qualifications are omitted, the result is both greater certainty and less professional deference, reflecting a different attitude to information and readers. However, while statements may be differently treated in the two genres, resulting in a lower density of forms, the distributions are broadly similar, with the soft fields containing more hedges, and boosters evenly spread among the disciplines.

The use of boosters are a means of treating observations as established facts, and we find examples of this in all the disciplines:

(9)   The virulence factors of *M. catarrhalis* are also under investigation because of the <u>demonstrated</u> pathogenicity of this species.   (Bio)

It <u>is a well-established fact that</u> if the mechanical resonance frequency occurs inside or near the servo bandwidth, the loop's stability is degraded ...   (ME)

<u>It is generally agreed that</u> the stigma attached to divorce has been considerably reduced. This, in itself, *will* make divorce easier.   (Soc)

They can also indicate the writer's assessment of information and their conviction in its reliability or truth, thereby projecting a strong, authoritative and credible authorial presence in the discourse. We tend to find this mainly in the softer fields:

(10)   <u>It is difficult to avoid the feeling that</u> many functionalists are committed to the institution of the family. <u>Indeed</u> their descriptions are often little short of an idealization of family life.   (Soc)

<u>Surely</u> we can know some things with certainty!   (Phil)

The view that older methods ignored comprehensible input is <u>surely</u> incorrect; <u>indeed</u>, most methods of the past 30 years insisted on ...   (AL)

This kind of authorial assertiveness is, of course, addressed as much to colleagues as to learners, contributing to a personal stamp on what peers might see as a recounting of disciplinary orthodoxy. Boosters, then, help writers to build a personal ethos through an impression of certainty, assurance and conviction in the views expressed, an image strengthened with the use of personal pronouns. An overt acceptance of personal responsibility for a judgement was quite rare in the hard science texts, but occurred often in the chapters from philosophy and applied linguistics:

(11)   But some of the features of human communication are becoming clearer, and <u>I believe</u> we are moving in positive and creative directions.   (AL)

<u>I am convinced, for my part, that</u> no ontology – that is to say, no apprehension of ontological mystery in whatever degree – is possible ...   (Phil)

<u>I think</u> there is a correct answer to the question 'Does God exist?'   (Phil)

<u>We believe that</u> this concept of the 'self' is not entirely appropriate as the basis for Asian communication.   (AL)

Here we see a confident and expert mind in full control of the material, making judgements and passing comment on issues of concern to the discipline.

The presence of hedges in this corpus strongly demonstrates that the genre is not simply a celebration of academic truths. Writers pick their way through the information they present, sorting the taken-for-granted from the still uncertain. This is particularly the case where authors speculate about the future or the distant past (12a), or when generalisations may attract challenges if presented baldly (12b):

(12a) ... earliest cells <u>could also have</u> obtained energy by chemoorganotrophic mechanisms, most <u>likely</u> simple fermentations. Photosynthesis is also <u>a possibility</u> but <u>seems less likely</u> than ... (Bio)

And it is <u>probably</u> impossible in the near future to describe the whole of human discourse. (AL)

The changes in retailing in the last 30 years have been rapid – and they <u>seem</u> to be continuing. Scrambled merchandising <u>may</u> become even more scrambled. (Mkt)

(12b) As unemployment increases, and new technological developments <u>seem</u> to herald a <u>possibly</u> permanent end to the need for full employment, then cuts in welfare expenditure <u>might be seen</u> as inevitable and necessary concomitants to changes in the industrial system. (Soc)

Women <u>appear to</u> use language that expresses more uncertainty (...) than men, <u>suggesting</u> less confidence in what they say. (AL)

In the hard knowledge textbooks, hedges are also used to give readers a clear picture of scientific progress, clearly distinguishing the ignorance or false assumptions of the past from the certainties of the present. The contrast of qualification and definiteness in the extracts below are typical of the ways that writers seek to establish a cognitive schema of growth and the increasing ability of their disciplines to describe the natural world. As we have seen, this view lies at the heart of the values and modes of inquiry of hard knowledge cultures:

(13) <u>It was argued</u> that the simple sporangiospores of the zygomycetes <u>could be</u> developed after only a short period, while the more elaborate fruit bodies of the ascomycetes <u>would</u> require a longer build-up, and the even larger basidiomata of the Coprini <u>would</u> need the longest preparation of all. (...)

<u>We now know that</u> the various components of the substrate are far from exhausted after the initial flushes of growth and sporulation. <u>What has really happened</u> is that Coprinus has seized control by suppressing most of the other fungi. Hyphae of Coprinus <u>are actually</u> ... (Bio)

Einstein suggested that <u>this might be possible</u>, and <u>indeed this has been experimentally</u> confirmed countless times and forms the basis for many important processes. (Phy)

But cases are not merely limited to either broad issues or ideological assumptions of progress. There appears to be a reluctance by writers in all disciplines to upgrade claims that might be considered tenuous by a more informed audience, displaying a clear orientation to students and a wider professional readership:

(14) Most observers would <u>probably</u> agree with the conclusions drawn by Richard Lewontin ... (Soc)

The folliicolous tropical lichen Strigula <u>possibly</u> affects plants adversely by shading leaf surfaces. (Bio)

If impact tests are performed on components or specimens under conditions that lead to multiaxial states of stress, <u>it appears that</u> the fracture strength ...

(EE)

...<u>in some cases</u> immersion <u>seems to</u> lead to a fossilised classroom pidgin.   (AL)

Textbook authors, then, appear to be very alive to the role of textbooks in introducing neophytes to the rhetorical practices of their disciplines, and in particular to an appropriately cautious attitude to knowledge as part of a scholarly cognitive schema. This expert handling of degrees of certainty, however, does not only convey a conceptual understanding of a discipline, it also helps to construct a social impression of the writer.

Another way in which textbook writers seek to construct a *persona* of disciplinary competence and authority is through attitude markers; a personal evaluation of material which serves to guide the reader's response to what he or she is reading:

(15)   <u>My own view is that</u> Krashen's hypotheses do not, on closer inspection, conform to the three linguistic questions.   (AL)

<u>It is interesting to note that</u> members of both of these groups have cell walls that lack peptidoglycan.   (Bio)

These markers mainly consisted of items which indicated surprise or importance, especially in the soft disciplines. The examples, however, suggest an interesting tendency of attitude markers in textbooks to function as signals of what the *reader* should find important or surprising, rather than the writer:

(16)   Two points are <u>particularly important</u>:...   (Mkt)

But <u>even</u> education works by conviction and persuasion as well as by compulsion, ...   (Phil)

<u>Yet, surprisingly</u>, the average amount of time spent on domestic work by women did not decline very markedly.   (Soc)

<u>Most importantly</u>, his perspective on these phenomena cannot be derived from statutes or precedent.   (Soc)

These are <u>extremely important</u> in academic writing where they are used to ...   (AL)

This is clearly an assertion of superior competence which would not be likely in purely peer interaction, a posture which is also evident in the most frequent instances of attitude, especially in the hard sciences, which expressly emphasise correct courses of action through necessity modals:

(17)   The other strand of DNA, however, <u>must be</u> synthesized discontinuously.   (Bio)

<u>Care must be taken to note that</u> when the external energy $W(h + y)$ exceeds ...   (ME)

... the transformer secondaries <u>should be</u> separated and the output voltage measured individually.   (EE)

At times, this relationship-constructing role of attitude resources sails close to the autocratic:

(18) T7 and T8 show a few rules <u>that should seem obvious</u>.   (EE)

<u>It must be remembered that</u> before Staudinger's macromolecular hypothesis in 1920, polymers and colloids were classed together.   (Phy)

<u>You should</u> encourage your local engineering chapters (...) to invite outside lecturers to discuss these topics with you. <u>It is important that</u> you learn how to ...

(ME)

Here are the introduction and instructions <u>you should read</u> to respondents, <u>practice reading</u> them beforehand until they sound fairly conversational. (Soc)

The unequal relationship between participants that allows writers to intrude into their texts and offer explicit advice and instructions, thus not only allows them to construe themselves as experts but, interactionally, to define the primary audience as novices – designation which seems to be reinforced, incidentally, in the legalistic and formally prescriptive style of advice in departmental guidelines on writing that are often offered to students in different fields (Lea and Street, 1999).

The most obvious manifestation of how writers negotiate an asymmetrical relationship of competence, however, is through the use of relational markers, which are far more prevalent in textbooks than in research articles (Hyland, 1998c, 1999a). These allow writers to intervene into the discourse to address readers directly. Questions, for example, are often seen as a means of treating readers as equal participants by drawing them into a dialogue (Webber, 1994: 264), although in this genre they are largely rhetorical and function to set up answers rather than invite them. This closely circumscribes the participant role of the reader:

(19) But how does such a reformist perspective seek to explain the contradictions of the period since 1979?   (Soc)

What does it mean to be a 'person'? What are the 'building blocks' of such an idea?   (Phil)

What then are 'lichenized fungi'?   (Bio)

More explicitly, these texts position the reader with the use of imperatives, principally *consider, see* and *note*, and mainly in the hard fields (cf. Swales et al., 1998). Such devices are risky face strategies in any encounter as they engage an audience by directing them to some action. In textbooks, however, one suspects that the degree of imposition on the reader is not a major consideration; on the contrary, their high frequency suggests a certain rhetorical effort to display authority rather than negotiate a shared relationship:

(20) <u>Recall</u> that translation always begins at a unique codon, the so-called start codon.   (Bio)

<u>Let us suppose</u> a person is on a train moving at a very high speed, ...   (Phy)

<u>Think about it</u>. What if we eventually learn how to communicate with some of this planet's intelligent mammals?   (Phil)

<u>As you read this excerpt, pay particular attention to</u> how the teacher sets up the structure of the student–student interaction.   (AL)

In highlighting an element of the discussion, then, imperatives in textbooks appear to represent an assumption of inequality that is closer to classroom than peer interaction. Indeed, the interpersonal tenor established by these imperative forms appears to correlate closely with the participant relationships often constructed by tutor feedback on written assignments (cf. Spinks, 1998).

Finally, inclusive and second person pronouns provided a significant means by which writers sought to negotiate role relationships through relational markers in these texts. These were over three times more frequent (per 1,000 words) in the textbook sample than in an article corpus of similar size (Hyland, 1999a), with the distinction between genres in the hard fields particularly marked. The dominant form was inclusive we, used to invite readers into the discussion by drawing on shared general knowledge or the previous discourse to lead the reader through an argument:

(21)   We are familiar with these results from our knowledge of pressure in a gas.
(ME)

We already know that the tiny chytrids and oomycetes live here, but we might not expect to find many of the typically terrestrial dikaryomycotan fungi.   (Bio)

Otherwise, all three dimensions are equivalent, a fact that we all accept today. Now we are asked to accept one more dimension, time, which we had previously thought of as being somehow different.   (Phy)

We adapt our talk to suit our audience and talk differently to children, customers and colleagues. We use language differently in formal casual contexts.
(AL)

In philosophy this is a particularly familiar strategy, and accounts for the very high use of relational markers in both textbook and peer expositions. It apparently operates to reduce the distance between participants and to stress participation in a shared journey of exploration, but it is always clear who is leading the expedition:

(22)   Don't think that we're finished, though. This is only the first step. Now, we have to revise this list in at least two ways   (Phil)

We cannot say that it is valid, since we have to use such rules in order to say that anything is valid. And we can't use a rule to prove itself.   (Phil)

We can appeal to intuition, but can we absolutely trust our intuitions? We can deduce some of these truths from other truths, but then how do we justify the truths that act as premises?   (Phil)

Interestingly, we also find a relatively large number of cases which do not simply refer to writers and readers. In (23), for example, the writers appear to be referring to disciplinary concepts and terms which should be familiar to practitioners and, by implication, the student reader:

(23)   We call these models mathematical models. In creating them it is our hope that we can find one which will simulate the real physical system very well.   (Phy)

In any complement number system, we normally deal with a fixed number of digits, say n.   (EE)

> Both of these features as <u>we</u> currently understand them require the develop-
> ment of a cell structure.   (Bio)

Here then, the writer is empowered by acting as a spokesperson for his or her community, while the student is constructed by the discourse as a member, albeit a junior one, of a shared discipline with particular understandings and practices. Embedded in this construction, of course, is the assumption that such understandings are differentially distributed, once more privileging the writer's expertise over the reader's more peripheral participation in the discipline.

This differentiation of status is equally clear in the heavy use of second person pronouns, rare in articles but comprising the second most frequent form in all disciplines after *we* in the textbooks. Ostensibly the most interactive of pronouns, as it explicitly acknowledges the presence of the reader, it is often avoided in discourses of peer parity because it detaches writers and readers (Kuo, 1999), separating the latter into a different category of knowledge or competence:

(24) <u>Perhaps now you can understand</u> why <u>I and many other teaching mycologists</u>
      ask <u>our</u> classes to put <u>their</u> culturally determined attitudes on hold, ...   (Bio)

      There is not space to illustrate all the possible contextual influences, but <u>you</u>
      might find it interesting to investigate some of them for <u>yourself</u> in <u>your own</u>
      <u>community</u>.   (AL)

      Helpful information on report writing, public speaking, and sketching or draft-
      ing is available from countless sources, and <u>you should take advantage</u> of these
      aids.   (ME)

The potentially negative impact of this interactional relationship on the pedagogical effectiveness of the discourse is frequently recognised, however, and writers often replace it with a less exclusive alternative to avoid such implications:

(25) Therefore, to reduce ground-loop interference, <u>we must</u> avoid establishing any
      complete ohmic ground-loop paths and break up any such loops that already
      exist.   (EE)

      Indeed, this very ability to look at a situation from the vantage points of compet-
      ing systems of interpretation is, <u>as we shall see more clearly later on</u>, one of the
      hallmarks of sociological consciousness.   (Soc)

Once more, then, there is a clear implication here that the writer is an expert in full command of the topic and the genre. Like the other interpersonal features we have examined, this choice of forms demonstrates to colleagues and students alike the confidence to handle both the material and the interactions involved in the cognitive and cultural reproduction of the discipline.

NEGOTIATING EXPERT STATUS: SOME TEACHING AND LEARNING ISSUES

In this chapter we have seen once again that viewing texts as interaction offers a powerful way of accounting for the rhetorical choices of academics, situating such choices as socially motivated communicative purposes. While a somewhat heterogeneous category, metadiscourse patterns provide another link between texts, writers and disciplinary cultures, helping to define the rhetorical context by revealing some of the writer's expectations and understandings of the audience for whom the text was written. The fact that we have examined a number of these features elsewhere in this book also helps to emphasise some generic variations as well as to demonstrate distinctions in community practices among textbook authors. Through metadiscourse, then, we see one more way in which acts of communication define and maintain social groups.

More specifically, metadiscourse in textbooks contributes to framing academic knowledge, both in terms of a pedagogic sequencing of content and a selection which commits the writer to a perspective of the discipline. These choices also display an orientation to both a professional and student audience, and to particular views of disciplinary socialisation and learning. By asking (mainly rhetorical) questions, varying their degree of certainty, confidently evaluating the assertions of others, issuing directives, providing definitions and leading readers to particular interpretations of material, writers massively intervene in these texts to constitute themselves as experts. They negotiate the right to speak both of and for the discipline, constructing an authoritative and coherent picture of their field for learners, and a relatively uncontroversial depiction of its central features for peers. So, while the role of textbook author may carry a strong implication of competence and authority, this has to be rhetorically accomplished and confirmed in the text.

The constitution of one participant in the interaction as an expert, however, is also a simultaneous construction of some other participants as less expert. In selecting these metadiscourse options to address different audiences, writers define one of those audiences as novices, subscribing to an 'apprenticeship' metaphor, which may also underlie many of the classrooms where the texts will be read. The roles constructed in this way may in turn influence the reader's acquisition of disciplinary precepts and principles, and impede his or her ability to eventually participate as independent producers of academic knowledge themselves. Indeed, defining students simply by their lesser knowledge opens a breach between student expectations and teacher behaviour that may actively obstruct this process (Bourdieu and Passeron, 1996). So, while writers draw on their knowledge of the discipline and many of its preferred discoursal patterns to create these texts, speaking as an expert in this way tends to widen the distance between one who knows and one who doesn't, and this is not the basis for successful communication with peers.

However, Vygotsky (1978), among others, has stressed that learning does not simply involve a passive transference of knowledge from the more to the less competent. On the contrary, it is seen by many as an interactive process in which learners increasingly participate in a community of social practice (Candlin and Plum, 1999; Lave and Wenger, 1991; Rogoff, 1990). In this view, learning is not an internalisation of what is external, but a social achievement within a community where a range of values, attitudes and ways of working are also developed and negotiated. Learning a disciplinary culture and learning its language are inseparable, as this is the only context in which the language has meaning. Students do not learn disciplinary knowledge independently of language; they become competent through an understanding of how language constitutes and is constituted by interaction within a discipline.

Because of this, the metadiscourse practices employed to facilitate knowledge transfer in textbooks might make them easier to read, but they may make it more difficult for students to use the research literature in their studies or to develop appropriate rhetorical skills in their writing. Textbooks are frequently the only models of disciplinary writing that first-year undergraduates encounter, and they rarely receive valuable literacy support from their department tutors (e.g. Candlin and Plum, 1998). Too close a familiarity with the ways that textbooks address readers, organise material, and present facts may mean that learners are poorly prepared to understand the meta-textual requirements of an academic audience composed of a relatively egalitarian community of peers. Of course, undergraduates are not expected to participate in professional dialogues, but they do have to gain control of appropriate forms of argument and interaction in genres other than textbooks.

Of concern here is the fact that learning a discipline through the linguistic forms of textbooks does not introduce students to the full range of conventions within which the socio-cultural system of the discipline is encoded. Because all language use is a social and communicative activity, addressing readers in this way means that textbooks develop a rather skewed view of disciplinary practice: offering explicit assistance in extracting information but providing only minimal training in the kinds of relations employed in research discourse and the social functions of academic argument. When writing in the discipline, an awareness of audience is recognised as crucial to the development of effective argument strategies (Johns, 1993; Park, 1986), but a lack of appropriate metadiscourse knowledge may mean that students produce prose which is seen as uncontextualised, incoherent and insufficiently reader-focused. Because many tertiary students experience difficulty in adapting their prose for readers (Redd-Boyd and Slater, 1989) it seems vital that they should receive appropriate models of argument to allow them to practise writing within the socio-rhetorical framework of a given discipline.

Textbooks are not blandly uniform, however, and in various ways represent the discourse of their parent cultures, so students will gain some understanding of the ways that meanings are encoded in their disciplines. The genre differences I have noted also remind us that discourse communities are not monolithic entities. They include individuals at various levels of experience and stages of membership, from newcomers to experts, who may participate at different degrees of engagement and in various genres of interaction. However, while textbook authors principally address the potential processing problems of an uninitiated readership in representing disciplinary subject matter, embedded in the conventions of this genre we also glimpse the ways that disciplinary writers perceive students and regard the process of leading them into the practices of their new disciplinary communities.

NOTES

1. The growing importance of distance learning and the increasing publication of inquiry-based textbooks such as those produced by the UK Open University may eventually impact on this view.
2. It should be noted that the calculation of devices according to a word count is not intended to represent the *proportion* of a text formed by metadiscourse. It is clear that metadiscourse typically has clause-level (or higher) scope and I have standardised the raw figures to a common basis merely to compare the *occurrence*, rather than the length, of metadiscourse in corpora of unequal sizes.

Chapter 7

Researching and teaching academic writing

In the preceding chapters I have considered some of the ways that academic disciplines are defined and distinguished from each other by their texts. In the process I have, often implicitly, sketched a methodology for investigating published academic writing as the outcome of social interactions. In this chapter I want to discuss this methodology in a little more detail and outline some of the implications of the approach for both teaching and research. My intention is to offer something of a practical guide for the extension of this perspective, exploring the research and pedagogic ramifications of viewing texts as discipline and genre-specific forms of social interaction.

As I have emphasised throughout, rhetorical action should be seen as situated in the historically-specific assumptions that community members make about reality and the ways they seek to influence that reality through writing. This means that the more we are able to understand the conventions, goals and assumptions of these communities, the better we can describe what it is writers are doing when they select one form or structure over another, and the better we can assist novices to evaluate and employ these devices effectively. In what follows, the focus turns to how we might reveal disciplinary repertoires more clearly, and how we might assist learners to gain greater control over them.

A SOCIAL APPROACH TO RESEARCHING TEXTS

The research discussed in this book has adopted a broadly social-based approach, an attempt to examine how, in the words of Faigley (1985: 235), 'individual acts of communication define, organize and maintain social groups'. I have examined this problem by bringing together a diverse range of linguistic and pragmatic features to see how they constitute a rhetorical link between writers and readers. A central aspect of this link is that social actors are aware of the need to ascertain each other's purposes and share assumptions about the ways that texts function to signal and represent them. These features direct attention from academic texts as sets of scholarly propositions, to texts as the interactions of people who are members of specific communities.

A number of different methods have been employed to study these relationships. Crudely, these methodological differences amount to a choice between either dematerialising texts and examining interaction as a packages of specific linguistic features, or rematerialising texts and examining interaction as a series of real, situated encounters (Myers, 1999: 58).

Ethnographic studies of academic writing, such as produced by Chin (1994), Haas (1994), Lea and Street (1999) and Prior (1998), are examples of the latter. Such analyses have adopted case study approaches to focus on particular writers or readers – what they do when they write or read. These studies are rich with the sense of human encounter, providing a detailed delineation of the context of composing that includes the personal and social histories of individual writers as they interact in specific socio-economic circumstances. By seeking to account for the ways that writers negotiate the immediate writing circumstances, such studies have provided valuable and fine-grained descriptions of dynamic, situated practices in which disciplines are portrayed as authentic, human moments. This kind of analysis Nystrand (1987) refers to as the *situation of expression*, as opposed to the contexts of eventual use for which written texts are composed.

One difficulty here, of course, is that context is a slippery concept and it is difficult to pin down precisely the impact of any particular event or writer experience which may help to shape the outcome of a given text. As a result, analysts have focused on a range of contextual dimensions to explicate the local influences on composing choices. These have included: the epistemological frameworks assumed in departmental undergraduate writing guidelines (Lea and Street, 1999); the authority of practitioner vs newcomer relationships in collaborative writing (Blakeslee, 1997); the design of the physical space in which composition may occur (Chin, 1994); and the restricted access to information or production technologies by third world scholars (Canagarajah, 1996). Clearly, not all of these features will be immediately relevant in all situations and, indeed, many peripheral features may be unconsciously influential and so not available for reconstruction by the researcher at all.

A second problem is that what is going on in any situation cannot be properly understood or interpreted unless we look beyond the local setting to the culture and event within which the action is embedded and which the discourse invokes. Participants, in their writing, conjure up institutional patterns that have an existence that extends beyond the immediate encounter, and these can only be perceived by viewing activity as socially and institutionally constituted modes of praxis. The genres and choices adopted by writers in the texts I have studied here are conventions in the sense of being socially ratified solutions to particular communication problems (Atkinson, 1991). They are not simply ad hoc choices but represent, through their regularity and repetition, institutionally recognised communicative preferences through which writers construct and engage in disciplinary realities.

The alternative approach to studying written interactions is to dematerialise texts. This involves removing them from their actual material circumstances of construction and making analytical assumptions about the relationships between linguistic forms and rhetorical effects as they operate within particular communities of writers and readers. Context here refers less to the actual contexts for the production of writing than to the larger world which lies beyond them, created by the purposes and uses that the finished text may potentially fulfil. Instead of detailing the actual situations that writers deal with when they write, this approach focuses on the goal-directed purposes and problems presented by particular rhetorical situations. It assumes that texts do not function communicatively at the time they are composed but only when they are read, anticipating particular readers and their responses to what is written. Looking at writing in this way therefore evokes the institutional frame within which the text is created, a social milieu which intrudes upon the writer and activates specific responses to recurring tasks.

As we have seen, one of the advantages of this approach is that it makes problematic the outsider's view that academic genres are simply written to tired, re-used formula. From an intensive study of large numbers of texts it is possible to see how much academic writing is the result of situated choices, and to identify the forms and patterns that writers typically select as being most likely to successfully negotiate their purposes with an anticipated audience. Such social practices can be seen as a skilled performance by social agents drawing on relevant knowledge and appropriate techniques. Moreover, by reconstructing the writer and reader from the text and making assumptions about the rhetorical functions of particular forms, this approach allows quantitative comparisons across genres, disciplines and times. In turn, as I shall discuss below, this can serve useful pedagogical purposes in introducing novices to unfamiliar genres.

Prior (1998) has criticised this perspective as being overdependent on structuralist assumptions of shared conventions and interaction patterns, while undervaluing the tenuous nature of intersubjectivity suggested by the varieties of contexts in which writing occurs. His ethnographic account regards action as mediated by personal, interpersonal and institutional histories which occur within complexly differentiated networks. From his perspective, then, to frame writing in terms of discourse communities is to reify the multiple meanings and practices of individual participants working within open and dynamic groups.

There is, of course, a great deal of truth in this argument for, as Lave and Wenger (1991) point out, and as we noted in the last chapter, there are varying degrees to which individuals are engaged in the fields of participation defined by a community. Communities are sets of relations and actions among people who are also members of other parallel and overlapping groups. It is obvious then that any social institution will contain varied ideological-discoursal formations, subjects who differ in their beliefs and practices. The extent to which they possess core norms and values is then open to question.

However, while writers may not always find themselves acting in forums that are completely predictable in terms of the conventions thought to be shared with others, we need to assume a certain overlap of interpretive practices in order to account for the ways that meanings are interactively created. Individuals have a sense of the roles and purposes of those with which they regularly engage and which others, in turn, appear to endorse. They recognise familiar discourses and relationships through which these roles and purposes are usually played out, and they perceive a common history through which these practices have evolved. While discourse communities undoubtedly develop and change through countless small acts of identification and interpretation of the kinds discussed by Prior and others, the influence of this identifiable sense of common endeavour and commonality must be recognised in explaining their discoursal practices.

Disciplinary discourses cannot be fully elucidated apart from the historically specific institutional modes of activity within which members operate. The knowledge and skills involved in academic research and communication form part of the structural properties of disciplinary collectivities, and we cannot ignore the reproduction of regularities which generate and sustain those collectivities. To focus on the contexts of individual acts of composition provides valuable detail about the practices of writing, but to neglect historical and structural properties makes it impossible to see the conditions writers require and employ to reproduce, and to change, such regularities (Bruffee, 1986; Geertz, 1983; Kuhn, 1970). While I agree that actors do not just conform to existing standards and routines, their exploitation of them demonstrates that they possess this knowledge for without it they would be unable to reproduce disciplinary activities. Put simply, institutions are the consequence of such routinised practices by community members. Without some reference to the trans-situational rules or shared expectations implied in the skills and procedures of discursive practice we could not account for the existence of disciplines at all (Hagstrom, 1965; Ziman, 1984).

To approach this point from a different direction, disciplinary interaction is possible because participants are linked by webs of intertextual knowledge as a result of their experience of similar texts and their expectations of how information and attitudes are likely to be expressed. In other words, writing and reading involve deploying a considerable amount of procedural and content knowledge to texts, and interlocutors have to suppose, even if only for the sake of economic processing, that what is salient, and therefore what is meaningful, is adequately encoded and recoverable. As Nystrand (1989: 75) observes:

> The process of writing is a matter of elaborating text in accord with what the writer can reasonably assume that the reader knows and expects, and the process of reading is a matter of predicting text in accord with what the reader assumes about the writer's purpose. More fundamentally, each presupposes the sense-making capabilities of the other. As a result, written communication is predicated on what the writer/reader each assumes the other will do/has done.

A common dictum of methodology texts is that the kind of research approach one adopts should depend on the kind of research questions one asks. It is equally true, however, that the kind of research model with which one operates predisposes one to ask certain types of questions and not others. This reciprocal relationship encourages us to reflect on the assumptions of our methods and recognise what they can tell us and what they ignore. While a social paradigm of the type I have outlined here is a powerful means of addressing the wider frames to which academics orientate when writing in their disciplines, it neglects issues arising from the local context or personal preciosity.

I subscribe to the view that a central constitutive feature of contexts are the culture-specific understandings of participants concerning how best to negotiate their purposes, accomplishing social order through routinely recognisable ways of communicating. To study discourse for insights into the beliefs and practices of the disciplines, we do not need to establish core values to see how this is achieved. We do, however, need to examine what is conventional and typical in the behaviour of skilled writers as they construct the meaning potential of their texts, constrained by their sense of a reader's expectations. This, unfortunately, does not always allow us to identify real writers or to hear the various voices that they hear. In ironing out the wrinkles of specifics and avoiding the untidy details that lie behind individual texts, we necessarily transform individuals into abstract actors making strategic choices. However, even although there are always local factors at work influencing how a text is constructed, academic writers are invariably seeking to achieve recognisable communicative purposes, and to do this they must rhetorically draw on a knowledge of their community of readers.

I have argued that by abstracting away from any specific writer to examine recurring features in large numbers of texts, we can infer more subtle relations between the various linguistic features than would be possible through the intensive studies of a few texts. Moreover, while this approach fails to offer insights into the local, contingent factors that might influence particular cases of situated academic writing, it is by no means merely an artefact of analysis. What these purposes are, the ways they are expressed and retrieved, and how individual practitioners respond to them can be recovered from those who write and read the texts under study. An important dimension of any analysis of academic or professional discourse is therefore to gather interview responses as a means of interpreting textual data as socially situated practice. I shall discuss below the methodology for undertaking this kind of research.

A METHODOLOGY FOR STUDYING ACADEMIC TEXTS

I have not set out to offer a new methodology but to employ techniques which focus on *discourse*, a process of social interaction, rather than just *texts*, by giving explicit attention to the perspectives of insiders and the social institutions within which they work. My goal has been to achieve a better understanding of social interactions as they are made manifest through repetition in academic writing, rather than in the practices of individual writers.

As I have suggested above, what this approach loses in human richness, it gains in providing a powerful description of community practices and a knowledge of academic disciplines. Moreover, it is a methodology that can be replicated and used by teachers wishing to learn more about the genres they are teaching, by researchers interested in professional discourse, or by students interested in pursuing a study of discourse for a final year project or a higher degree. Because of this, I shall set out the approach in some detail and offer suggestions for research directions that interested readers might wish to follow.

The method employs both quantitative analysis and pragmatic interpretation to describe patterns in language features in texts. The quantitative studies allow us to see the extent of variation and similarity in texts and to examine the complex interactions among linguistic features, while the more qualitative interpretations encourage us to understand the communicative functions they serve for the users of these texts.

The research approach offers a systematic means of tying generic practices to situated cognition, examining texts while obtaining the views of those who use the genres in question. This broadly follows the model set out by Bhatia (1993: 22–34). While Bhatia's book largely focuses on schematic structure, the steps he recommends clearly emphasise the importance of situated research, of locating texts in contexts. His steps are:

1. Placing the genre-text in a situational context in order to understand why the genre is conventionally written the way it is.
2. Surveying the existing literature for other perspectives and insights into the situated working of the genre and its conventional form.
3. Refining the situational/contextual analysis to more clearly identify the goals, participants, network of surrounding texts, and the extra-textual reality that the text is trying to represent.
4. Selecting an appropriate corpus to ensure that it is sufficiently representative of the focus genre to allow the research questions to be explored adequately.
5. Studying the institutional context in which the genre is used in order to better understand the implicit conventions most often followed by participants in that communicative situation.
6. Selecting one or more levels of analysis (lexico-grammatical, textualisation, move structure) to best address the motivating problem.
7. Obtaining information from specialist informants to confirm findings, validate insights, add psychological reality, and open areas of further exploration.

Different types of research methods lead to different types of understanding, but this outline provides a useful research recipe, whether starting from an analysis of linguistic features or an inquiry into how particular functions are expressed through forms, to reveal disciplinary preferences of expression and meanings.

To draw some valid conclusions about published writing in different fields

I sought to maximise the quality and quantity of data I collected. I did this by developing a stratified, randomly selected corpus of texts from research journals, textbooks and quick reports in eight academic fields and conducting interviews with senior academics in those disciplines at a number of universities. The next few subsections briefly explore the details of this methodology, set out in programmatic rather than retrospective form to better display its generalisability.

SOURCES AND ANALYSIS OF DATA

The analyst needs multiple sources of evidence, and a combination of techniques to analyse them, to increase the construct validity of his or her study. Three kinds of data appear to be necessary.

- First a corpus of representative texts is needed which can be searched for repeated uses of features that might reveal routine interactions with readers. From this corpus examples of linguistic decisions can be associated with particular social purposes and relations which might, in turn, point to aspects of disciplinary knowledge.
- A second source of data is interview transcripts from disciplinary informants. This material is necessary to provide an understanding of how insiders view their literacy practices and how they see their participation in their disciplines. This data is best collected through a series of wide-ranging and relatively unstructured interviews with a researcher from each discipline.
- The third source of information also involves expert self-reports, but of a more focused kind, concentrating on particular texts and text features. This data provides a greater understanding of how the actual users of the focus genres, those who write, read and review them, see and respond to the target features. Here interviews focus informants on particular texts, and examine their own writing where practicable.

Textual data

The value of corpus-based approaches to linguistic description has been convincingly demonstrated in recent years, revealing how items which recur in particular contexts fulfil particular functions (e.g. Kennedy, 1998; Thomas and Short, 1996). Malcolm (1987), Gosden (1993) and Swales et al. (1998), for example, have illustrated through corpus analysis the specific importance of tense, theme and imperatives in disciplinary writing. As my study has shown, such an approach brings a distributional perspective to linguistic analysis by providing quantitative information about the relative frequency of use of particular elements in different contexts, pointing to systematic tendencies in the selection of meanings. The use of corpora therefore reduces the burden that is often placed on individual texts (or on intuitions) and dramatically shows how particular grammatical and lexical choices are regularly made. It is this regularity, the continuous reinforcement of repetition and consistency, which helps to construct and maintain social reality, and gives meaning to social institutions such as academic disciplines.

A huge number and variety of texts are, of course, produced by the academy and, as noted earlier, it is this production which largely helps to define disciplines and members' participation in them. This fertility also provides numerous ways for the researcher to approach academic interactions through texts and gives many opportunities to break new ground, for few genres have been adequately described or explored. It is relatively easy to compile a corpus of texts, either electronically or via the photocopier, and academics are normally happy to talk about their writing. In addition, the compilation of corpora has been made considerably easier in recent times by the availability of a great deal of material on the internet. A number of websites offer written corpora for linguistic analysis and many journals are now in electronic form.

Data selection is generally influenced by subjective criteria and is validly determined in any number of ways. We might select texts because of the respective value of the genre to our target community, because of our interests, or because of the convenience of collection. Teachers may find it easier to collect samples of work from their students (e.g. Gosden, 1996), conference organisers might have access to abstract submissions (e.g. Kaplan et al., 1994), successful researchers to reprint requests (Swales, 1990) and journal editors to submission letters (Swales, 1996). My own preference here, however, has been with published writing. This was partly because of the straightforward access to such data, but also because I felt this was the high stakes area which would yield the best examples of social interactions about which I was curious.

If an individual's engagement in the discourses of his or her discipline comprises membership of that discipline, then there would seem to be considerable value in examining published texts as the most public, successful and highly regarded examples of the ways in which such engagements are configured. The importance of published texts lies in their status as accredited disciplinary artefacts. These are writings that have completed professional and institutional rites of passage and gained legitimacy in the eyes of community gatekeepers. They are what disciplines most obviously produce. They are its public face and its life force. They are at the heart of its institutional goals of furthering knowledge and consolidating influence, and central to its members' professional goals of establishing reputations. While other forms of writing clearly play a critical role in supporting the research and publication process, such 'occluded' genres (Swales, 1996) are hidden from public scrutiny and so do not directly contribute to the reputation of the writer or the validation of knowledge.

It is important to gather the recommendations of subject specialists when assembling the corpus to ensure a sample of representative texts. In this study my informants nominated ten journals each as sources for the reviews, articles and abstracts, and I took the textbook sample from the core material on the reading lists for introductory undergraduate courses. The letter genre is restricted to the sciences and the texts studied here were selected by experts in physics, chemistry and biology.

In most cases these texts were examined using two text analysis programs, *Wordsmith Tools* (Scott, 1996) and *WordPilot* (Milton, 1999) to retrieve lexical expressions and graphic symbols, and to examine target items in their sentential contexts. Among other things, these programs can search a corpus of texts and display all examples as keyword-in-context (KWIC) concordanced lines, thus providing information on both paradigmatic and syntagmatic behaviour of language use. This means that all instances of a particular feature in a collection of texts constitute the evidence for sociolinguistic and pragmatic generalisations. In most cases I was principally interested in lexical expression, searching for forms of hedging and boosting, metadiscourse signals or explicit citation markers; sentence analysis was sufficient to determine these functions. Occasionally, however, it was necessary to go beyond the concordance sentence to retrieve a fuller context and establish the category used.

In Chapters 3 (reviews) and 4 (abstracts) I also employed non-computerised procedures. Concordance techniques are unhelpful when dealing with move structure analyses and these larger rhetorical stages in texts have to be identified manually. This is because the schematic structure that writers employ to shape their purposes for a particular readership are not always explicitly marked linguistically, but more often draw on pragmatic understandings. Paltridge (1994, 1995), for example, points out that there are generally non-linguistic reasons for generic staging in texts and that structural or move boundaries depend more on convention, appropriacy and content than, say, patterns of lexical cohesion or other linguistic patterning. Analysts therefore draw on content-based terms such as 'indicating a gap' (Swales, 1990), 'establishing credentials' (Bhatia, 1993) or 'value for a particular readership' as in Chapter 3, or 'product' as in Chapter 4. The methodology required here therefore involves a careful analysis of each text in its entirety, examining the relationship between text stages guided by a cognitive rather than purely linguistic sense of divisions.

Chapter 4 also includes a comparison with a sample of generically similar texts from 1980, providing a brief illustration of how disciplinary writers mediated reality with their peers at a slightly earlier time. Much of this book examines how academics treat their literatures, their topics, their audiences and themselves in the published disciplinary discourses we find today, but this may tend to give the impression of professional language and its use as a timeless and inevitable means of communicating knowledge. The study of community practices from a diachronic perspective, however, is an important way of looking at the constitutive relationships between writers and their texts, to show that language and communities are mutually entailed and constituted. While my discussion of this is a simple comparison, studies of this kind typically sample texts in period blocks over regular intervals of the life of a publication (e.g. Atkinson, 1996; Bazerman, 1988; Valle, 1997). Using many of the procedures of rhetorical and register analysis outlined above, these historical studies are then able to reveal important changes in the target genre and the rhetorical strategies it contained as a response to the needs, conceptions and practices of the many writers who contributed to its evolution.

With the kind of functional coding of items undertaken in this book, it is important to validate the reliability of one's judgements by comparing them with those of a second rater working independently, and preferably to seek the independent views of an expert informant on a sample of items where this is possible. Both methods were used in this study and revealed a strong correlation in almost all cases.

A further decision is whether to apply statistical analyses to the quantitative results of frequency counts. Unfortunately there seems to be no clearly reliable way of demonstrating significance with this kind of data. Frequency data does not meet the stringent conditions to apply multiple *t*-tests, although these are sometimes used, and the use of ANOVA procedures to compare means for every feature across every field is extremely unwieldy and time consuming. On the other hand, discourse analysts are often less interested in establishing detailed non-parametric comparisons than in discovering broad distributional differences of items between groups. Frequencies are thus used as a springboard to more qualitative study, using the quantitative findings as a basis for characterising broad similarities and differences in the genres produced by particular communities. The numbers, in other words, are intended to fill some gaps in our knowledge of the subject, and are preliminary to the development of viable candidate explanations of underlying communicative purposes and interactional practices.

One important point should be emphasised concerning the analysis of text data, mainly because it is often either ignored or denied. It should be clear that research is never totally open-ended and undirected but always, at the very least, guided by an intention to understand the workings of some aspect of language. In the case presented in this book, it was the nature of social interactions in academic writing. Contrary to some views on research, analysis can never be exhaustive and comprehensive. It always involves some focus of attention and selectivity and in some ways mirrors the interpretive processes of discourse participants. De Beaugrande (1998: 91) has recently made this point in responding to Widdowson's argument that we should account for everything in a discourse:

> I can see no way to determine, much less 'account' for, 'everything that is encoded', much of it probably tedious and irrelevant in any case. Instead, we all 'decide to select certain features to attend to'; and we do so not in any 'arbitrary' fashion but in alliance with what I have termed the 'cognitive interests' of the discipline.

My research therefore began with assumptions about what interaction is and the idea that traces of it could be found by matching repeated forms to the purposes of strategic actors sharing communicative goals. This meant that while I was open to discovering the unanticipated, I nevertheless had a basic framework of analysis which meant I looked for certain features and not others, drawing on the literature, my own understandings, and my informants' comments to do so.

The role of subjectivity in this process should not be underemphasised or tucked away behind numbers. All data analysis involves making connections and developing categories, and this is not, and cannot be, some kind of objective, pre-theoretical exercise. The ways that researchers generate constructs through identifying specific phenomena as instances of larger patterns in data involves a degree of intuition, inspiration and luck (see Doheny-Farina and Odell, 1985). Essentially and inevitably, however, it relies most heavily on the emergence of what they see as a result of their training and experience. No less than in the hard sciences, observations are theory-laden and therefore fallible. Contrary to any kind of naive inductivism, all explanations are underdetermined by evidence because observation statements are always made in the language of some theory. In discourse analysis, as in physics, we cannot reach a kind of transcendental truth because the only thing an analyst really has direct contact with is his or her own experiences.

Ultimately, our explanations are only as reliable as the theories they presuppose. Academic knowledge, like all knowledge, is at least partly socially determined and relative to the context in which it is generated. So, because reasoning concerns the relationships between statements, rather than between reality and statements, we need to be aware of the mediation of our expectations when searching for constructs and connections, and to make these connections as clear and as coherent as we possibly can. This means being frank about the problem and explicit about the constraints of our theory. It also means that we are not cheating if we draw on our own insider knowledge of the contexts we investigate, or if we allow these understandings to guide our research.

In understanding texts, therefore, we draw on theoretical presuppositions about what writers are trying to achieve in their choice of genres and language. We select from a repertoire of intepretations rather than hit on the truth. Explanation involves selecting texts and items which we believe will be most fruitful given our research interests. It involves filtering out from the statements of our subjects the ways that their interests, beliefs, affiliations, experiences, values and practices appear to influence their writing. It also involves making decisions about how these perceptions carry traces of wider participation frameworks not immediately accessible in the composing context. These are clearly not observational issues as the researcher has to determine what constitutes the relevantly operative factors in that context to explain the discourse; but nor is it pure speculation if these decisions are made plausible by grounding them in written and oral data.

Interview data

Oral data is generally collected by focus group discussions and various types of interview. In this study I used focus groups, unstructured interviews, and discourse-based interviews with 12 subject specialists from these disciplines in four universities. The informants comprised a group of experienced and well-published researchers, typically an associate or full professor. They regularly read the journals studied here and frequently contributed to them and acted as reviewers. The sessions lasted between 40 and 90 minutes, and were often followed up by a shorter conversation to check interpretations and follow leads. All interviews were taped and written up as a summary immediately after the session and subsequently returned to several times, often with the assistance of the subjects.

Myers (1998: 85) points out that 'the effectiveness of focus groups depends on a tension between the moderator's constraints and participants' interactions' which works as a collaborative project of opinion display. This methodology has been popular in the social sciences and public survey research for many years, but has not been widely used in discourse studies. I conducted three such groups with between two and four different combinations of informants from various disciplines. These worked best when groups were relatively disciplinary heterogeneous, and yielded useful comparisons of particular practices such as citing and criticising.

Both the focus groups and the first part of the one-to-one interviews were conducted using a semi structured format (Cohen and Manion, 1994). This involved a series of open-ended prompts which focused broadly on the characteristics of the discipline and its literacy practices. This method is a productive means of learning about respondents' views of how their fields are structured, their epistemology and the role of theory and empiricism in them, the criteria for recognition and success of members, and, most centrally, about their communication and publication practices. It is important to avoid imposing any kind of hypotheses on interviewees here, and in my sessions I simply told them I was interested in how academics communicated with each other and how this related to their disciplines. These discussions generated a lot of material about professional beliefs and practices and raised issues concerning intentions, previous encounters with discoursal resources, experiences of institutional conventions, and the pressures to conform to them. Here, then, the focus was on the informants' views of the social and ideological perspectives of their disciplines.

In the second stage of the interviews I employed what Odell, et al. (1983) call a 'discourse based interview', which involves detailed discussions about particular pieces of writing. This format requires participants to respond to features in selected corpus articles as members of the readership for whom the texts were composed, allowing them to employ their specialist knowledge as community members to interpret meanings, reconstruct possible writer motivations, and evaluate rhetorical effectiveness. It is also helpful if subjects can examine and discuss, as far as possible, the reasons for their choices at specific points in published examples of their own work. I therefore asked respondents to consider a paper they had written and to try to explain what they had had intended to achieve by their choice of particular forms. In this way it is possible to obtain something of the perspectives of insiders acting in their authentic disciplinary roles as both consumers and creators of texts, capturing both sides of the practices of negotiation which create meanings.

It is important to note that the use of participants' perspectives as data must recognise the manner in which these perspectives are themselves socially constructed. In other words, such perceptions and opinions are not fixed objects, but may change according to the interview situation itself (e.g. Littlejohn, 1988). However, while I am aware of the possible meaning-constructing effects of interviewing, it seems to be the most effective way of bringing the insider's perspective to the analysis, taking us nearer to a description of cultural practices in terms of its members' understandings. Participant accounts are not simply checks on the analysis but are a feature in their own right, indicators of members' experiences of the situated activities of their disciplines. Human agency is involved in the reproduction of texts and of social institutions, and while actors may be unaware of the effects of their practices, their understandings are important in providing a fuller picture of what these effects might be.

Such accounts, therefore, are not only essential for an interpretive and explanatory analysis of texts, allowing us to see the factors that might contribute to disciplinary coherence and meanings, they also offer invaluable insights into the relationship between individuals and institutions, allowing us to go beyond the discourse processes that participants are aware of. I have therefore used the spoken material not as problematical sociological data, but at face value as insiders' perspectives of what they do when they read and write in their disciplines. While I acknowledge that this data may well be examined in other ways, I am interested mainly in situating texts through members' frames of reference which are formed from broadly common naturalised ideologies.

This, then, is how I collected and analysed the data, the assumptions I made and the steps I took to explore it. In the next section I want to look at some of these assumptions in greater detail by turning to the implications the approach has for teaching.

DISCIPLINES, TEXTS AND TEACHING

There often seems to be an implicit assumption in ESP (English for Specific Purposes) and EAP (English for Academic Purposes) that academic writing is a limited textual practice, a set of steps which, if executed correctly, produces successful text genres. By appropriately setting out the expected moves novices can, near enough for their purposes, approximate the writing of experts. Such a perspective implies that effective texts involve applying a set of monolithic rules and that learning genres involves developing conformity to these rules. In reality, as I hope the previous analyses have suggested, disciplinary conventions are both subtle and complex, offering a guiding framework for writers as they struggle to present their arguments in the ways that are most likely to gain their readers' acceptance. Writing is produced and mediated through writers' experiences of prior discourse, rather than explicit knowledge of rules, and involves making rational choices based on an understanding of how texts work within and for specific contexts and audiences.

Learning to write academic genres essentially means developing an understanding of the social practices of one's discipline, becoming aware of the functions of texts and how these functions are conventionally accomplished. It means taking on certain roles and using, for individual meaning-making, the resources that one's discipline and its genres make available. This does, of course, involve students contending with issues of form and structure, and with public contexts for writing. To be successful, however, it must also involve them in acquiring a metacognitive awareness of these forms and contexts and a familiarity with the discoursal strategies they need to perform roles, engage in interactions, and accomplish goals in the target community. In sum, it requires that students gain an awareness of the discipline's symbolic resources for getting things done by routinely connecting purposes with features of texts.

The approach to disciplinary discourses I have taken in this book has a number of implications for teaching academic writing and it is perhaps worth setting them out here.

First, it is clear that academic literacy is unlikely to be achieved through an orientation to some general set of trans-disciplinary academic conventions and practices. I have consistently argued that writing cannot be understood solely in terms of either immediate situations of writing or from individual texts; rather, it reflects, and in turn constitutes, social and institutional practices derived from contexts which are principally disciplinary. This means that while academic knowledge is frequently represented in style guides, ESP materials and University 'enhancement courses' as attending to transferable writing skills, students actually have to readjust to each discipline they encounter. Paraphrasing, citing, reviewing the literature, and other standard features of EAP courses are not uniform practices reducible to generic advice. The varied academic practices of writing and reading cannot be seen as general skills that can be taught in marginalised university 'Language Centres' by anyone with a reasonable grasp of English and a textbook. They are the core of each discipline; 'ways of being in the world' (Geertz, 1983: 155).

We have seen in these analyses that the conventions of writing are always embedded in deeper epistemological frameworks that are frequently discipline specific. Each discourse community has unique ways of identifying issues, asking questions, solving problems, addressing its literature, criticising colleagues and presenting arguments, and these make the possibility of transferable skills unlikely. Composition theorists, sociolinguists and rhetoricians have repeatedly stressed that critical differences exist in academic argument forms, style and graphical representation (e.g. Bartholomae, 1986; Bazerman, 1988; Bizzell, 1992) and, indeed, that these form the major means by which we are able to recognise disciplinary behaviour.

Similarly, there is now considerable empirical research which underlines and documents these differences. MacDonald (1994), for instance, points to the epistemic reasons behind the high incidence of particularised sentence subjects in literature, Bloor (1996) to the hypothetical argument strategies of philosophy, McKenna (1997) to distinctive theme choices in engineering, Channel (1990) to imprecision in economics and Halliday (1998) to nominalisation in physics. Work reported in Jolliffe (1988) and Braine (1995) demonstrates the wide variety of genre characteristics which masquerade under common labels such as 'experimental lab report', 'research paper' and 'the student essay' in different disciplines. Comparative studies of research writing have, among many other features, demonstrated disciplinary differences in evaluative focus (Thetela, 1997), patterns of tense and voice (Hanania and Akhtar, 1985), use of imperatives (Swales et al., 1998) and modal qualification (Butler, 1990). Perhaps it is unnecessary to labour the point further.

A second implication, closely related to the first, is that viewing academic writing in this way brings the importance of multiple literacies sharply into focus. The term literacy itself draws attention to the relative nature of academic writing, encompassing as it does the wide range of experiences, practices and ways of knowing that individuals carry to a writing task (Street, 1995). 'Literacy' refers to different strategies for conceptualising, organising and producing texts; it implies variations in the contexts and communities in which they are written, and the roles of reader and writer that they invoke. Unfortunately, as Street observes, there has been a tendency to acknowledge this complexity and diversity in the spoken medium, yet to maintain faith with a traditional view which reifies the written language as an autonomous abstraction.

The issue is relevant here because in acquiring disciplinary knowledge and skills students simultaneously encounter a new and dominant literacy, often finding their own writing practices to be marginalised by the academy and regarded as failed attempts to approximate the standard forms (Pardoe, 1999). In institutional contexts where a unitary and autonomous model of literacy prevails, such as many university environments, literacy is seen as an independent variable detached from its social consequences. In such circumstances it is easy for teachers and students to see writing difficulties as learners' own weaknesses.

Tertiary study is often a challenging experience for students. Not only does it confront them with a more complex and relativistic style of learning than they knew at school, but they also have to 'employ cultural and discourse literacies very different from those of "standard English" varieties' (Bizzell, 1987: 131). These difficulties are compounded for second language speakers, particularly as success is principally judged by the display of competence in a specialist written register. This is most vividly illustrated in situations such as that experienced by Aboriginal Australians whose experiences of educational literacy conflict alarmingly with their familiar community-based oral communication patterns (Malcolm, 1999).

Less dramatically, but more commonly, Ballard and Clanchy (1991) and Bloor and Bloor (1991) show that Australian and British universities rarely take into sufficient account the home academic cultures of overseas students, who are often unprepared for the type and volume of writing expected. Unfortunately, like their native counterparts, they are then required to suppress or deny elements of their cognitive and linguistic repertoire and adopt those of their new disciplines. This is often referred to as 'fixing up' their language problems, which is fondly believed to then facilitate learning, allowing them to take on the academic knowledge of their fields.

While it may seem self-evident to faculty what writing at the university entails, this is rarely explicitly conveyed to students. Even where they are presented with writing guidelines these rarely seek to provide them with a means of conceptualising the epistemological frameworks within which they have to study, nor do they offer ways of recognising that there are also different practices within the academy itself (Lea and Street, 1999).

The fact of multiple literacies within the academy is a further burden to students, particularly if they lack the vocabulary and analytical skills to distinguish the heterogeneity of the discourses and practices typical of the different disciplinary cultures they encounter. Presenting academic skills as universal and transferable does a serious disservice to learners as it disguises variability, and misrepresents academic writing as naturalised, self-evident and non-contestable ways of participating in academic communities. A large literature testifies to the enormous variability of academic writing tasks required of students across disciplines (Braine, 1989; Bridgeman and Carlson, 1984; Horowitz, 1986) and the specific expectations demanded may actually be contradictory (Candlin and Plum, 1999). Students that are working in interdisciplinary programmes, of course, are doubly disadvantaged, as they are confronted with multiple, and wholly different, discourses, content and assumptions about the nature of writing and about disciplinary participation.

A major task of EAP teaching is therefore to address the perceptions and practices of writing that students may bring with them, and thereby seek to provide a bridge to the assumptions about writing that are embedded in their disciplines. By making students aware of how literacy practices are grounded in social structures, undermining the 'single literacy' view, we can make transparent those practices that otherwise seem objective, reified and universal. We have to reveal writing as relative to particular groups and contexts, and reject a teaching approach which implicitly accepts EAP as a remedial exercise. We are not correcting a deficit in students' writing weaknesses, but helping them to unpack the requirements of their disciplines. The challenge is to show that the forms and structures revealed by analysis and presented in teaching materials are simply ways of organising arguments and knowledge within particular communities. What appears as a dominant and superior academic form of discourse can then be seen as simply one practice among many, and thus open like others to scrutiny and contestation.

A third related implication is that training in academic writing becomes a process of raising students' consciousness of the choices they can make and the consequences of making those choices in particular contexts. ESP teaching often rests on the presentation of linguistic facts based on frequency counts and on the features that have been identified as common in the target discipline. This has proved extremely useful in moving language teaching away from unhelpful 'process/expressivist' practices towards the socio-cultural realities of university settings. However, such an orientation often promotes the impression that there is a correct way of presenting arguments and neglects the purposes that these features are used to accomplish. Description then becomes prescription, and students become slaves of convention, able only to fit texts into formal requirements (Miller, 1994). To avoid this our methods should help learners to explore authentic examples of relevant genres and assist them to make choices informed by professional frameworks.

The goal, then, is for learners to acquire the skills needed to create their own meanings using the socially recognised discursive practices drawn on by full community members. This involves developing a generative capacity rather than an adherence to rules, an exploitation of forms rather than a compliance to them. Bhatia (1999: 38) refers to this as 'genre knowledge':

> In the context of actual classroom teaching, the tension between conventional form and individual expression can be resolved by considering generic conventions not simply as a blueprint for further replication in similar rhetorical contexts, but more as a resource to develop an understanding of the generic conventions which make the genre possible.

We need then to find ways to incorporate contextual factors such as purpose and audience into the formal and functional descriptions of texts that students are often given.

Such methods need to emphasise a conscious awareness of recurrent and useful patterns in the target genre repertoire and the need to reflect on the motives behind their use. There are a number of possible ways of approaching this.

- Allow data to drive learning by guiding students' exploration of authentic models. An invaluable tool in this kind of consciousness raising is a concordancer, which can turn students into researchers by helping them to search, isolate and sort particular features in large amounts of computer-readable text (Wichmann et al., 1997).
- Give students intertextual writing experiences through the use of mixed-genre portfolios (Purves et al., 1995).
- Invite students to use a personal voice in their oral and written texts to allow them to position themselves to their work and consciously establish an identity in their writing (Cadman, 1997).

- Encourage students to reflect, perhaps through diaries, on their own practices and those that they observe in their lectures, labs and subject tutorials (Johns, 1990).

In these ways students might come to understand the conventions of their communities and more readily view these conventions as possibilities rather than constraints. While biologists or engineers are not linguists, we might succeed in developing their curiosity about language use in their disciplines and encourage them to ask questions about the purposes and potential effects of the features they encounter.

A final, and related, implication is, of course, that the study of academic writing alone is insufficient to understand the ways individuals create, communicate and gain acceptance for their ideas within their communities. We need to move beyond the pages of the genres we teach to examine disciplinary activities more generally. As we have seen, the process of 'becoming literate' in the practices of a discipline means relating successfully to its texts and the roles they play for particular audiences. Bazerman (1988: 323), for example, argues that knowledge of the aims and assumptions of a community is crucial for selecting situationally appropriate rhetorical forms.

Disciplinary writing is a form of social action in which the communicative purpose of the writer is a defining feature. We should, then, not view EAP teaching too narrowly to exclude the institutional and social practices in which these purpose are embedded. Instead we have to strengthen textual analysis with the insights gained from examining how writing is constructed, interpreted, and used by experienced members of the community in their everyday lives. In other words, students need to research not only the profession's principal discourses, but also the profession itself.

To control the features of the texts they must write, it is helpful if students see how these features are related to the beliefs and practices of initiated members. Equally importantly, if they are not to sacrifice their home cultures in taking on the values and discourses of the new one, they need to recognise the relativity and hybridity of disciplinary practices, and distinguish the authority of academic cultures as simply another set of literacy conventions. It is, then, important for students to stand back from their disciplines and analyse the cultures in which they are becoming immersed. Ann Johns has long championed this approach, and puts the argument succinctly in her recent book:

> What I am advocating then, is an approach in which literacy classes become laboratories for the study of texts, roles, and contexts, for research into evolving student literacies and developing awareness and critique of communities and their textual contracts.

> (Johns, 1997:19)

Geertz (1983: 155) reminds us that disciplinary communities are not simply bundles of discourse conventions, but ways of being in the world, and this implies the use of specific ways of conceptualising problems, devising taxonomies, selecting data and presenting claims through established genres. ESP has long recognised this, although it has rarely endorsed an investigative approach to communities as well as texts. But successful writing requires social explanation, to assist students to learn the skills to reproduce it and the awareness to demystify its dominant status.

What I have tried to show in this section is that a social perspective encourages us to focus both on texts and on individuals acting as members of groups. It invites us to go beyond a view of academic writing as only a textual practice confined within the pages of journals, reports or textbooks, and to return to those pages for linguistic evidence of such practices. It cautions us, as teachers, against reifying the genres we teach by overemphasising conventional form–function relations at the expense of opportunities for expressing purposes in creative ways. Finally, it encourages us to assist our students to gain and employ insights into how communal meanings are typically signalled by examining not only texts but also the communities that use them.

MOVING ON: SOME DIRECTIONS FOR RESEARCH

My arguments in this chapter lead in a clear direction: that research is central to our understanding of disciplines and our teaching of their genres. The analyses in this book indicate my own interests and orientations, but they merely scratch the surface of a large and complex topic. While not quite virgin territory, disciplinary writing is nevertheless a rich and diverse area and the opportunities for adding to our knowledge of texts, communities, institutions and disciplinary practices are enormous. In this section I want briefly to sketch how we might take a few more steps into this territory, suggesting some directions that teachers, researchers and students may like to follow.

Text analysis

One obvious area for further study is the linguistic analyses of discourses and texts. While recent years have seen a tremendous growth of interest in the genres of the academy, the sheer diversity and complexity of these genres means that the structures and features of even apparently familiar text-types often remain unexplored or opaque.

I have focused on published genres, but other genres are equally important in disciplinary life: lab reports in biology, equipment reports in engineering, software manuals in computer science, feasibility studies in business, case summaries in law, and so on (e.g. Bargiela-Chippini and Nickerson, 1999; Bhatia, 1993; McKenna, 1997). Outside of these there is an abundance of curriculum genres such as first-year essays, final-year projects, progress reports, theses and dissertations (e.g. Cadman, 1997; Martin and Christie, 1997). This is not to mention the relative neglect of such genres as circulated preprints, internet newsgroup discussions, faxes, grant proposals, or other forums of academic discussion (Lewenstein, 1995). Generally we know little about how these genres are cognitively structured, about their typical text patterns and features, about how prominent functions are expressed in them, how they are changing, or how they vary both within and between disciplines.

Such linguistic analyses have tremendous value for ESP and EAP teaching as we obviously need reliable and validated analyses of the texts we teach. As noted above, the availability of concordancing software and scanners means that it is relatively easy to compile corpora and produce frequency counts and concordance lines for analysis. This approach, as earlier chapters indicate, is helpful not only for quantitative analyses, identifying preferred means of expression and meanings, but also for generating new lines of inquiry, uncovering unexpected patterns, and suggesting taxonomic hypotheses that can be explored further with disciplinary experts. The approach to methodology that I have set out above, together with Bhatia's summarised guidelines, offer a clear strategy for this kind of linguistic analysis which students might care to follow.

Genre variability

In addition to genre description, another important issue is the extent of genre variability. This concerns the degree to which particular forms are conventionalised and how far a genre in a particular discipline allows, or encourages, the writer freedom to innovate. Participation in the genres of a discipline not only involves a linguistic knowledge of its rhetorical staging and the conventional ways that forms express purposes, but also the acceptable limits on creativity.

Prefabricated patterns and routines are features of all genres as a result of users previous repeated encounters with them, but while these conventions and rhetorical expectations impose some constraints on writers to conform, they also allow experienced and established practitioners to exploit them to create new forms (Bhatia, 1997, 1999). We are interested here, then, in the permissible versatility of genres:

- How far can writers go in pushing the boundaries of the form to achieve their purposes?
- What is the strength of the consensus regarding characteristic discourse patterns in particular communities and genres?
- Which genres and features have the greatest propensity for innovation?
- Who may legitimately manipulate the conventions?
- What does generic integrity actually mean in specific cases?

Intertextuality and interdiscursivity

A third major area of text-focused research, closely related to the notion of innovation, is that of intertextuality and interdiscursivity (Chapter 6): the extent that genres overlap or writers borrow from one form of discourse to create another. An intertextual approach focuses on the heterogeneity of texts and how far particular genres incorporate elements of other discourses or represent a relatively inconsistent construction of relations between writer and readers (Fairclough, 1995: 8). Fairclough (1992: 221) has argued that local discursive norms and conventions have become increasingly 'fragmented' as a result of 'commodification'. Fairclough sees here the transfer of promotional and advertising features from the domain of commodity marketing to a variety of other domains, accompanying a growing encroachment of entrepreneurial tendencies and values into academic genres.

This hypothesis is, of course, entirely plausible and many of the features I have identified as central to academic relationships appear to reflect promotional values. However, the extent to which these features represent a borrowing from other discourses or a reconstruction of professional identities and practices is unclear and needs to be confirmed empirically.

The notion of mixing or embedding discourses and genres presupposes the possibility of 'pure' and independent generic forms, that research articles, for example, might once have carried neutral informational messages that then became modified with persuasive or promotional features. It implies that there are representative discourses unsullied by external changes in discursive practices or colonisation by external orders of discourse. To describe genres as hybrid forms then, we need to establish what an actual 'homogenous' text looks like and go on to examine the links between such a text and other text types. For most genres this has not yet been done and such colonisation remains a hypothesis:

- Are, for example, promotional features creeping in to all academic genres in all disciplines?
- Are some disciplines and genres more susceptible to this process than others?
- In what ways are different genres affected and what features are changing?
- How are the socially sanctioned purposes of the community influenced by these forces?

Cross-cultural variation

A final area for fruitful text-oriented research is that of cross-cultural variation. Academic genres and preferred patterns of exposition, interaction and argument differ enormously across cultures and languages. The books by Connor (1996), Connor and Kaplan (1987) and Purves (1988) give a good overview of important studies in this area, and academic writing in Finnish (Mauranen, 1993; Ventola, 1992), Chinese (Li, 1996), Swedish (Gunnarsson, 1997) and Korean (Eggington, 1986) appear to differ in important ways from English. Some writers have attributed these differences directly to predominant patterns of social relationships within the particular communities involved. Hinds (1987) and Clyne (1987), for example, argue that rhetorical differences are related to expectations concerning the extent of reader involvement in different cultures, while Scollon and Scollon (1995) trace variations in argument strategies to the cultural structuring of participant roles related to interpersonal face considerations.

The field of contrastive rhetoric is a contested area, however, and its findings raise interesting, and often conflicting, issues for our understanding of disciplinary discourses which can only be resolved through further research. While there has been considerable interest in academic writing in European languages (e.g. Gunnarsson, 1995; Schröder, 1991), the hegemony of English in international research settings has led to a general sorry neglect of professional academic writing in non-European cultures, and for the restricted awareness of those studies which are not written in English. Apart from the contributions of a few notable studies, this field is overdue for intensive and serious consideration.

- What are the major intercultural variations in the rhetorical preferences of different national academic cultures?
- How is academic writing learnt in different cultural contexts?
- What cultural and linguistic differences in writing practices make cross-cultural academic writing problematic?
- What are the relative roles of 'interference' and developmental factors in cross-cultural academic writing?
- What practices characterise professional research writing in different cultures?

I have focused here on texts as a starting point for research, how their features and organisation reflect certain preferences and constraints that can be traced back to professional, institutional and cultural ideologies and beliefs. In practice, of course, texts and contexts are inseparable and interdependent, and it is therefore equally possible to begin with people and work towards texts. This involves investigating practices and contexts to see how disciplinary norms and values may be reflected in the ways members write. This more ethnographically oriented approach emphasises the dimensions of the target culture which influence the genre under study. Developing a picture of the ways genres are instantiated remains the objective, but it is achieved through shifting the focus to the activities surrounding their creation and interpretation.

The non-linguistic aspects of a genre – that is, the beliefs, values, goals and relevant social structures of the community that uses it – are likely to be more easily accessible to established members of the discourse community than to outsiders such as applied linguists. Through the use of observation, case studies, verbal protocols and various kinds of interviews, more can be learnt about what participants understand by the genres they use and how they construe their participation in them. Information about the different emphases placed on particular genres in different disciplines, the part those genres play in the processes of research and career, the roles of epistemology, institutional structures, collaboration and interactional networks on writing practices, and much more, can be obtained in this way. I have found that most academics, irrespective of discipline, enjoy talking about their research and their writing and need little encouragement to do so.

There is, then, much more we need to learn about the ways particular groups organise their lives and their communication, and gathering the reflections of experienced and established academics can offer invaluable insights into professional practices. It should also be noted, however, that this kind of introspective data can also tell us something of how members at various stages of induction and at different levels of involvement see their discourses and relevant domains of inquiry. Tapping into the personal beliefs and experiences of learners, for example, provides a way of understanding not only the practices of a discipline, but also how novitiates struggle to gain an academic and professional fluency. This greater emphasis on context, of course, does not neglect the linguistic instantiation of disciplinary genres; on the contrary, it offers a complementary perspective of interpretation, drawing on the thoughts and actions of writers to better understand what they write.

Chapter 8

Power, authority and discourse change

In this book I have focused on academic genres to determine how communicative practices contribute to the social relations that organise disciplinary realities. We have seen that what writers essentially do in pursuing their professional goals and constructing knowledge is to engage with others, and because of this, discourses carry assumptions about knowledge, relationships and how these should be structured and negotiated. As a result, disciplines are also sites of power and authority which influence differential access to resources for creating knowledge and which define discipline approved realities. My analyses demonstrate that social context always impinges on the discourses of the academy; by extension, this also implies that there is a political dimension underlying academic practices.

It should be clear from my discussion that particular genres and conventions play a privileged role in ratifying meanings and legitimising certain forms of interaction. Less obvious perhaps is the fact that these discourses also act to determine the influence of the discipline with outsiders and define its position in the wider social world. We need to understand academic knowledge then as a cultural product mediated by a wider social context, and to examine how discursive practices shape beliefs, define identities and structure relationships in ways that serve particular interests. In this chapter I first sketch some background and central concepts in approaching these issues, and then situate the authority of academic discourses, both in the wider secular community and in the webs of relations that tie individuals to their disciplines. In the final section I briefly examine the consequences that these issues have for the possibility of discursive and genre change.

ANALYSING DISCOURSE AND POWER

The notion of power as an organising concept in the relationship between discourse and social groups has been explored by those working within a linguistic perspective often labelled 'critical discourse analysis' (CDA), and by social theorists, particularly those emerging out of a broadly post-structuralist framework. While incorporating several diverse positions, much of this work is underpinned by a view which emphasises the importance of culture and ideology, rather than economics, in reproducing capitalist social relations.

CDA includes a diverse body of work which essentially highlights the role of power relations in social institutions as ideologically shaping how language is used in them. Discourse is a form of social practice, implying a dialectical relationship between a particular event and the institutions and social structures within which it occurs (e.g. Fairclough, 1992, 1995; Wodak, 1996). A number of writers in this area therefore follow Giddens' (1987) concept of *structuration* and regard discourse as shaped by situations and also constituting them, so the languages of the academy work as social practices to reproduce and transform the identities and relationships of the disciplines. This has important ideological consequences as discourses can reproduce unequal power relations through the ways in which things and people are represented and positioned (Kress, 1989; van Dijk, 1997).

A number of eminent social theorists also contribute towards establishing this link between language and power. In particular, post-structuralism rejects a representational view of language and sees language use as inherently involving domination, referring to different ways of structuring knowledge and social practice. Not only are all our perceptions and understandings filtered through the medium of language, but the way in which this works serves the purposes of regulation and control. The idea that language can be used to represent things outside itself is essentially ideological, and academic discourses are the leading exponents of this ideology. Bakhtin (1981: 289), for example, argues that genres are inherently ideological and imbued with the value judgements of particular professions and social elites, and Bourdieu (1991) links social power to the ability to employ institutional discourses expertly.

In addition, postmodern discourse theorists such as Laclau, Mouffe and Zizek (Torfing, 1999) also give a primary role to discourse, insisting on its role of shaping social relations. Like post-structuralism, this work also moves beyond constructionist perspectives in seeking to marry post-structuralism with post-Marxism, interweaving the semantic aspect of language with the pragmatic aspects of action. Once more, social interaction can only be understood in terms of its discursive context, which is seen as constituting a coherent framework for what can be said and done, bridging the distinction between thought and reality. Discourse here, then, is taken to influence the cognitive scripts, categories and rationalities that are central to any kind of action; in its ideological role it conceals the contingent and unstable character of discursively constructed realities.

From within these important perspectives on the relationship between language and society, three key concepts offer considerable potential for insights into the power exercised by disciplinary discourses.

One is Bakhtin's (1981) view of intertextuality that I have discussed earlier (Chapters 2 and 6). Discourses are always related to other discourses, both as they change diachronically and in terms of their congruity and contrariety at any point in time. This links text users to a network of prior texts depending on their group membership, and provides a system of coding options for making meanings. Because they help to instantiate or construe the meaning potential of a disciplinary culture, the conventions developed in this way fore-close certain options and make some predictions about meanings possible (Martin, 1998).

The notion of intertextuality is particularly useful as a means of under-standing disciplinary interactions against a background of community practices, and as a means of seeing these practices as responding to the changed circumstances and values of the group. The idea of intertextuality also suggests the potential for semiotic and cultural change through the notions of mixing and embedding of texts (Chapter 6). The concept shows that while some genres are valued by the discipline and that individual dis-courses can only be understood in relation to many others, the conventions are neither immutable nor strait-jacketing. The individual actor is neither completely subject to the structures of power of the discipline nor subjugated by its particular forms of communication. Innovation is always possible and the impact of wider societal influences may be important sources of change.

Bourdieu's (1991) notion of symbolic capital is also important here as it draws attention to the value attached to particular forms of discourse in social and economic life. We have seen in earlier chapters (especially Chapters 4 and 6) how the expert use of specialist language defines someone as belonging to an exclusive group which, in turn, helps to form the individ-ual's identity and exclude others who do not have the same experience and training. What is secured between members of disciplinary communities as a means of effective communication can therefore reinforce the legitimacy of certain practices and imbue them with authority; they become capital in an asymmetrically structured symbolic marketplace. Connected to the notion of cultural capital is that of 'habitus' (1977), a set of dispositions that leads peo-ple to adopt certain practices and to anticipate the value that their linguistic practices will have in other markets, such as the labour market. Thus our dis-courses are integrated into wider aspects of our lives, social identities and lifestyles, and these are, again, socially evaluated according to the symbolic value attached to them.

Finally, the notion of 'Orders of Discourse' (originating with Foucault and taken up by Fairclough, 1992), discussed earlier in Chapter 7, is also a useful way of looking at the power relationships embedded in the discourses of the disciplines. The term refers to the relatively stabilised, but often contested, configurations of discourse practices and conventions found in particular social domains or institutions. These are the resources for creating ideational meanings, offering templates for interaction which have symbolic value in institutions and which are intimately linked to the values and beliefs of domi-nant groups within them. Disciplinary orders of discourse, then, are ideologically shaped by those who exercise authority, the powerbrokers and gatekeepers of the field, and serve the interests of the powerful within the discipline. Outside the group its orders of discourse work to articulate these ideological interests and mediate the links between the discipline's knowledge-creating practices and the wider society, constructing a political acceptance of its significance and its interpretations of the world.

It should be noted that while one dimension of these frameworks suggests the hegemonic influence of particular forms of discourses which result from the current relations of power in disciplinary communities, another dimension emphasises change. Particular literacy practices, discourses and genres possess symbolic capital because they are underpinned by dominant ideological positions and carry the interests and beliefs of the powerful, but they exist in a climate of alternatives. The historical evolution of communities and their discourses demonstrate clearly that social actions are characterised by multiplicity and contestation, and that there are invariably many options for representing relationships and realities. So, while particular sets of conventions and practices of a discipline may be dominant in a given age, they are not permanent.

The concepts of intertextuality, symbolic value and orders of discourse are therefore important as they encourage us to consider the social and the individual in texts, and to look at the belief systems of communities and the responses and interests of individuals within them. Together they point to the important role played by community ideologies and how these are acted out through personal cognition in textual practices. This is a position recognised by genre analysts such as Bhatia (1993, 1999), in characterising genre patterns as cognitive structures, and by Miller (1994) when she talks of genres helping individuals to carry out purposes within spatio-temporal communities and reproducing the virtual communities that we carry in our minds. Discourses are both texts and contexts, the work of individuals and institutions, and require a socio-cognitive as well as a textual explanation. In terms of the discourses of the academy, this means looking at both the relationship of such discourses to the wider social environment, and the part they play for individuals within professional contexts.

Academic discourses are a powerful cultural form in modern society, influencing and being influenced by the societies of which they are part. On the one hand, they originate in disciplines that depend on the wider secular culture for material and social resources, the funding and prestige they need to exist, and, on the other hand, they work to reconstruct society in their own image, mediating our understandings of the world. Because disciplines reflect the cultures they are part of, these social forces selectively facilitate and constrain the knowledge created, shaping the discourses of the academy. Socio-political dynamics influence the questions disciplines ask, the conceptual frameworks they employ and the methodologies they follow. At the same time, truth-claiming discourses themselves exercise social authority, possessing considerable prestige in the wider world.

These discourses do not, then, function in isolation from a wider moral, political and economic context but are, on the contrary, very much part of that context. In the next two sections I look at how academic discourses claim external authority through their central roles in the processes of ideological and economic reproduction. Following these I look at authority within disciplines themselves and the mechanisms of discourse change.

THE IDEOLOGICAL POWER OF ACADEMIC DISCOURSES

While my analyses in earlier chapters have largely focused on textual interactions between academics, it is clear that the discourses of the academy are not merely credible systems of making meaning within sealed disciplines. Rather, they are extremely valued and influential ideological systems in the wider community. In *Science as Power*, for example, Stanley Aronowitz (1988) argues that science is the 'discourse of the late capitalist state':

> Science is a language of power and those who bear its legitimate claims, i.e., those who are involved in the ownership and control of its processes and results, have become a distinctive social category equipped with a distinctive ideology and position in the post-war world.

These discourses promote a universe in which the domination of nature is linked to the domination of humans, and is used to justify power relations and conflate a particular view of knowledge as *truth*. Disciplinary discourses are therefore essentially ideological as they obscure the contradictions between material and social processes.

Lemke (1995: 178) points out that science, together with the domains of art and politics, are the three prestige orders of discourses of our culture. Each separate domain resists synthesis with the others and represents a major disjunct in how we see the world: 'Science speaks the language of truth, art the language of beauty, and politics the language of good.' The discourses of science, including the humanities, technology and social sciences, are the discourses of 'Truth', presenting statements which provide an objective description of what the natural and human world is actually like. They carry an assurance and an authority that compel our belief because of their apparent ability to answer our questions about the world, explain its intricacies, satisfy our curiosities, and improve our futures. The languages of science and technology are momentous because they are means of producing truth, and in every society power is based on truth.

Importantly, then, academic discourses possess cultural and political authority because of the control they afford over the physical and intellectual circumstances of our lives. They are the guarantors of reliable knowledge, providing objective representations of reality, unbiased and uncorrupted, that can be transformed into practical effect. Their power rests on an ideology which clearly demarcates them from the everyday discourses of politics, commerce, religion or common sense. They embody a rationality apparently free from vested interest, emotional conviction or political and economic values. However, as the Frankfurt school writers repeatedly warned, while academic rationality may produce an understanding of nature, it also alienates human beings through the social relations which attend it: the discourse of reason appears to benefit everyone, and so 'all contradiction seems irrational and all counteraction impossible' (Marcuse, 1972: 22).

So while the view that academic practices are independent of societal influences continues to hold considerable currency inside and outside disciplinary communities, the theoretical frameworks and explanatory discourses of the disciplines are closely interconnected with socio-political arrangements in the secular community.

The languages of the academy have, in fact, reshaped our entire world view, becoming the dominant mode for interpreting reality and our own existence. They exert a considerable, although often unnoticed, influence on all aspects of our everyday lives:

> Every text, from the discourses of technocracy and bureaucracy to the television magazine and the blurb on the back of the cereal packet, is in some way affected by the modes of meaning that evolved as the scaffolding for scientific knowledge. In other words, the language of science has become the language of literacy.   (Halliday and Martin, 1993: 11)

Halliday also suggests that the influence of scientific discourses has spilled into other disciplines and to government and public administration, influencing the control of both material and human resources. The discourse practices of a powerful social group has therefore become a dominant force in many walks of life, increasingly providing a model for communication and a filter for perception.

Of particular importance is the role of academic disciplines in constructing how we, scientists and lay observers alike, understand the world, offering schemata of what is known and how it can be known. These schemata have typically relied heavily on an explanatory discourse which facilitates a mechanically materialist view of the world directed to utility (e.g. Gibbons and Wittrock, 1985). Influentially elaborated by Descartes in the social realm, the explanation of all phenomena, from the molecular to the social, as special cases of a few overarching laws is the culmination of a programme for the mechanisation of living phenomena that began in the seventeenth century (Lewontin, 1998: 117). The academy has promoted an influential discourse of universal laws, analytical procedures and controlled experiments which removes organisms from the systems in which they exist and represents them as incapable of novel and flexible responses to their environment (e.g. Taylor, 1986).

Postmodern analysts have argued that ideological effects are not generally systematically encoded in a single way, but that they draw on very limited explanatory repertoire (Torfing, 1999). Disciplines contain alternative, even deviant perspectives, but dominant ideologies have tended to promote a view of the world as composed of individuals passively subject to forces outside their control. In his excellent *Biology as Ideology*, for example, Richard Lewontin (1991) examines the doctrine of genetic determinism, biology's view that all human traits, all that we are, are encoded in our DNA from birth. He attributes this reductionist view to an ideology of oppression, that puts the individual at the mercy of laws which we confront but cannot influence. Such narratives of human and natural phenomena successfully obscure the social relations behind them because elements are abstracted from their social contexts, thereby offering little threat to existing social relations. In this way academic knowledge is implicated in political structures and, to the extent that they embody social premises in their concepts, values and explanations, academics reinforce and legitimate a social perspective. To put the position starkly: disciplinary discourses are not, and cannot be, neutral.

The ways that new socio-political formations give rise to new ways of conceptualising problems and new discourses of inquiry clearly illustrate these connections between the political and academic realms. The Copernican revolution, which represented a radical new view of the natural order, for example, did not involve new data or new technology, but a conceptual reconstruction which was only possible because of the changing class structure of sixteenth-century Europe (Diamond, 1986). Copernicus' cosmology, which essentially argued the novel idea that rotating planets circled the sun, occurred in the period of cultural flourishing of the Renaissance and was grounded in a long period of stagnation and decline. Copernicus drew on a newly developing world view brought about in response to conflicts between classes and social groups and a climate in which old certainties and political hierarchies were being seriously challenged. Its success lay in the fact that it brought terrestrial knowledge down from the level of theology into the realm of human understanding.

Closer to our own age, Darwin's theories of biological evolution both borrowed from, and gave a strong impetus to, the nineteenth-century ideology of competitive individualism. What today is known as 'social Darwinism' – that the fittest individuals and races will flourish socially and economically if just left alone to do so – was endemic in much of the popular and philosophical thinking in mid-nineteenth-century Britain. Darwin was deeply influenced by this current of thought and *Origin of Species*, which forms the basis of modern biological thought, owed a great deal to it (Moore, 1986).

Today the popular discourse which sees evolution as a predictable progression to a human apex further demonstrates this connection between political and scientific ideologies. Stephen Jay Gould (1998) has pointed to the strength of an iconographic depiction of evolution in discourses from museum exhibits and textbook plates to cartoons and advertisements, where diversity and stability are suppressed to represent a fixed progression. Such representations are influential as they help to construct an analogous picture of social and technological evolution as a march of uninterrupted progress to the present. This supports an ideology of comfortable progress and predictability, justifying current political and social realities and humankind's rightful ascendancy, natural superiority and ultimate control over the physical environment. These representations are achieved, however, only by suppressing alternative positions and reproducing one particular view. Very often popular scientific discourses depict a positivist and technicist orientation that downplays the humanist and social elements that would emerge by setting work within historical contexts.

In sum, the application of scientific discourse to justify social relations is inherently ideological as it serves to endow those relations with nature's authority. It is our experiences of modern social existence that define our assumptions about science and academic inquiry and restrict the range of available interpretations of its work. Foucault (1972) famously observed that what people see and understand is conditioned by the contemporary intellectual climate. The conventions of academic argument, the ways that research is discursively reconstructed for social agreement, draw on community values influenced by the ideologies and power relations which dominate current socio-economic realities. For science's publics, as for scientists, what is accepted depends on the conceptual frameworks they employ – and these are social, not abstract, intellectual constructs.

Disciplinary discourses then, are not only powerfully authoritative accounts of human and natural phenomena, they also have profoundly significant political consequences as they desensitise us to the socially situated nature of expert pronouncements. The ways that these discourses represent reality, express probability, and enact social relations play an important part in establishing how we perceive the world. Many of the features I have examined in this book work to disguise what is contingent, competitive and contentious in academic debate. Hedging claims, citing previous work, mitigating criticism, displaying metadiscoursal cooperation, signalling membership and rapport, drawing on shared understandings, and boosting collegiality are strategies of rhetorical persuasion with peers, but they also act to erase most traces of conflict and division with them. Collectively, the products of the academy, a discipline's research papers, reviews and textbooks, present a narrative of progress towards current belief, accepted, for the moment, as true.

The fact that the disciplines have successfully sought to decouple the political and methodological dimensions of their discourses demonstrates that they have not been entirely innocent in this relationship. Haberer (1972) argues that from Galileo to Bacon to the death camps and the Manhattan Project, science has adopted a tactic of 'prudential acquiescence' to secular authority. This has allowed academics institutionally to isolate fact and value through a discourse of methodological purity, emphasising the neutrality of the procedures which generate knowledge, while abstaining from comment on their use. This authority and apparent independence of expert discourse has important effects in the public sphere where such discourse is translated into policy. Here the prestige of disciplinary knowledge can be presented as value free and neutral, dictated by facts rather than interests.

The discourses of the academy have been singularly successful in persuading the public of their value and independence, and none has been more successful than the hard sciences. The public largely accepts science's claims that it offers an understanding of natural realities that are externally extant and knowable through correct disciplinary procedures. Academic, and again particularly scientific, knowledge is generally held to be governed by transcendental canons of rational argument, to be most effectively policed by the disciplines themselves, and to work best when it remains undisturbed by outside interference. We accept as a general precept of democratic cultures that scientists should be autonomous and left free to determine what to study, how to study it, and how to distribute the material rewards of success.

This is not to say that all disciplines have enjoyed the same status, of course, and it is clear that public opinion has been especially unforgiving of those liberal fields engaged in professional welfare. Overall, however, the power of disciplinary discourses is largely unchallenged; confirmed in their ability to attract state and commercial funding, in the established curricula of schools and universities, and in their priestly status in public opinion.

To the outsider then, to write science is to engage in an impersonal, empirical and cumulative enterprise whose methodological standards are rigorously monitored by the disciplines. This popular impression is supported by the mass media and popular stereotypes: the absent-minded professor working alone surrounded by bubbling test-tubes. We may be amused by TV advertisers' use of actors in lab coats to endorse toothpaste or biological soap-powder, but we recognise the authority that lies behind it. These are powerful discourses that demand our assent. Myers (1990) has shown how popular science texts support a definite, naively empiricist view of science that contradicts the picture embodied in scientific articles, and held by most scientists:

> In this view the scientist is alone and proceeds without concepts or methodology, by simple observation of nature. There are no choices to make about the course of research, which proceeds from given questions to unambiguous answers. Just as scientists have an interest in promoting scientific expertise, the public, and those who edit journals with the public in mind, have an interest in this view, which minimizes expertise and emphasizes the unmediated encounter with nature.
> (Myers, 1990: 189)

In this way scientific knowledge is made intelligible as everyday reasoning, disguising both the social construction of science and the interests which lay behind disciplinary practices. A science providing a mirror of nature, unaffected by gender, class, cultural differences or political bias. A critical orientation to the discourses of the academy can thus help to reveal these relations between knowledge and social structure. As Thompson (1984: 131) observes:

> The analysis of ideology is fundamentally concerned with language, for language is the principal medium of the meaning (signification) which serves to sustain relations of domination.

Treating meanings as contingent on their social contexts involves questioning their claims to represent 'truths' about the world and ways of knowing it.

THE ECONOMIC POWER OF ACADEMIC DISCOURSES

The relationship between academic communities and the societies with which they interact are not, of course, only seen in the hegemonic perspectives they make available for understanding the world. They are also integrally related to the industrial base of modern society, and the hierarchical relations of those who participate in it. A principle reason for the power of academic, and particularly scientific, discourse is the control they provide over our physical environment through technology. This control lies at the centre of economic development and therefore at the heart of power in western societies.

Lenoir (1997: 47), for example, argues that disciplines are principally dynamic structures for assembling and channelling the social and technical practices 'essential to the functioning of the political economy and the system of power relations that actualize it'. He therefore proposes that disciplines are, firstly, political institutions which support current social arrangements. Embedded in, and actualised through disciplinary research and discursive practices, are the interests of modern capitalism. This link is also clearly spelt out by Rose (1998: 237) in his contextualisation of the growth of science:

> Modern science would not have happened without the evolution of industrial capitalism. From Chaucer's *Treatise on the Astrolabe*, to the astronomy, mathematics and physics of Galileo, Descartes and Newton, the impetus and application of scientific discovery was in the maritime expansion of European trading and colonisation, and warfare between imperial powers. From Priestley to the present day, physical, chemical and geological sciences have developed in tandem with the beginnings, expansion and technologisation of mass industrial production, for which mercantile and imperial expansion provided the capital.

These changes have occurred in wider social processes of knowledge production in which discovery, application and use have become closely integrated. Most western countries spend up to 3 per cent of their GDP on scientific research, for example, and a great deal of additional business money has flowed into university research (Bridgestock, 1998). This is the result of an expanded market for knowledge driven by the intensification of international business competition beyond a capacity which in-house research can sustain. The science parks in Europe, and the large military projects involving MIT, Berkeley and Stanford in the USA, for instance, represent intensified interactions between industry and universities and the closer bonding of economics and knowledge production. This expansion of output appears to be as pronounced in the humanities as in the sciences (Gibbons et al., 1994), and the fact that these disciplines are increasingly influenced by IT and are moving into contexts of application, such as the image production industry, means that they are linked ever closer to the commercial web.

In sum, because of the connections with economic development and production, academic discourses influence every level of education, technical training and shopfloor manufacturing, establishing a workforce stratified by the access it has to such discourses (Rose, 1998).

Within this context, disciplines can be seen sociologically as political institutions that demarcate academic territory and constitute, and also comprise, rival interest groups engaged in a constant struggle for power and status. The discourses of different disciplines, and of different research programmes within the disciplines, stake out different definitions of reality and often compete to gain acceptance for them. Lenoir (1997), for example, shows through a number of case studies how competing disciplinary programmes prosper or perish within the shifting fortunes of the economy. This competitiveness thus largely results from their dependence on external funding. Continuing research, and the prestige that accompanies it, is often contingent on persuading powerful bodies in the non-academic sphere to provide resources. Thus, although this disciplinary quest for status is driven partly by an intrinsic tribal pride, it is mainly motivated by 'an extrinsic need to justify their existence and maintain their collective livelihood' (Becher, 1989: 142).

Gibbons et al. (1994) argue that a new form of knowledge, evaluated by standards of applied usefulness, is replacing traditional academic knowledge based on standards of truth and interest. Typically, then, such justifications are increasingly established through a discourse of social utility, whether current or potential. Physics, for example, originated in the Cambridge Moral Sciences Tripos in sets of problems designed to develop clear thinking, but it subsequently emerged as a discipline largely through the application of its mathematical technologies to the solution of problems in engineering, electricity and magnetism.

More recently, molecular genetics, environmental biology and information technology have achieved considerable academic distinction, partly riding our culture's preoccupation with such issues, but mainly by persuading us of their socio-economic value. In the 1960s almost every application to the US National Institutes of Health emphasised the importance of their project for cancer research; in the 1990s it was for AIDS. Through effective and well-organised political lobbies these promotional strategies have paid off handsomely. The hard knowledge disciplines have been very successful in articulating research with the priorities of government, military and business elites.

This success, however, has been purchased at a high cost in terms of the socio-political arrangements under which much of science is produced. President Eisenhower recognised this even in 1961:

> The free university, historically the fountainhead of free ideas and scientific discovery, has experienced a revolution in the conduct of research. Partly because of the huge costs involved, a government contract becomes virtually a substitute for intellectual curiosity. (Quoted in Redner, 1987: 15)

Research in medicine, genetics, neuroscience, military and space technology, and 'big science' generally, requires massive public investment and a clear harnessing of research to secular goals. Since the 1940s the pursuit of basic research into problems inherently arising from the intrinsic development of scientific theories has increasingly been replaced by mission-oriented research (e.g. Laurent, 1998).

To summarise, disciplines acquire their value in relation to the functions they perform and, because commercial values predominate, they are valued for the role they play in production. The success of these disciplines – the expansion of their power – has been achieved by following the path of utility: negotiating knowledge as a commodity valued by societal paymasters (Gibbons and Wittrock, 1985).

Utility tends not to be a strong point of humanities disciplines, although once again wide differences are evident, but the kind of knowledge soft fields create is often respected by outsiders as 'scholarship'. The ideology that learning should be pursued for its own sake, however, is now perhaps archaic; it tends, moreover, to be too personal and limited to reap significant funding. Softer disciplines have therefore tried to gain external credibility by promoting a strong academic image, either through a rhetoric of intellectual rigour or of social relevance. Moreover, not only have the resources they need for research and professional structures increased – witness the costs of linguistic research due to the introduction of new technologies for example – but the expansion of higher education, with a rate of publication expanding as rapidly as in sciences,[1] demonstrates their success in persuading government departments of their usefulness.

The social sciences have also sought to increase their prestige by engaging in policy-oriented research or by developing general laws of human understanding, but while less characterised by public relations and political lobbying, this has not increased the autonomy of the softer fields. The role of external political agencies in the social sciences in particular has been tremendous, and the research practices of soft applied fields, such as social work, business studies and education, have been extremely susceptible to commercial and political influences (e.g. Gibbons et al., 1994). As Whitley (1984) observes, when defined by government or commercial clients, the notion of 'relevance' is particularly persuasive in approving topics and strategies in these disciplines. Even applied linguistics has become increasingly implicated in the socio-cultural struggles of the end-users of its research (Pennycook, 1994; Rampton, 1995).

Attracting research funding, consultancy contracts and students is a highly competitive business and this kind of competition invariably brings Mammon closer to the academy, and marketing norms into university discourses (Fairclough, 1995). Because of this, neither academics nor their discourses can remain neutral. As Taylor (1986: 93) observes:

> Once they have rejected any explicit commitment, scientists are 'free' to follow 'a path of least resistance', thereby responding implicitly to dominant social relations. Facilitated by those relations, scientists incorporate them unwittingly into their science.

It also, of course, poses a serious threat to the professional authority of academics. This increasing external interference challenges the ways disciplinary communities govern themselves, ask questions, decide research problems, reward success and value the pursuit of knowledge (Rothblatt, 1985). In other words, the unrelenting pressures of external social forces may ultimately undermine academic cultures and any independent power they can exercise in the wider society.

Already the credibility of the academy's ideological representations have been seriously eroded, both by an increasing recognition of the socio-political processes at work in the discourses of public science and in lay constructions of increasing risk and hazard. The sociology of science has documented how the optimism of technological expansion has increasingly turned to public resistance to many scientific claims. Public concerns about genetic engineering (Frewer et al., 1997), human embryo research (Mulkay, 1995) and the export of toxic waste (Jones, 1986), for example, have fuelled growing unease concerning science's destructive power and its apparent inability to control the forces that most threaten the quality of our lives.

Perhaps more damagingly, there is a growing public reconstruction of the claims of science and the academy more widely as a result of well-publicised scandals of dubious practices and the close associations between academics and powerful interests. Jones (1981), for example, relates the public horror at the unfolding of the Tuskegee project in the USA, where syphilis patients suffered agonising degeneration as part of a government health department experiment which denied them accepted medical treatment for 40 years. In more recent times Higgins (1994) has catalogued an eruption of academic fraud cases, which undermines the right to self-policing. Moreover, the discourses of scientists have been criticised or rejected on various issues – e.g. the risks of radon gas (Cole, 1993), the threat of BSE in beef in the UK and Alar toxins in apples in the USA (Gregory and Miller, 1998), and genetic engineering projects in Germany (Gottweis, 1995) – because of the alignment of science with powerful secular forces.

Writing in a Royal Society report, academics have ascribed the public's suspicion of scientific expertise to its ignorance of scientifically validated knowledge and a failure to appreciate how this will benefit society (Irwin and Wynne, 1996). More realistically however, the role of academic discourses in legitimating social ideologies and economic advances is now clearly under threat. The power of the academy to provide knowledge regarded by the public as universal, objective and socially beneficial is waning. Academic claims are increasingly seen as socially contingent and dependent on political and economic patronage.

THE AUTHORITY OF DISCOURSES IN DISCIPLINARY PRACTICES

In this section I turn to another aspect of discursive power, the power that enables individuals to exercise control over participation in disciplinary discourses and regulates individual influence within a community. In fact I return, rather than turn, to this issue, for this has been an undercurrent of the entire book. The social interactions in the writings of academics not only negotiate community knowledge and credibility, but help to produce and sustain status relationships, exercise exclusivity and reproduce interests which lead to an unequal distribution of influence and resources. This is the power to engage with one's peers and to have one's opinions heard, considered and accepted. This is also the power that accrues to those who have tangibly demonstrated their credibility within the discipline and achieved substantial recognition in it. In short, it is the power to act effectively in one's field and to make a difference.

Here, then, we are less concerned with the ideological impact of expert discourses or the relationships between disciplines and the wider community. Instead the focus will be on the voices used by academics when addressing one another rather than outsiders, the voices that define disciplinary boundaries, exclude outsiders and authorise contributions as new knowledge. I am talking about the power to use, manipulate, innovate and control particular generic forms valued within a disciplinary community and which subsequently create particular kinds of hierarchical social organisation. Once again, knowledge is power, but this is the knowledge to make one's way in one's discipline and claim authority.

As I have argued throughout this book, academic communities are fields of practical activity, and to participate in one is to employ its conventions and speak its language. Earlier chapters have sought to elaborate how successful participation in a discipline requires a display of disciplinarity, the command of a tacit set of procedures which recontextualise local work within a framework of interest to the community. Simultaneously these conventions help to define and protect a coherent definition of reality and group identity by restricting the ways that knowledge is produced. In other words, group discourses help members to create, acquire and sustain an ideology, 'an interface between collective group interests and individual social practices' (van Dijk, 1997: 27). Power in academic disciplines has to do with the ways that these ideologies influence and constrain individuals within the contexts of certain practices, social roles and purposes.

At the heart of this interface between the individual and the discipline is the institutionalised system which creates knowledge and distributes rewards: the system of publication. A paper is judged as a contribution to a particular field by an audience of colleagues who are potentially in a position to make use of it. If editors, referees, proposal readers, conference attendees and journal readers regard it as original and significant, allow it to be published, cite it in their own work, and develop it further, then the writer receives the reward of recognition. This can take the form of promotion, substantiation, or simply a reputation among one's peers. At higher levels it may mean a Nobel Prize, a Royal Society Fellowship, or greater access to grants and commercial consultancies.

Hagstrom (1965) has analysed this process as a form of barter where the recognition that motivates individual academics is exchanged for a contribution of information. Latour and Woolgar (1979), in a well-known variant of this market metaphor, and echoing Bourdieu's (1991) notion of symbolic value, see academics as engaged in converting different kinds of 'credit' in a cycle of moves designed to maximise their credibility. A successful publication may help a researcher to gain credit that can be converted into a research grant to finance equipment and recruit colleagues; this, in turn, generates more data that can be converted to arguments, fresh publications, and so on. Credibility thus helps academics to progress through the cycle:

> For example, a successful investment might mean that people phone him, his abstracts are accepted, others show interest in his work, he is believed more easily and listened to with greater attention, he is offered better positions, his assays work well, data flow more reliably and form a more credible picture.
>
> (Latour and Woolgar, 1979: 204)

Both views see academic success as largely measured by recognition and, in turn, the process of acquiring recognition as dependent on the capacity to produce papers valued by one's colleagues.

This picture may attribute an unrealistically high degree of autonomy to the individual practitioner. It presents writers as independent actors in a closed system and ignores the important interactions of academics with the kinds of outside political and economic forces that I discussed in the previous section. A professional reputation, however, is likely to facilitate greater access to these outside forces. Academics who excel in the publication process often gain appointments to key positions, access to economic resources, and the occupation of major gatekeeping roles, not only achieving social power within their disciplines, but tending to form an elite as greater resources flow to them to further their work. Such people often exercise great influence in setting standards, directing strategies and determining what is considered good or important in their disciplines (Cole, 1983). They are also more likely to gain greater influence as spokespeople for their colleagues, and more likely to become members of government and foundation committees which decide the fate of funding applications and research contracts (Becher, 1989; Mulkay, 1976).

The interpersonal approval of peers and the institutional recognition of one's discipline are significant motivating forces. While my informants spoke of advancing knowledge and genuine curiosity about specific research issues, most admitted that recognition was an important source of professional gratification for them. However, because reputation becomes translated into concrete consequences, and because both material and symbolic capital are scarce, participation in the system of academic exchange is often fiercely competitive. Bourdieu (1975: 19), sees it like this:

> The scientific field is the locus of a competitive struggle, in which the specific issue at stake is the monopoly of scientific authority, defined inseparably as technical capacity and social power, or to put it another way, the monopoly of

scientific competence, in the sense of a particular agent's socially recognized capacity to speak and act legitimately in scientific matters.

This institutionally sanctioned competition is frequently claimed to be a spur to the advancement of knowledge, but is, in fact, now inseparable from the process by which prestige and credibility are assessed. Moreover, institutional competition is also now governmentally sanctioned in many countries, with regular research assessment exercises and the publication of university league tables. Thus 'productivity' is a crude measure of worth, and haste to publish is a condition of survival in institutions that confer promotion and substantiation on the length of personal bibliographies. James Watson, Nobel laureate and a member of the biology establishment, spells this out:

> It starts at the beginning. If you publish first, you become a professor first; your future depends on some indication that you can do something by yourself. It's that simple. Competitiveness is very dominant. The chief emotion in the field.
>
> (Quoted in Judson, 1995: 194)

Competition is increasingly important with the growth of commercial incentives which, in technological fields in particular, may be even stronger than intellectual ones.[2]

In sum, through peer review and editorial intervention, disciplines seek to ensure that accounts of new knowledge conform to the broad generic practices they have established, while writers are often willing to employ these practices because of a desire to get published and achieve recognition. This desire to gain a reputation therefore acts as a system of social control as it encourages conformity to the approved discursive practices of the discipline. To put it bluntly, the ideological and discursive system which reproduces knowledge also reproduces a particular arrangement of social relations.

The importance of appealing to readers from within the boundaries of a disciplinary discourse, of projecting an insider ethos, has been stressed throughout this book as a means of displaying credibility and 'membership', but the practices and strategies I have examined also contain traces of the power relationships which exist within communities because, through such displays of intimacy with cultural knowledge, writers are also implicitly orientated to particular hierarchical arrangements. The doctrinal knowledge of a field does more than define allegiance to a body of truths and practices; it also, by raising issues of heresy, controls topics of discourse, and so defines who might speak with credibility and who has public authority (Foucault, 1972).

This kind of power has been vividly illustrated in the literature. Berkenkotter and Huckin's (1995) study of editorial control at a major US composition conference, for example, showed how successful abstracts strongly reflected the interests of the programme chair and addressed topics of current community concern in novel ways. Such a rhetorical construction of a valued disciplinary ethos is obviously difficult to achieve for newcomers or other cultural outsiders. Sacks's (1998) interesting review of the ways that even brilliant insights from outsiders may be neglected by scientific hierarchies underlines this general picture, while Paul and Charney (1995) detail the complex rhetorical strategies needed to gain a community hearing for the radical new idea of chaos theory. At a more everyday level, Myers (1990) shows the vulnerabilities of two scientists seeking to publish in new areas of research with neither the advantages of a conventional background in the field nor an established social network. This process of negotiation, of course, is particularly fraught for writers whose native language is not English and whose academic norms may not be those of the discipline in the metropolitan 'centre' (Flowerdew, forthcoming; Gosden, 1992).

It would seem then, that hierarchical relationships within disciplines are, at least in part, a consequence of one's ability to manipulate, exploit and perhaps innovate its generic and rhetorical conventions effectively. As a result, academic disciplines are highly stratified. Mulkay (1976) argues that a small elite of scientists enjoys a disproportionate share of grant resources and peer recognition and Becher (1989: 58) notes that this profile spans the social sciences, the humanities and the professional disciplines.

This exercise of power may be beneficial to the discipline, promoting its interests in the secular community or contributing to its coherence and development internally. It can also, however, have the opposite effect. Cases of fallibility or partiality in the exercise of power are legion, and all my informants were able to cite examples where funding or publication had been denied for reasons they believed to be based on autocratic fiat rather than intellectual merit. Less common, but more celebrated, are cases of obstruction or attack by authority. The theory of stellar degeneration and 'black holes', for example, was delayed for 30 years by the unquestioned authority of the leading theoretical astrophysicist of the time, A.S. Eddington, who protected his own cosmological theory by preventing the development and publication of the idea. Fifty years passed before Chandrasekar was awarded the Nobel Prize for this work. Similarly, the authority of Felix Klein, the great German mathematician, allowed him to persecute Georg Cantor, the originator of infinite sets.

More generally, academic advances have often been delayed by the entrenched orthodoxies of its leading figures, rather than personal attack. Virtually all the key pioneers in cancer research met resistance, for example, with work on viral transmission and tumour development only attracting serious attention when authoritative figures began replicating the experiments of more junior researchers (Kelves, 1998).

Publication, then, drives career, position and professional influence and this provides a powerful motivation for writers to draw from the discourse practices routinely available in their disciplines. However, while the published writings of community members express social interactions which realise unequal relationships of authority and status, they also provide a cultural identity for all those within the discipline. Several of my informants spoke of their sense of belonging to a discipline – a community with a history, conceptual structure and mode of inquiry. This identification of distinct knowledge domains and collective behaviours can therefore serve to reinforce community ideologies and the discoursal conventions in which they are embedded. The appeal to members using insider discourse, however, also excludes those not privy to its practices and understandings. The stamp of legitimacy bestowed on those familiar with the conventions simultaneously works to withhold it from outsiders, thus enforcing a linguistic apartheid and the increasing separation of the disciplines.

Power is exercised by restricting access to different discourses and this is perhaps an inevitable consequence of social life. In any community access to privileged discourse is controlled by conditions of membership, and without this distinction between insiders and outsiders there would be little hope of describing social structures at all (e.g. Giddens, 1987). Group identification does not therefore simply satisfy shadowy psychological needs; it has real social, political and economic benefits in terms of the status and advantages that result from membership of an influential and prestigious discipline. Members gain from the independent authority that their discipline may possess in the secular community, and from the fact that such status attracts material advantages, ensuring their continuing flow of students, resources and employment.

Thus, because a discipline's discoursal resources are not ordinarily available to outsiders, conditions of homogeneity tend to be created within communities which increases the social distance between members and others. This is a process which clearly works against cooperation and integration:

> As the work and the points of view grow more specialised, men in different disciplines have fewer things in common, in their background and in their daily problems. They have less impulse to interact with one another and less ability to do so.   (Clark, quoted in Becher, 1989: 23)

The idea of interdisciplinarity – almost universally held to be a positive aspect of knowledge and research – often therefore amounts only to the accumulation of knowledge gleaned from more than one field. Relentless diversification and specialisation appear to be more common, with ever new academic journals exploiting more specialised intellectual market niches. While disciplinary genres may display an interdiscursive hybridity by drawing on other orders of discourse, the myriad ways they do this may well lead to the growing mutual incomprehensibility of academic communities.

WRITER VARIATIONS, SOCIAL SHIFTS AND DISCOURSE CHANGE

In this section I want to examine briefly the modes and possibilities for change in the dominant valorised genres of academic disciplines. These changes may occur as a result of influences originating at the institutional/societal levels, or at the level of discursive practices (Fairclough, 1995), and both tendencies will have effects in published disciplinary discourses. As we have seen, genres are dynamic constructs closely linked to both individual purposes and wider social and cultural practices. These interactions suggest that changes at either level are likely to bring about changes in discourse practices. Essentially, there are three main sources of change: from users inside the discipline manipulating conventions; from peripheral members seeking to assert new practices; and from macro-level developments within the discipline or wider culture.

First, genres may change from the inside, from the small acts of individual writers giving expression to their intentions using innovative forms within the boundaries of generic convention. Although academic genres tend to be identified by their conventional surface features, which generally exhibit regular and standardised patterns, they are actually forms of social action designed to accomplish socially recognised purposes with some hope of success. These purposes are, of course, framed within the institutional processes of the academic world, but they are coloured by personal ambition, private intentions and individual experience, and are therefore subject to subtle manipulation and exploitation.

Writers always have options: choices concerning the extent to which they should rely on the conventions and expectations associated with the genre, or how much they can be innovative and exercise creativity. Individual writers are, as I noted earlier, members of multiple communities and experience a range of discourses as a result of their age, gender, race, professional subculture, political orientation, and so on. As a result, they have the potential to read situations differently and to employ these other discourses in constructing their own, moving outside the standardised communicative behaviour of the genre-at-hand to introduce new elements which subtly transform it. Similarly, texts are not monolithic and homogeneous, they are combinations of other texts and other genres and these combinations similarly work to slowly change the prevailing practices.

One might expect that the ability of writers to exploit routine practices, and to impose an individual stamp on their texts, has increased as they learn more about the contingency of rhetorical forms. Genre analysis, critical discourse analysis, and the sociology of scientific knowledge have played important roles in deconstructing the taken-for-granted 'naturalised' discourses of social institutions. The research in English for Specific Purposes has had some influence in raising practitioners' metacognitive awareness of the conventions of disciplinary literacy. Spurred on by university ranking tables and the importance of publication to career, many institutions now offer in-service courses in research writing to their staff, developing their ability to engage effectively in professional forums. This rhetorical consciousness clearly has the potential to initiate change for it gives writers the power to question, to experiment, and to exercise options.

Options, however, carry risks. As we have seen, an understanding of conventions is an important means of demonstrating membership and identification with the group, and the most effective way of being heard as competent and plausible. Manipulation is therefore generally subtle and realized within the boundaries of what is conventionally recognized as typical practices, what Bhatia (1993) calls 'generic integrity'. It also involves a good grasp of the resources available within the discipline for creating meanings and a certain confidence to depart from the conventional. So while an important dimension of community membership is the knowledge of when to follow and when to innovate, neither the knowledge nor the right to do so is equally distributed. Bhatia (1997: 359) makes this point:

> Unfortunately, however, this privilege to exploit generic conventions to create new forms becomes available only to those few who enjoy a certain degree of visibility in the relevant professional community; for a wide majority of others it is more of a matter of apprenticeship in accommodating the expectations of disciplinary cultures.

While we may want to question the kinds of participant relationship assumed in the concept of 'apprenticeship', established membership seems to be a prerequisite for generic exploitation, and indeed, is often a marker of the authority of those who successfully exercise this practice. In Bourdieu's (1991: 72–6) terms, only those possessing sufficient 'symbolic capital' in the field can effectively see through innovative practices. So while change occurs, it is always driven by those with authority in the discipline.

A second source of change is through the literacy conventions brought to the discipline by those more familiar with academic conventions outside its western metropolitan centres. Disciplines are always evolving through the affiliation of new members, the retirement of authority figures, the expansion or contraction of lines of research and so on, but a major element of change over the past few decades has been the massive increase in the participation of non-native English speakers in their discourses. Publication in English is now often a prerequisite for professional success for academics throughout the world, but the different epistemological traditions in which these writers have been trained, and in which their identities as chemists, engineers or lawyers are rooted, poses new challenges to disciplinary membership and its expression in generic conventions (cf. Pennycook, 1994).

Various studies have shown that considerable cultural and linguistic differences exist between the source and target languages in the writing practices of academics from many backgrounds (e.g. Ventola and Mauranen, 1996). Institutional power, however, continues to remain principally in the large universities and industrial research labs of the west, and disciplinary gatekeepers have successfully resisted the encroachment of alternative conventions into the mainstream. It is still the case, for example, that professional polishing/pre-editing is often sought by L2 writers submitting papers (Chandler-Burns, 1996) and in many disciplines editors may insist on having submissions vetted by native English speakers (Gosden, 1992).

However, many writers from other backgrounds may be unwilling to suppress elements of their native cognitive and linguistic repertoire, and may seek to extend them into their submissions in a different cultural setting. Moreover, the notion of linguistic variation is becoming increasingly respectable among some members of the dominant communities. Many journals now actively encourage submissions from all over the world to reflect an international status, and as a result have begun to accommodate a 'World Englishes' perspective in the papers they accept, tolerating a certain level of non-standard forms.[3]

However, the manipulation of a convention on a particular occasion of use is one thing, getting these changes to stick is quite another. Academic communities have a stake in maintaining the distinctiveness of their prestigious discourses; after all, they are the principal means by which disciplines assess and authorise knowledge, distinguish members from outsiders and legitimate its authority in the world. Discursive innovations are therefore unlikely to be readily incorporated without some resistance, but, as we observed in Chapter 1, they do occur. Atkinson's (1996) rhetorical history of scientific norms from the seventeenth century show the incremental effect of modest routine innovations. Historically, early science employed a dialogic form and argued much the same as theology and philosophy had argued previously; today's rhetorical conventions have emerged from very different earlier practices based on author-centred genteel conduct and virtual witnessing of experiments.

Kress (1987: 42) argues that new generic forms are unlikely to be successfully accepted into the community's practices without changes in either social structure or in the social contexts within which texts are produced:

> That is why childish innovations fail; not because they do not constitute perfectly plausible solutions to particular textual/cognitive problems, but because they are supported neither by a stable social occasion, nor by 'authority'. This latter is of course the case where a writer of 'authority' creates a new generic form, which, seemingly because of the writer's authority alone, succeeds in establishing a new generic convention.

Once again, the power to bend the rules is therefore largely in the hands of established figures in the disciplines, rather than novices or journeymen. Shapin (1984) and Bazerman (1988), for example, show the significant impact that Boyle, Newton and Edison had on shaping the research article in science. For Kress, challenging genres means challenging cultures, and the powerful are in the best position to do this.

A further source of discursive change, which may also be initiated by powerful members of the discipline, is that related to developments in the wider social and cultural environment. New discursive forms can result from users' reconceptualisation of their purposes or how to best accomplish them due to social changes in a particular period. As I have discussed above, academic disciplines are intimately connected with aspects of secular cultures and are susceptible to the dominant relations and orders of discourse within them. Fairclough (1989: 198) has suggested that instrumental discourses are powerful influences in the modern age, and has identified the discourses of advertising and bureaucracy as particularly prominent models that are widely drawn upon. He argues that text users, influenced by these changes, begin to incorporate them into their writing, combining discursive conventions and elements in new ways, and thereby cumulatively restructuring institutional hegemonies (Fairclough, 1993: ch. 7).

In academic settings we have noted an increasingly competitive professional environment, dominated by the need to publish, to get claims accepted, to secure funding and promotion, and to gain a reputation among one's peers. This is a very different picture to earlier academic values and practices. For several centuries academic communities were loose collections of individuals who tended to lack a wholly shared intellectual purpose or recognisable career structure. Science, for example, did not become a professional activity oriented towards original discovery until the late nineteenth century, and it is only in this century that scientists have been able to speak as professional experts (e.g. Gibbons, 1985; Rothblatt, 1985).

The structure and roles of industry, business, government and education have changed dramatically over the last 100 years. This has fostered an increasing mutual dependence of state and academy which has increased the extent to which academics are enmeshed in the dominant value systems of the secular world. Put succinctly, and no doubt oversimply, the increasing market for knowledge of all kinds has had a direct influence on the increasing marketisation of the discourses of its producers.

The overwhelmingly intrusive nature of promotional discourses, which are insinuating themselves into every corner of our lives, are clearly making inroads into the published genres of the academy (see, for example, Chapters 4 and 5 above). My analyses have shown the importance that academics attach to highlighting novelty, foregrounding relevance, and demonstrating credibility, thereby indicating the extent to which promotional elements are helping to construct discourses often considered non-promotional (Fairclough, 1995). The purposes of writers, the ways they negotiate knowledge, and the social relations between members of disciplinary communities, are not immune from societal ideological and political trends. Tendencies towards the competitive, self-motivating, 'entrepreneurial' self in political life are reflected in the interactional features of published academic texts shown in earlier chapters.

Clearly the actual impact of these broad social changes will be variable, affecting different disciplines, individuals, and genres in different ways on different occasions. However, they are pervasive. Over time, the conventions of disciplinary discursive practices become naturalised and taken-for-granted along with the ideological assumptions they carry, constantly shifting in response to changes in the dominant socio-cultural forces in society.

ENDWORDS

I would like to close this book by making a few brief remarks on some of the main points that have been raised. Principally I have tried to elucidate the view that it is through the ways that writers promote their ideas and stake their claims that they sustain their communities and define themselves as members of those communities.

I believe an understanding of how this membership is accomplished is important not only for the practical pay-offs it may have for training outsiders and newcomers in the skills of writing and reading specialist texts, but also because of the importance of the social, political and economic centrality of academic discourses in most advanced industrialised societies. Disciplinary discourses can have a local and a more societal relevance, and the former is often produced and understood in terms of the latter. We live in a world substantially influenced by the privileged discourses of the academy, and it is important for an understanding of this world that we are able to reconstruct the social contexts within which such discourses are produced and which they largely conceal.

At the local level I hope my analyses have shown that disciplinary texts form relatively tightly-knit intertextual sets, drawing on each other to address similar problems about a similarly conceived external world. Their unity of purpose and themes, their adoption of similar approaches and questions, their preferences for particular argument forms, lexical choices and discourse structures, all display their writer's professional competence in discipline-legitimated discursive practices. My main point has been that it is these practices, and not abstract and disengaged beliefs and theories, that manifest disciplines and construct their realities, authorise particular beliefs and social relations and, gradually, lead to social and discursive change.

The decisions writers make at different points of composing – to employ dialogical resources to minimise or foreground claims, to appeal to community knowledge or spell out assumptions, to point to writer inferences or let facts speak for themselves – are all strategic choices. They are part of a repertoire of preferred practices among members which help to construct knowledge and the relationships that constitute membership. As should be clear, there are no strictly epistemological reasons why these particular strategies and forms should have evolved to express disciplinary knowledge; they are not in themselves value-free, neutral reportage. Nor could they possibly be, for all language use reflects the social and epistemological positions of its users as they engage with others in common endeavours.

However, academic discursive practices are not merely a cynical manipulation of a disinterested ethic, a socio-political agenda dressed in empirical clothing. No institution, set of practices, or forms of discourse can be completely objective, disinterested and free of rivalries or ideological interest, but these can be openly recognised and their worst effects minimised. While no doubt there are many academics, some of them among my informants, who take an extreme realist and empirical view of research activity, many acknowledge that their work involves negotiation with colleagues and persuasion through texts. This involves neither subterfuge nor fabrication; it is simply what it means to engage in disciplinary discourses.

Finally, I hope that the kinds of analysis I have presented here can tell us something about published texts, academic practices and the relationships which constitute doing science in its broadest sense. An awareness that academic concepts are socially contingent demystifies them and makes it possible not only to learn and teach others to employ them effectively, but also to identify the apparently neutral and commonsensical premises these discourses presuppose. To see knowledge-creating discourses as the product of social interactions means understanding both texts and ideas as historically situated cultural products – i.e. forms of knowledge that are not simply given, but which we can redefine as socially valued ideologies. This, in turn, allows us to question the social relations that underlie them, develop strategies for understanding their persuasive rhetorical forms and open up greater possibilities for change.

NOTES

1. Gibbons et al. (1994: 94) report 30,000 doctoral theses on modern literature completed each year in western universities.
2. Competition in technology has long been fierce. Rawlence (1990), for example, shows how Edison's ruthlessness and dishonesty in dealing with competitors not only delayed the development of power-transmission technology and motion pictures, but also secured him a substantial share of the profits.
3. Several journals in TESL and applied linguistics operate a selection procedure which favours non-native researchers, while journals in agriculture and astrophysics appear to exercise very liberal practices in accepting non-standard grammatical expressions.

Appendix 1

Corpora

1.1   RESEARCH ARTICLES

Cell biology (Bio)

Journal of Cell Biology (1997), **136** (4): 845–57
Mycological Research (1997), **101** (5): 625–31
The Plant Cell (1997), **9**: 283–96
Plant Molecular Biology (1997), **33**: 467–81
Plant, Cell and Environment (1997), **20**: 425–37
Molecular and Cellular Biology (1997), **17** (3): 1236–43
Mycologia (1997), **89** (1): 163–72
The New Phytologists (1997), **135**: 575–85
Canadian Journal of Botany (1997), **75** (5): 699–710
Plant Physiology (1997), **115** (1): 129–35

Electrical engineering (EE)

International Journal of Microwave and Millimeter-Wave CAE (1997), **7**: 149–66
Microsystem Technologies (1997), 53–60
IEEE Transactions on Microwave Theory and Techniques (1997), **45** (1): 58–71
Journal of Microelectomechanical systems (1997), **6** (1): 10–17
Solid-State Electronics (1997), **41** (4): 635–41
Microelectronics Journal (1997), **28**: 247–62
Analog Integrated Circuits and Signal Processing (1997), **12**: 179–99
Journal of Manufacturing Science and Engineering (1997), **119** (2): 151–60
International Journal of Production Research (1997), **35** (7): 1857–74
International Journal of Industrial Engineering (1997), **4** (2): 73–80

Mechnical engineering (ME)

Mechanism and Machine Theory (1997), **32** (4): 419–32
Energy Sources (1997), **19**: 233–43
Journal of Process Mechanical Engineering (1997), **210**: 159–69
Mechanics and Material Engineering (1997), A, **40** (1): 65–74
Journal of Engineering Manufacture (1997), B, **211**: 29–41
International Journal of Mechanical Sciences (1997), **39** (7): 819–28

Journal of Mechanical Engineering Science (1997), C, **211**: 77–87
Energy Engineering (1997), **94** (4): 16–30
International Journal of Energy Research (1997), **21** (13): 1215–21
Journal of Energy Resources Technology (1997), **119** (3): 164–70

Applied linguistics (AL)

Applied Linguistics (1997), **18** (1): 27–42
TESOL Quarterly (1997), **31** (1): 121–39
Second Language Research (1997), **13** (1): 34–65
System (1997), **25** (1): 103–12
English for Specific Purposes (1997), **16** (1): 27–46
World Englishes (1997), **15** (2): 159–70
Journal of Second Language Writing (1997), **6** (1): 45–60
Journal of Pragmatics (1997), **28** (1): 69–101
Written Communication (1997), **14** (2): 221–64
International Journal of Applied Linguistics (1997), **7** (1): 49–56

Marketing (Mkt)

Journal of Marketing Management (1997), **12**: 695–706
International Journal of Research in Marketing (1997), **14**: 19–33
Journal of Marketing Research (1997), **34**: 13–23
Journal of Marketing (1997), **61**: 68–84
Journal of the Academy of Marketing Science (1997), **25** (1): 18–30
Journal of Marketing Communication (1997), **3**: 21–32
Journal of International Consumer Marketing (1997), **9** (1): 83–103
Journal of Consumer Research (1997), **24** (1): 15–42
Journal of Retailing (1997), **73** (1): 135–59
Marketing Science (1997), **16** (2): 97–111

Philosophy (Phil)

Mind (1997), **106** (422): 245–61
The Journal of Philosophy (1997), **XCIV** (4): 165–87
Analysis (1997), **57** (1): 51–9
The Philosophical Quarterly (1997), **47** (187): 195–211
Philosophy (1997), **72** (279): 85–104
Erkenntnis (1997), **45** (1): 253–43
Inquiry (1997), **39** (3): 343–58
Political Theory (1997), **25** (3): 347–76
Ethics (1997), **107** (3): 410–26
Philosophy and Public Affairs (1997), **26** (1): 3–30

Sociology (Soc)

American Journal of Sociology (1997), **102** (4): 1113–42
The Sociological Review (1997), **45** (1): 24–41
Current Sociology (1997), **44** (3): 153–76

International Journal of Comparative Sociology (1997), **37** (3–4): 231–51
Sociology (1997), **30** (4): 701–16
International Sociology (1997), **12** (1): 47–60
British Journal of Sociology (1997), **48** (1): 54–70
British Journal of Criminology (1997), **37** (2): 362–88
Criminology (1997), **35** (2): 277–306
International Journal of the Sociology of Law (1997), **25** (1): 21–44

Physics (Phy)

Journal of Magnetism and Magnetic Materials (1997), **167**: 209–22
Bulletin of Magnetic Resonance (1997), **18** (1–2): 65–70
Applied Magnetic Resonance (1997), **12**: 103–117
Electromagnetics (1997), **17**: 25–39
Journal of Magnetic Resonance (B) (1997), **113**: 228–35
Journal of Electromagnetic Waves and Applications (1997), **11**: 297–313
Journal of Material Science (1997), **32** (13): 3457–62
Journal of Applied Physics (1997), **82** (4): 1521–4
Physical Review B (1997), **56** (5): 2680–7
American Journal of Physics (1997), **65** (7): 605–14

1.2 BOOK REVIEWS

Cell biology (Bio)

The New Phytologists, **137**: 371–2, 539–42, 563–7 and 703–7

Electrical engineering (EE)

Microelectronics Journal, **28**: 101–4, 199–202, 359–63, 595 and 601–5

Mechnical engineering (ME)

Energy Sources, **18**: 345–6 and 743; **19**: 89
Journal of Engineering Manufacture, **209**: 327–8; **210**: 99; 11: 251
Journal of Mechanical Engineering Science, **206**: 75–7; **211**(C): 89–90, 173, 251–2, 323, 489
   and 490

Applied linguistics (AL)

Applied Linguistics (1997): 558–60, 560–4 and 564–6
TESOL Quarterly, **30** (3): 641–6 and 177–81
Second Language Research, **13** (2): 170–86
System, **25** 113–15, 116–18 and 435–7
English for Specific Purposes, **16**: 153–8 and 245–7
World Englishes, **15**: 125–9; **16**: 153–6
Journal of Pragmatics, **29**: 205–10
International Journal of Applied Linguistics, **7**: 106–16 and 266–9

Marketing (Mkt)

Journal of Marketing Management, **13**: 327–30 and 601
International Journal of Research in Marketing, **14**: 291–300 and 397–8
Journal of Marketing Research, **34**: 537–44; **35**: 128–9
Journal of Marketing, **61**: 92–7 and 112–16

Philosophy (Phil)

Mind, **106**: 167–76 and 800–3
The Journal of Philosophy, (1997): 156–64 and 584–7
The Philosophical Quarterly, **47**: 382–6 and 519–23
Philosophy, **72**: 317–23 and 602–4
Erkenntnis, **46**: 127–31 and 397–400
Political Theory, **25**: 289–301 and 761–5
Ethics (1997): 208–15

Sociology (Soc)

American Journal of Sociology, **103**: 763–9
The Sociological Review (1997): 325–30 and 704–9
International Journal of Comparative Sociology, **38**: 151–6
Sociology, **31**: 625–7 and 806–10
British Journal of Sociology, **48**: 701–4
British Journal of Criminology, **37**: 131–4; **38**: 171–2

Physics (Phy)

Applied Magnetic Resonance, **12**: 393–4
American Journal of Physics, **65**: 258–61, 355, 452–4, 675–7, 801–2, 1124–6 and 1218–19;
    66: 92–4

1.3 SCIENTIFIC LETTERS

Cell biology (Bio)

Biotechnology Letters, **19**: 221–3, 229–32, 245–9, 719–26, 755–8, 961–5, 967–9, 999–1004,
    1063–5, 1067–71, 1103–7, 1193–5, 1205–8 and 1223–5
Letters in Applied Microbiology, **25**: 24–9, 63–9, 186–90, 197–201, 202–6, 233–8, 239–42,
    249–53, 316–20, 321–4, 345–8, 353–8, 419–25, 435–6 and 437–41

Physics (Phy)

Physics Letters B, **415**: 15–23, 24–30, 39–44, 75–82, 149–55, 170–4 and 193–9
Physical Review Letters, **79**: 4083–7, 4131–4, 4190–3, 4230–3, 4522–4, 4546–9, 4589–92
    and 4645–8
Europhysics Letters, **40**: 245–50, 263–8, 293–8, 311–16, 601–6, 619–24 and 661–6

Applied Physics Letters, **71**: 3054–6, 3078–80, 3093–5, 3111–13, 3471–3, 3501–3, 3531–3 and 3561–3

Chemistry (Chem)

Tetrahedron Letters, **38**: 6959–60, 6985–8, 7033–6, 7087–90, 8939–42, 8977–80, 8997–9000 and 9027–30

Chemistry Letters (1997): 7–8, 19–20, 49–50, 1205–6, 1237–8, 1261–2 and 1295–6

Chemistry Communications (1997) 1705–6, 1725–6, 1755–6, 1775–6, 2347–8, 2369–70, 2389–90 and 2403–4

Chemistry Physics Letters, **275**: 469–76, 506–12, 513–18 and 419–422; **280**: 459–63, 535–8 and 551–5

1.4 TEXTBOOKS

Cell biology (Bio)

Brock, T. and Madigan, M. (1994). *Biology of micro-organism* (7th edn), (pp. 692–716). Prentice Hall.

Kendrick, B. (1992). *The fifth kingdom* (2nd edn), (pp. 180–91). Focus Information Group.

Koneman, E. et al. (1992). *Colour atlas and textbook of diagnostic microbiology* (4th edn), (pp. 370–83). Lippincott.

Onions, A., Allsopp, D. and Eggins, H. (1981). *Smith's introduction to industrial mycology* (7th edn), (pp. 50–61). Edward Arnold.

Atlas, R.M. (1989). *Microbiology: fundamentals and applications* (2nd edn), (pp. 171–80). Macmillan.

Alexopoulos, C. and Mims, C. (1993). *Introductory mycology* (3rd edn), (pp. 575–87). Wiley.

Moore-Landecker, E. (1990). *Fundamentals of the fungi* (3rd edn), (pp. 377–89). Prentice Hall.

Electronic engineering (EE)

Allocca, J.A. and Stuart, A. (1983). *Electronic instrumentation* (pp. 473–517). Reston, VA: Reston.

Jones, L. D. and Foster, C. (1983). *Electronic instruments and measurements*, (pp. 57–84). New York: Wiley.

Lander, C.W. (1993). *Power electronics* (3rd edn), (pp. 181–241). London: McGraw-Hill.

Nashelsky, L. (1994). *Introduction to digital technology* (4th edn), (pp. 48–92). Englewood Cliffs, NJ: Prentice Hall Career and Technology.

Rashid, M.H. (1993). *Power electronics: circuits, devices, and applications* (2nd edn), (pp. 262–302). Englewood Cliffs, NJ: Prentice Hall.

Wakerly, J. F. (1994). *Digital design: principles and practices* (2nd edn), (pp. 21–72). Englewood Cliffs, NJ: Prentice Hall.

Wolf, S. (1983). *Guide to electronic measurements and laboratory practice* (2nd edn), (pp. 387–414). Englewood Cliffs, NJ Prentice Hall.

Mechanical engineering (ME)

Collins, J. A. (1993). *Failure of materials in mechanical design: analysis, prediction, prevention* (2nd edn), (pp. 526–582). New York: Wiley.

Edwards, K. S. and McKee, R. B. (1991). *Fundamentals of mechanical component design* (pp. 524–57). New York: McGraw-Hill.

Klafter, R. D., Chmielewski, T. A. and Negin, M. (1989). *Robotic engineering: an integrated approach* (pp. 101–201). Englewood Cliffs, NJ: Prentice Hall.

Knight, C. E. (1993). *The finite element method in mechanical design* (pp. 181–200). Boston: PWS-Kent.

Shigley, J. E. and Mitchell, L. D. (1983). *Mechanical engineering design* (4th edn), (pp. 3–27). New York: McGraw-Hill.

Steidel, R. F. (1989). *An introduction to mechanical vibrations* (3rd edn), (pp. 164–195). New York: Wiley.

Crandall, S. H., Dahl, N. C. and Lardner, T. J. (1978). *An introduction to mechanics of solids* (2nd edn) (pp. 143–86). New York: McGraw-Hill.

Applied linguistics (AL)

Bloor, T. and Bloor, M. (1995). *The functional analysis of English: a Hallidayan approach* (pp. 86–106). London and New York: Arnold.

Brown, H. D. (1994). *Principles of language learning and teaching* (pp. 226–50). Prentice Hall Regents.

Cook, V. J. (1993). *Linguistics and second language acquisition* (pp. 51–68). Macmillan Press.

Holmes, J. (1992). *An introduction to sociolinguistics* (pp. 285–305). Longman.

Johnson, K. (1995). *Understanding communication in second language classrooms* (pp. 111–28). Cambridge: Cambridge University Press.

Schiffrin, D. (1994). *Approaches to discourse* (pp. 49–60). Blackwell.

Scollon, R. and Scollon, S. (1995). *Intercultural communication: a discourse approach* (pp. 33–49). Blackwell.

Marketing (Mkt)

Cateora, P. (1990). *International marketing* (7th edn), (pp. 459–83). Boston, MA: Irwin.

Kotler, P. and Armstrong, G. (1994). *Principles of marketing* (pp. 185–95). Englewood Cliffs, NJ: Prentice Hall.

Lovelock, C. (1991). *Services marketing* (2nd edn), (pp. 109–17). Englewoods Cliffs, NJ: Prentice Hall.

Luck, D., Ferrell, O.C. and Lucas, G. (1989). *Marketing strategy and plans* (3rd edn), (pp. 392–407). Prentice Hall.

Lusch, R. and Lusch, V. (1987). *Principles of marketing* (pp. 180–200). Boston, MA: Kent Publishing.

McCarthy, J. and Perreault, W. (1990). *Basic marketing: a managerial approach* (pp. 299–320). Homewood IL.: Irwin.

Stanton, W., Etzel, M. and Walker, B. (1994). *Fundamentals of marketing (10th edn)*, (pp. 89–113). New York: McGraw-Hill.

Philosophy (Phil)

Barcalow, E. (1992). *Open questions: an introduction to philosophy* (pp. 153–72). Wadsworth: California.

Deutsch, E. (1997). *Introduction to world philosophies, with introductions and commentaries* (pp. 170–200) (Part II). Upper Saddle River, NJ: Prentice Hall.

Gill, J.H. and Rader, M. (1995). *The enduring questions: traditional and contemporary voices* (6th edn), (pp. 178–201). Fort Worth, TX: Harcourt Brace College Publishers.

Gould, J. A. (1992). *Classic philosophical Questions* (5th edn), (pp. 132–42). New York: Macmillan.

Solomon, R.C. (1997). *Introducing philosophy: a text with integrated readings* (pp. 257–88). Fort Worth: Harcourt Brace College Publishers.

Stumpf, S.E. (1993). *Elements of philosophy: an introduction* (pp. 372–395). New York: McGraw-Hill.

White, T.I. (1991). *Discovering philosophy* (pp. 52–67). Englewood Cliffs, NJ: Prentice Hall.

Sociology (Soc)

Berger, P.L. (1966). *Invitation to sociology: a humanistic perspective* (pp. 37–67). Harmondsworth: Penguin.

Giddens, A. (1993). *Sociology* (pp. 160–207). Cambridge: Polity Press.

Haralambos, M. and Holborn, M. (1995). *Sociology: themes and perspectives* (4th edn), (pp. 325–68). London: Harper Collins.

Lenski, G., Nolan, P. and Lenski, J. (1995). *Human societies: an introduction to macrosociology* (7th edn), (pp. 272–96). New York: McGraw-Hill.

Levin, W. (1988). *Sociological ideas: concepts and applications* (4th edn), (pp. 157–73). New York: Wadsworth International.

Morales, A. and Sheafor, B.W. (1992). *Social work: a profession of many faces* (pp. 193–219). Boston: Allyn & Bacon.

Sullivan, M. (1987). *Sociology and social welfare* (pp. 29–61). UK: Allen & Unwin.

Physics (Phy)

Boresi, A.P. and Sidebottom, O.M. (1985). *Advanced mechanics of materials* (4th edn), (pp. 492–524). New York: Wiley.

Flinn, R.A. and Trojan, P.K. (1990). *Engineering Materials and Their Applications* (4th edn), (pp. 591–622). Boston: Houghton Mifflin.

Giancoli, D.C. (1984). *General physics* (pp. 744–70). Englewood Cliffs, NJ: Prentice Hall.

Serway, R. A. (1996). *Physics for scientists and engineers, with modern physics* (4th edn), (pp. 144–62). Philadelphia: Saunders College Pub.

Skoog, D.A., Holler, F.J. and Nieman, T.A. (1998). *Principles of instrumental analysis* (5th edn), (pp. 116–40). Philadelphia: Saunders College Pub.

Smith, W.F. (1990). *Principles of materials science and engineering* (2nd edn), (pp. 559–628). New York: McGraw-Hill.

Sperling, L.H. (1992). *Introduction to physical polymer science* (2nd edn), (pp. 65–115). New York: Wiley.

1.5 ABSTRACTS FROM 1980

Cell biology (Bio)

Mycologia (1980), **72**: 55, 110, 159, 229, 288, 378, 472, 689, 737, 759, 791, 988, 1065, 1077 and 1103
The New Phytologists (1980), **84**: 19, 139, 251, 465 and 603; **85**: 33, 173, 235, 351 and 451; **86**: 17, 57, 155, 329 and 365

Electronic engineering (EE)

Solid-State Electronics (1980), **23**: 35, 87, 117, 289, 345, 377, 441, 621, 715, 741, 831, 875, 893, 1107 and 1197
International Journal of Production Research (1980) **18**: 11, 43, 57, 143, 179, 295, 335, 411, 455, 479, 583, 597, 619, 699 and 723

Mechanical engineering (ME)

Adv. Manufact. Sci. and Tech. (1980) **43**: 144, 263, 270, 351
Ball-and-Roller-Bearing-Engineering (1980), **19** (1), 16
Chem. and Petro. Eng. (1980), **16** (3–4): 207
Chem. and Tech. Fuels and Oils (1980), **16** (3–4): 212 and 258
Coast. Eng. Japan. (1980): 121
Data Process (1980), **23** (8): 12 and 14
Energy from Biomass and Wastes IV (1980): 423
Engineering Cybernetics (1980), **18** (4): 68
Fluid Mech. Sov. Res. (1980), **9** (3): 117
Health Effects of Diesel Engine Emissions: Proceedings Int. Symp. (1980), **1**: 358
International Journal of Fracture (1980) **16** (6): 499 and 563
J. Hydraul. Div. ASCE. (1980) **106** (HY11): 1915
J. Mecaniq (1980), **19** (4): 663
J. Inst. Eng. India (1980), **61** (EN1): 8
Marine Tech. Soc. J. (1980), **14** (5): 12
Maritime Policy and Management (1980) **7** (3): 185
Nat. Safety (1980), **40** (5): 10
NTIS, Springfield (1980): 50 and 94
Remote Sensing Environment (1980), **10** (3): 175
Scientific Basis for Nuclear Waste Management (1980), **2**: 403 and 681
Soviet Physics: Doklady (1980), **25** (4): 273
The character and origins of smog aerosols (1980), **9**: 215

Applied linguistics (AL)

TESOL Quarterly (1980), **14** 17, 27, 53, 81, 157, 165, 189, 221, 285, 345, 353, 443, 469, 483 and 489
Journal of Pragmatics (1980), **4**: 1, 15, 43, 121, 137, 147, 213, 233, 253, 301, 321, 341, 351, 367 and 413

Marketing (Mkt)

Journal of Marketing Research (1980), **17**: 212, 253, 294, 316, 323, 341, 359, 385, 407, 432, 450, 460, 470, 524 and 531
Journal of Marketing (1980), **44** (winter): 10, 19, 26 and 36; **44** (spring): 9, 36, 48, 56, 65, 78 and 82; **44** (summer): 17, 36, 40 and 70

Philosophy (Phil)

American Philosophy Quarterly (1980), **17**: 301
Bull. Sect. Log. (Dec. 80), **9**: 189
Can. J. Phil. (1980), **6**: 119
Fran. Stud. (1980), **40**: 265
Grazer. Phil. Stud. (1980), **11**: 1
Hist. Phil. Log. (1980), **1**: 95, 187 and 231
Hist. Polit. Thought (Summer 1980), **1**: 301
History Poli. Thought (Fall 1980), **1**: 517
Humanitas (Mexico) (1980), **21**: 41
Independ. J. Phil. (1980), **4**: 31 and 79
Inform. Log. (1980), **3**: 2
International Studies in Philosophy (1980) **12**: 41
J. Relig. Ethics (Fall 1980), **8**: 330
Journal of the History of Philosophy (1980), **18**: 23
Logique en analyse (1980) **23**: 263 and 431
Logos (1980), **1**: 45
Phil. Inq. (spr–sum 80), **2**: 496
Philosophical Topics (Supp. 80), **1980**: 133
Proc. Phil. Educ. (1980), **36**: 372
Process Stud. (Fall/Wint 80), **10**: 120
Rep. Phil. (1980), **4**: 17
Rev. Univ. Ottawa (JL-O 80), **50**: 411
Social Praxis (1980), **7**: 219
Synthese (1980), **44**: 13 and 241
The Journal of Mind and Behavior (Autumn 1980), **1**: 247

Sociology (Soc)

British Journal of Sociology (1980), **31**: 1, 28, 46, 78, 204, 246, 265, 401, 419, 463, 507 and 544; **32**: 39, 111 and 224
Sociology (1980), **14**: 29, 49, 69, 183, 217, 247, 261, 345, 363, 401, 417, 525, 551, 567 and 581

Physics (Phy)

Journal of Applied Physics (1980), **51**: 5816, 5838, 5926, 5954, 6010, 6030, 6130, 6141, 6202, 6265, 6279, 6292, 6337, 6348 and 6356
American Journal of Physics (1980), **48**: 739, 760, 807, 837, 850, 868, 926, 933, 945, 956, 962, 1020, 1038, 1063 and 1080

Items expressing doubt and certainty investigated

BOOSTERS

actually
always
assured(ly)
certainly
certainty
certain that
clear(ly)
conclude
conclusive(ly)
confirm
convince
convincingly
couldn't
of course
decided(ly)
definite(ly)
demonstrate
determine
doubtless
is essential
evidence
expect

in fact
the fact that
we find
given that
impossible(ly)
improbable(ly)
indeed
inevitable(ly)
we know
it is known that/to
(at) least
manifest(ly)
more than
must
necessarily
never
no doubt
obvious(ly)
particularly
patently
perceive
plain(ly)

precise(ly)
prove
(without) question
quite
reliable(ly)
show
sure(ly)
surmise
we think
true
unambiguous(ly)
unarguably
undeniab(ly)
undoubted(ly)
unequivocal(ly)
unmistakab(ly)
unquestionabl(ly)
well-known
will
won't
wouldn't
wrong(ly)

HEDGES

about
admittedly
almost
(not) always
apparently
appear
approximately
argue

around
assume
assumption
basically
my/our belief
I believe
a certain X
certain extent

I/we claim
conceivab(ly)
conjecture
consistent with
contention
could
deduce
discern

doubt
essentially
estimate
evidently
formally
frequently
(in) general
generally
guess
hypothesise
hypothetically
ideally
(we) imagine
implication
imply
indicate
infer
interpret
largely
likely
mainly
may
maybe
might
more or less
most
not necessarily
normally

occasionally
often
ostensibly
partly
partially
perceive
perhaps
plausible
possibility
possible(ly)
postulate
predict
prediction
predominantly
presumably
presume
probable(ly)
probability
provided that
propose
open to question
questionable
quite
rare(ly)
rather
relatively
seen (as)
seem

seemingly
seldom
(general) sense
should
shouldn't
somewhat
sometimes
speculate
suggest
superficially
suppose
surmise
suspect
technically
tend
tendency
in theory
theoretically
typically
uncertain
unclear
unlikely
unsure
usually
virtually
would

Appendix 3

Metadiscourse items investigated

TEXTUAL METADISCOURSE

Logical connectives

and
but
therefore / thereby
so / so as to
in addition
similarly
equally
likewise
moreover
furthermore
in contrast / by contrast
as a result / the result is / result in
since
because
consequently / as a consequence
accordingly
on the other hand
on the contrary
however
besides
also
whereas
while
although
even though / though
yet
nevertheless
nonetheless
hence
thus
leads to

Frame markers

sequencing

to start with
first(ly), second(ly), etc.
next
to begin
last(ly)
finally
subsequently
numbering (1, 2, 3, etc.)
listing (a, b, c, etc.)

label stages

to conclude
in conclusion
to sum up / in sum / summarise
overall
on the whole
all in all
so far / by far / thus far
to repeat

announce goals

my purpose / the aim
I intend
I seek
I wish
I argue
I propose

I suggest
I discuss
I would like to
I / we will focus on / emphasis
my goal is
in this section / in this chapter
here I do this / I will

topic shifts

well
now
so
to move on
to look more closely
to come back to
in regard to / with regard to
to digress

Code glosses

for example / say
for instance
e.g.
i.e.
that is / that is to say
namely
in other words
this means / which means
( )
--
in fact
viz
specifically
such as
or X
put another way

known as / defined as
called

Endophoric markers

see / noted / discussed below
see / noted / discussed above
see / noted / discussed earlier
see / noted / discussed later
see / noted / discussed before
Section X
Chapter X
Fig. / Figure X
Table X
Example X
page X

Evidentials

(date)
according to X
cite
quote
established
said
says
X points out / to
X indicates
X argues
X claims
X believes
X suggests
X shows
X proves
X demonstrates
X found that
studies / research / literature

INTERPERSONAL METADISCOURSE

Attitude markers

!
admittedly
I agree
amazingly
appropriately
correctly

curiously
disappointing
disagree
even x
fortunately
have to
hopefully
important(ly)

interesting(ly)
like (prefer)
glad
pleased
must (obligation)
ought (obligation)
prefer / preferable
remarkable
should (obligation)
surprisingly
unfortunate(ly)
unusually
understandably

Hedges

about
almost
apparently
appear to be
approximately
assume
believed
certain extent / amount / level
could / couldn't
doubt
essentially
estimate
frequently
generally / in general
indicate
largely
likely
mainly
may
maybe
might
mostly
often
perhaps
plausible
possible(ly)
presumably
probable(ly)
relatively
seems
should

sometimes / somewhat
suggest
suspect
unlikely
uncertain
unclear
usually
would / wouldn't
little / not understood

Emphatics (boosters)

actually
always
apparent
I believe
certain that
certainly
certainty
clearly / it is clear
conclusively
decidedly
definitely
demonstrate
determine
doubtless
essential
establish
evidently
in fact / the fact that
find / found that
indeed
(we) know
it is known that
must
never
no / beyond doubt
obvious(ly)
of course
prove
we show
sure
(we) think
true
undoubtedly
well-known
will / won't

Relational markers

()
?
incidentally
by the way
determine
consider
find
imagine
Let x = y
Let's / let us
note (that)
notice
our (inclusive)
recall

us (includes reader)
we (includes reader)
you / your
one / one's
assume
think about

Person markers

I
we
me
my
our
mine

References

Achtert, W. and Gibaldi, J. (1985). *The MLA style manual.* New York: Modern Language Association.

Ahmad, U.K. (1995). *Academic language and culture: some observations on scientific Malay and scientific English.* Exploring language, culture and literature in language learning, RELC Conference: Singapore.

Alred, G.J. and Thelen, E.A. (1993). Are textbooks contributions to scholarship? *College Composition and Communication,* **44** (4), 466–77.

Aronowitz, S. (1988). *Science as power: discourse and ideology in modern society.* London: Macmillan.

Atkinson, D. (1991). Discourse analysis and written discourse conventions. *Annual Review of Applied Linguistics* (1990), **11**, 57–76.

Atkinson, D. (1996). The Philosophical Transactions of the Royal Society of London, 1675–1975: a sociohistorical discourse analysis. *Language in Society,* **25**, 333–71.

Bakhtin, M.M. (1981). In M. Holquist (ed.), *The dialogic imagination.* Austin, Texas: University of Texas Press.

Ballard, B. and Clanchy, J. (1991). Assessment by misconception: cultural influences and intellectual traditions. In L. Hamp-Lyons (ed.), *Assessing second language writing in academic contexts.* Norwood, NJ: Ablex.

Bargiela-Chiappini, F. and Nickerson, G. (eds) (1999). *Writing business: genres, media and discourses.* London: Longman.

Bartholomae, D. (1986). Inventing the university. *Journal of Basic Writing,* **5**, 4–23.

Barton, E.L. (1995). Contrastive and non-contrastive connectives. *Written Communication,* **12** (2), 219–39.

Bazerman, C. (1984). The writing of scientific non-fiction. *Pre/Text,* **5** (1), 39–74.

Bazerman, C. (1988). *Shaping written knowledge.* Madison: University of Wisconsin Press.

Bazerman, C. (1993). Foreword, in N. Blyler and C. Thralls (eds), *Professional communication: the social perspective* (pp. vii–x). Newbury Park, CA: Sage.

Beaugrande, R. d. (1998). On 'usefulness' and 'validity' in the theory and practice of linguistics. *Functions of Language,* **5** (1), 85–96.

Beauvais, P. (1989). A speech-act theory of metadiscourse. *Written Communication,* **6** (1), 11–30.

Becher, T. (1989). *Academic tribes and territories: intellectual inquiry and the cultures of disciplines.* Milton Keynes: SRHE/OUP.

Beebe, L. and Takahashi, T. (1989). Sociolinguisic variation in face-threatening speech acts. In M.Eisenstein (ed.), *The dynamic interchange: emprirical studies in second language variation* (pp. 199–218). New York: Plenum Press.

Bereiter, C. and Scardamalia, M. (1987). *The psychology of written composition*. Hillsdale, NJ: Lawrence Erlbaum.

Berkenkotter, C. and Huckin, T. (1995). *Genre knowledge in disciplinary communication*. Hillsdale, NJ Lawrence Erlbaum.

Bhatia, V.K. (1993). *Analysing genre: language use in professional settings*. London: Longman.

Bhatia, V.K. (1997). The power and politics of genre. *World Englishes*, **17** (3), 359–71.

Bhatia, V.K. (1999). Integrating products, processes, processes and participants in professional writing. In C.N. Candlin and K. Hyland (eds), *Writing: texts, processes and practices* (pp. 21–39). London: Longman.

Biber, D. (1988). *Variation across speech and writing*. Cambridge: CUP.

Biglan, A. (1973). The characteristics of subject matter in different scientific areas. *Journal of Applied Psychology*, **57** (3), 204–13.

Bizzell, P. (1982). Cognition, convention and certainty: what we need to know about writing. *Pre/Text*, **3**, 213–41.

Bizzell, P. (1987). Language and literacy. In T. Enos (ed.), *A sourcebook for basic writing teachers*. New York: Random House.

Bizzell, P. (1992). *Academic discourse and critical consciousness*. Pittsburgh: University of Pittsburgh Press.

Blakeslee, A. (1994). The rhetorical construction of novelty: presenting claims in a letters forum. *Science, Technology, and Human Values*, **19** (1), 88–100.

Blakeslee, A. (1997). Activity, context, interaction, and authority: learning to write scientific papers in situ. *Journal of Business and Technical Communication*, **11**, 125–69.

Bloor, M. and Bloor, T. (1991). Cultural expectations and socio-pragmatic failure in academic writing. In P. Adams, B. Heaton and P. Howarth (eds), *Socio-cultural issues in English for Academic Purposes*. *Review of ELT*. Basingstoke: Modern English Publications/British Council.

Bloor, T. (1996). Three hypothetical strategies in philosophical writing. In E. Ventola and A. Mauranen (eds), *Academic writing: intercultural and textual issues* (pp. 19–43). Amsterdam: John Benjamins.

Bourdieu, P. (1975). The specificity of the scientific field and the social conditions of the progress of reason. *Social Science Information*, **14** (6), 19–47.

Bourdieu, P. (1977). *Outline of a theory of practice*. Cambridge: CUP.

Bourdieu, P. (1980). The production of belief: contribution to an economy of symbolic goods. *Media, Culture and Society*, **2**, 261–93.

Bourdieu, P. (1991). *Language and symbolic power*. Oxford: Polity Press.

Bourdieu, P. and Passeron, J.-C. (1996). Introduction: language and relationship to language in the teaching situation. In P. Bourdieu, J.-C Passeron and M. de Saint Martin (eds), *Academic discourse* (pp. 1–34). The Hague: Mouton.

Braine, G. (1989). Writing in science and technology: an analysis of assignments from ten undergraduate courses. *English for Specific Purposes*, **8**, 3–15.

Braine, G. (1995). Writing in the natural sciences and engineering. In D. Belcher and G. Braine (eds), *Academic writing in a second language: essays on research and pedagogy*. New Jersey: Ablex.

Brenton, F. (1996). Rhetoric in competition: the formation of organizational discourse in conference on College Composition and Communication abstracts. *Written Communication*, **13** (3), 355–84.

Bridgestock, M. (1998). The scientific community. In M. Bridgestock, D. Burch, J. Forge, J. Laurent and I. Lowe (eds), *Science, technology and society*. Cambridge: CUP.

Bridgman, B. and Carlson, S. (1984). Survey of academic writing tasks. *Written Communication*, **1**, 247–80.

Brown, J., Collins, A. and Duguid, P. (1989). Situated cognition and the culture of learning. *Educational Researcher*, **18**, 32–42.

Brown, P. and Levinson, S. (1987). *Politeness: some universals in language usage*. Cambridge: CUP.

Brown, R. and Gilman, A. (1989). Politeness theory and Shakespeare's four major tragedies. *Language in Society*, **18**, 159–212.

Brown, V. (1993). Decanonizing discourses: textual analysis and the history of economic thought. In W. Henderson, T. Dudley-Evans and R. Backhouse (eds), *Economics and language* (pp. 64–84). London: Routledge.

Bruffee, K. (1986). Social construction: language and the authority of knowledge. A bibliographical essay. *College English*, **48** , 773–9.

Bruner, J. (1994). From joint attention to the meeting of minds: an introduction. In C. Moore and P. Dunham (eds), *Joint attention: its origins and role in development*. Hillsdale, NJ: Lawrence Erlbaum.

Butler, C.S. (1990). Qualifications in science: modal meanings in scientific texts. In W. Nash (ed.), *The writing scholar: studies in academic discourse* (pp. 137–70). Newbury Park, CA: Sage.

Cadman, K. (1997). Thesis writing for international students: a question of identity? *English for Specific Purposes*, **16** (1), 3–14.

Canagarajah, A.S. (1996). 'Nondiscursive' requirements in academic publishing, material resources of periphery scholars, and the politics of knowledge production. *Written Communication*, **13** (4), 435–72.

Candlin, C.N. and Hyland, K. (eds) (1999a). *Writing: texts, processes and practices*. London: Longman.

Candlin, C.N. and Hyland, K. (1999b). Introduction: integrating approaches to the study of writing. In C.N. Candlin and K. Hyland (eds), *Writing: texts, processes and practices* (pp. 1–18). London: Longman.

Candlin, C.N. and Maley, Y. (1997). Intertextuality and interdiscursivity in the discourse of alternative dispute resolution. In B.-L. Gunnarson, P. Linell and B. Nordberg (eds), *The construction of professional discourse* (pp. 201–22). London: Longman.

Candlin, C.N. and Plum, G.A. (eds), (1998). *Framing student literacy: cross cultural aspects of communication skills in Australian university settings*. Sydney: NECLTR, Macquarrie University.

Candlin, C.N. and Plum, G.A. (1999). Engaging with challenges of interdiscursivity in academic writing: researchers, students and teachers. In Candlin, C.N. and K. Hyland (eds), *Writing: texts, processes and practices* (pp. 193–217) London: Longman.

Chalmers, A.F. (1978). *What is this thing called science?* Milton Keynes: OUP Press.

Chandler-Burns, R.M. (1996). Value of editing vs. research. *Linguist List* **7**, 627.

Channell, J. (1990). Precise and vague expressions in writing on economics. In W. Nash (ed.), *The writing scholar: studies in academic discourse*. Newbury Park, CA: Sage.

Chargaff, E. (1974). Building the Tower of Babel. *Nature*, **248** (26 April), 778.

Cheng, X. and Steffensen, M. (1996). Metadiscourse: a technique for improving student writing. *Research in the Teaching of English*, **30** (2), 149–81.

Cherry, R. (1988). Politeness in written persuasion. *Journal of Pragmatics*, **12**, 63–81.

Chin, E. (1994a). Redefining 'context' in research on writing. *Written Communication*, **11**, 445–82.

Clyne, M. (1987). Cultural differences in the organisation of academic texts. *Journal of Pragmatics*, **11**, 211–47.

Čmejrková, S. (1996). Academic writing in Czech and English. In E. Ventola and A. Mauranen (eds), *Academic writing: intercultural and textual issues* (pp. 137–52). Amsterdam: Benjamins.

Coates, J. (1983). *The semantics of the modal auxiliaries*. Beckenham: Croom Helm.

Cohen, M. and Manion, L. (1994). *Research methods in education* (4th edn). London: Croom Helm.

Cole, L.A. (1993). *Element of risk: the politics of radon*. Washington, DC: AAAS Press.

Cole, S. (1983). The hierarchy of the sciences. *American Journal of Sociology*, **89** (1), 111–39.

Connor, U. (1996). *Contrastive rhetoric*. Cambridge: CUP.

Connor, U. and Kaplan, R. (eds) (1987). *Writing across languages: Analysis of L2 text*. Reading, MA: Addison-Wesley.

Connors, R. J. (1986). Textbooks and the evolution of the discipline. *College Composition and Communication*, **37**, 178–94.

Cooper, M.M. (1989). Why are we talking about discourse communities? Or, foundationalism rears its ugly head once more. In M.M. Cooper and M. Holzman (eds), *Writing as social action* (pp. 203–20). Portsmouth, New Hampshire: Boyton/Cook.

Crick, F. (1990). *What mad pursuit*. London: Penguin Books.

Crismore, A. (1989). *Talking with readers: metadiscourse as rhetorical act*. New York: Peter Lang.

Crismore, A. and Farnsworth, R. (1989). Mr. Darwin and his readers: Exploring interpersonal metadiscourse as a dimension of ethos. *Rhetoric Review*, **8** (1), 91–112.

Crismore, A. and Farnsworth, R. (1990). Metadiscourse in popular and professional science discourse. In W. Nash (ed.), *The writing scholar: studies in academic discourse* (pp. 118–36). Newbury Park, CA: Sage.

Crismore, A., Markkanen, R. and Steffensen, M. (1993). Metadiscourse in persuasive writing: a study of texts written by American and Finnish University Students. *Written Communication*, **10** (1), 39–71.

Crowley, P. (1999). Review article: linguistic diversity in the Pacific. *Journal of Sociolinguistics*, **3** (1), 81–103.

D'Amico-Reisner, L. (1983). An analysis of the surface structure of disapproval exchanges. In N. Wolfson and E. Judd (eds), *Sociolinguistics and language acquisition* (pp. 103–115). Rowley, MA: Newbury House.

Daiker, D. A. (1989). Learning to praise. In C. Anson (ed.), *Writing and response* (pp. 103–13). Urbana, IL: NCTE.

Dant, T. (1991). *Knowledge, ideology and discourse*. London: Routledge.

Diamond, N. (1986). The Copernican revolution: social foundations of conceptualization in science. In L. Levidow (ed.), *Science as politics* (pp. 7–37). London: Free Association Books.

Doheny-Farina, S. (1992). *Rhetoric, innovation, technology: case studies of technical communication in technology transfers*. Cambridge, MA: MIT Press.

Doheny-Farina, S. and Odell, L. (1985). Ethnographic research on writing: assumptions and methodology. In L. Odell and D. Goswami (eds), *Writing in non-academic settings*. New York: Guilford.

Dubois, B. (1987). 'Something of the order of around forty to forty four': imprecise numerical expressions in biomedical slide talks. *Language and Society*, **16**, 527–41.

Dubois, B. (1988). Citation in biomedical journal articles. *English for Specific Purposes*, **7**, 181–94.

Eggington, W. G. (1986). Written academic discourse in Korean: implications for effective communication. In U. Connor and R.B. Kaplan (eds), *Writing across languages: analysis of L2 text*. Reading, MA.: Addison-Wesley.

Eurin Balmet, S. and Henao de Legge, M. (1992). *Pratiques du français scientifique*. Hachette: AUPELF.

Faigley, L. (1985). Nonacademic writing: the social perspective. in L. Odell and D. Goswami (eds), *Writing in non-academic settings* (pp. 231–48). New York: Guilford Press.

Faigley, L. (1986). Competing theories of process: a critique and a proposal. *College Composition and Communication*, 48, 527–42.

Fairclough, N. (1989). *Language and Power*. London: Longman.

Fairclough, N. (1993). *Discourse and social change*. Cambridge: Polity Press.

Fairclough, N. (1995). *Critical discourse analysis*. London: Longman.

Flowerdew, J. (forthcoming). *Publication and Cantonese speakers of English: problems, practices and strategies*.

Foucault, M. (1972). *The archaeology of knowledge*. London: Tavistock Publications.

Frewer, L., Howard, C. and Shepherd, R. (1997). Public concerns in the United Kingdom about general and specific applications of genetic engineering: risk, benefit and ethics. *Science, Technology and Human Values*, 22 (1), 98–124.

Gambier, Y. (ed.) (1998). *Discours professionnels en français*. New York: Peter Lang.

Garvey, W. (1979). *Communication: the essence of science*. Oxford: Pergamon.

Gebhardt, R.C. (1993). Scholarship, promotion and tenure in composition studies. *College Composition and Communication*, 44, 439–42.

Geertz, C. (1983). *Local knowledge: further essays in interpretive anthropology*. New York: Basic Books.

Gibbons, M. (1985). The changing role of the academic research systems. In M. Gibbons and B. Wittrock (eds), *Science as a commodity* (pp. 2–20). Harlow: Longman.

Gibbons, M., Limoges, C., Nowotny, H., Schwartzman, S., Scott, P. and Trow, M. (1994). *The new production of knowledge*. London: Sage.

Gibbons, M. and Wittrock, B. (eds) (1985). *Science as a commodity*. London: Longman.

Giddens, A. (1987). *Social theory and modern sociology*. Cambridge: Polity Press.

Gilbert, G. (1976). The transformation of research findings into scientific knowledge. *Social Studies of Science*, 6, 281–306.

Gilbert, G. (1977). Referencing as persuasion. *Social Studies of Science*, 7, 113–22.

Gilbert, G. and Mulkay, M. (1984). *Opening Pandora's Box: a sociological analysis of scientific discourse*. Cambridge: CUP.

Goffman, E. (1967). *Interaction ritual*. Garden City, NY: Anchor Books.

Gosden, H. (1992). Research writing and NNSs: from the editors. *Journal of Second Language Writing*, 1 (2), 123–39.

Gosden, H. (1993). Discourse functions of subject in scientific research articles. *Applied Linguistics*, 14 (1), 56–75.

Gosden, H. (1996). Verbal reports of Japanese novices' research writing practices in English. *Journal of Second Language Writing*, 5 (2), 109–28.

Gottweis, H. (1995). German politics of genetic engineering and its deconstruction. *Social Studies of Science*, 25, 195–235.

Gould, S.J. (1998). Ladders and cones: constraining evolution by canonical icons. In R. Silvers (ed.), *Hidden histories of science* (pp. 37–67). London: Granta.

Graetz, N. (1985). Teaching EFL students to extract structural information from abstracts. In J.M. Ulijin and A.K. Pugh (eds), *Reading for professional purposes* (pp. 123–35). Leuven, Belgium: ACCO.

Gregory, J. and Miller, S. (1998). *Science in public: communication, culture and credibility*. New York: Plenum Press.

Grice, H. (1975). Logic and conversation. In P. Cole and J. Morgan (eds), *Syntax and semantics, Vol. 3: Speech acts*. New York: Academic Press.

Griffith, B.C. and Small, H.G. (1983). *The structure of the social and behavioural sciences literature*. Mimeo: Royal Institute of Technology Library, Stockholm.

Gunnarsson, B.-L. (1997). On the sociohistoric construction of scientific discourse. In B.-L. Gunnarsson, P. Linell and B. Nordberg (eds), *The construction of professional discourse*. London: Longman.

Gunnarsson, B.-L. (1995). Studies of language for specific purposes: a biased view of a rich reality. *International Journal of Applied Linguistics*, 5 (1), 111–34.

Haas, C. (1994). Learning to read biology: one student's rhetorical development in college. *Written Communication*, 11 (1), 43–84.

Haberer, J. (1972). Politicalisation in science. *Science*, 178, 721–5.

Hagge, J. and Kostelnick, C. (1989). Linguistic politeness in professional prose. *Written Communication*, 6 (3), 312–39.

Hagstrom, W.O. (1965). *The scientific community*. New York: Basic Books.

Halliday, M.A.K. (1973). *Explorations in the functions of language*. London: Edward Arnold.

Halliday, M.A.K. (1978). *Language as a social semiotic: the sociological interpretation of language and meaning*. London: Edward Arnold.

Halliday, M.A.K. (1988). On the language of physical science. In M. Ghadessey (ed.), *Registers of written English* (pp. 162–78). London: Pinter.

Halliday, M.A.K. (1994). *An introduction to functional grammar* (2nd edn). London: Edward Arnold.

Halliday, M.A.K. (1998). Things and relations: regrammaticising experience as technical knowledge. In J.R. Martin and R. Veel (eds), *Reading science* (pp. 185–235). London: Routledge.

Halliday, M.A.K. and Martin, J.R. (1993). *Writing science: literacy and discursive power*. London: Falmer Press.

Halloran, S. (1984). The birth of molecular biology: an essay in the rhetorical criticism of scientific discourse. *Rhetoric Review*, 3, 70–83.

Hanania, E.A.S. and Akhtar, K. (1985). Verb form and rhetorical function in science writing: a study of MS theses in biology, chemistry and physics. *ESP Journal*, 4, 49–58.

Harris, J. (1989). The idea of a discourse community in the study of writing. *College Composition and Communication*, 40, 11–22.

Harris, R.A. (1989). Rhetoric of science. *College English*, 53 (3), 282–307.

Harris, W.H. (1977). Teacher response to student writing: a study of the response patterns of high school English teachers to determine the basis for teacher judgements of student writing. *Research in the Teaching of English*, 11, 176–85.

Hawking, S. (1993). *Black holes and baby universes and other essays*. New York: Bantam.

He, A. (1993). Exploring modality in institutional interactions: cases from academic counselling encounters. *Text*, 13 (2), 503–28.

Herbert, R. (1990). Sex-based differences in compliment behaviour. *Language in Society*, 19, 201–24.

Hewings, A. (1990). Aspects of the language of economic textbooks. In A. Dudley-Evans and W. Henderson (eds), *The language of economics: the analysis of economic discourse* (pp. 109–27). London: Modern English Publications.

Higgins, A.C. (1994). *Bibliography of scientific fraud*. Albany, NY: Exams Unlimited.

Hinds, J. (1987). Reader versus writer responsibility: a new typology. In U. Connor and R.B. Kaplan (eds), *Writing across languages: analysis of L2 text.* Reading, MA: Addison-Wesley.

Holmes, J. (1983). Speaking English with the appropriate degree of conviction. In C. Brumfit (ed.), *Learning and teaching languages for communication: applied linguistics perspectives.* London: BAAL.

Holmes, J. (1984). Modifying illocutionary force. *Journal of Pragmatics,* **8,** 345–65.

Holmes, J. (1988). Doubt and certainty in ESL textbooks. *Applied Linguistics,* **91,** 20–44.

Holmes, J. (1990). Hedges and boosters in women's and men's speech. *Language and Communication,* **10** (3), 185–205.

Holmes, J. (1995). *Women, men and politeness.* London: Longman.

Hood, S. and Forey, G. (1999). Research to pedagogy in EAP literature reviews. *TESOL '99,* 10–14 March 1999, New York.

Horowitz, D.M. (1986). What professors actually require: academic tasks for the ESL classroom. *TESOL Quarterly,* **20** (3), 445–62.

Hoye, L. (1997). *Adverbs and modality in English.* London: Longman.

Hunston, S. (1993). Evaluation and ideology in scientific writing. In M. Ghadessy (ed.), *Register analysis: theory and practice* (pp. 57–73). London: Pinter.

Hyland, K. (1996a). Writing without conviction? Hedging in science research articles. *Applied Linguistics,* **17** (4), 433–54.

Hyland, K. (1996b). 'I don't quite follow': making sense of a modifier. *Language Awareness,* **5** (2), 91–9.

Hyland, K. (1997). Scientific claims and community values: articulating an academic culture. *Language and Communication,* **16** (1), 19–32.

Hyland, K. (1998a). *Hedging in scientific research articles.* Amsterdam: John Benjamins.

Hyland, K. (1998b). Exploring corporate rhetoric: metadiscourse in the Chairman's letter. *Journal of Business Communication,* **35** (2), 224–45.

Hyland, K. (1998c). Persuasion and context: the pragmatics of academic metadiscourse. *Journal of Pragmatics,* **30,** 437–55.

Hyland, K. (1998d). Boosting, hedging and the negotiation of academic knowledge. *Text,* **18** (3).

Hyland, K. (1999a). Disciplinary discourses: writer stance in research articles. In C. Candlin and K. Hyland (eds), *Writing: texts, processes and practices* (pp. 99–121). London: Longman.

Hyland, K. (1999b). Talking to students: metadiscourse in introductory textbooks. *English for Specific Purposes,* **18** (1), 3–26.

Hyland, K. and Milton, J. (1997). Hedging in L1 and L2 student writing. *Journal of Second Language Writing,* **6** (2), 183–206.

Intaraprawat, P. and Steffensen, M. (1995). The use of metadiscourse in good and poor ESL essays. *Journal of Second Language Writing,* **4** (3), 253–72.

Irwin, A. and Wynne, B. (1996). *Misunderstanding science? The public reconstruction of science and technology.* Cambridge: CUP.

Johns, A. (1990). Coherence as a cultural phenomenon: employing ethnographic principles in the academic milieu. In U. Connor and A. Johns (eds), *Coherence in writing: research and pedagogical perspectives* (pp. 209–26). Alexandria, VA: TESOL.

Johns, A. M. (1993). Written argumentation for real audiences: suggestions for teacher research and classroom practice. *TESOL Quarterly,* **27** (1), 75–90.

Johns, A. M. (1997). *Text, role and context: developing academic literacies.* Cambridge: Cambridge University Press.

Johnson, D. M. (1992). Compliments and politeness in peer review texts. *Applied Linguistics*, **13**, 52–71.

Johnson, D. M. and Roen, D. H. (1992). Complimenting and involvement in peer reviews: gender variation. *Language in Society*, **21**, 27–57.

Jolliffe, D. A. (ed.) (1988). *Writing in academic disciplines*. Norwood, NJ: Ablex.

Jones, J. H. (1981). *Bad blood: the Tuskegee syphilis experiment*. New York: Free Press.

Jones, T. (1986). Hazards for export: double standards? In L. Levidow (ed.), *Science as politics* (pp. 119–38). London: Free Association Books.

Judson, H. (1995). *The eighth day of creation: the makers of the revolution in biology*. Harmondsworth: Penguin Books.

Kaplan, R., Cantor, S., Hagstrom, C., Lia, D., Shiotani, Y. and Zimmerman, C.B. (1994). On abstract writing. *Text*, **14** (3), 401–26.

Kaufer, D. and Geisler, C. (1989). Novelty in academic writing. *Written Communication*, **6** (3), 286–311.

Kellenberger, E. (1989). Origins of molecular biology. *Plant Molecular Biology Reporter*, **7**, 231–4.

Kelves, D. J. (1998). Pursuing the unpopular: a history of viruses, courage and cancer. In R. Silvers (ed.), *Hidden histories of science* (pp. 69–114). London: Granta.

Kennedy, G. (1987). Expressing temporal frequency in academic English. *TESOL Quarterly*, **21**, 69–86.

Kennedy, G. (1998). *An introduction to corpus linguistics*. Harlow: Longman.

Killingsworth, M. J. (1992). Discourse communities local and global. *Rhetoric Review*, **11**, 110–22.

Killingsworth, M.J. and Gilbertson, M.K. (1992). *Signs, genres and communication in technical communication*. Amityville, New York: Baywood.

Knorr-Cetina, K. (1981). *The manufacture of knowledge*. Oxford: Pergamon Press.

Kolb, D. A. (1981). Learning styles and disciplinary differences. In A. Chickering (ed.), *The modern American college* (pp. 232–55). San Francisco: Jossey Bass.

Kress, G. (1987). Genre in a social theory of language: a reply to John Dixon. In I. Reid (ed.), *The place of genre in learning: current debates*. Geelong, Australia: Deakin University Press.

Kress, G. (1989). *Linguistic processes in sociocultural practice*. Oxford: Oxford University Press.

Kress, G. and Van Leeuwean, T. (1996). *Reading images: the grammar of visual design*. London: Routledge.

Kuhn, T. (1963). The function of dogma in scientific research. In A.C. Crombie (ed.), *Scientific change* (pp. 347–69). London: Heinemann.

Kuhn, T. (1970). *The structure of scientific revolutions*. (2nd edn). Chicago: University of Chicago Press.

Kuo, C.-H. (1999). The use of personal pronouns: role relationships in scientific journal articles. *English for Specific Purposes*, **18** (2), 121–38.

Latour, B. and Woolgar, S. (1979). *Laboratory life: the social construction of scientific facts*. Beverly Hills: Sage.

Laurent, J. (1998). Science, technology and the economy. In M. Bridgestock, D. Burch, J. Forge, J. Laurent and I. Lowe (eds), *Science, technology and society* (pp. 132–58). Cambridge: CUP.

Lave, J. and Wenger, E. (1991). *Situated learning: legitimate peripheral participation*. Cambridge: Cambridge University Press.

Lea, M. and Street, B. (1999). Writing as academic literacies: understanding textual practices in higher education. In C.N. Candlin and K. Hyland (eds), *Writing: texts, processes and practices* (pp. 62–81). London: Longman.

Lemke, J. (1995). *Textual politics: discourse and social dynamics*. London: Taylor & Francis.

Lemke, J. (1998). Multiplying meaning: visual and verbal semiotics in scientific text. In J. Martin and R. Veel (eds), *Reading science: critical and functional perspectives on discourses of science* (pp. 87–113). New York: Routledge.

Lenoir, T. (1997). *Instituting science: the cultural production of scientific disciplines.* Stanford, CA.: Stanford University Press.

Lerat, P. (1995). *Les langues spécialisées*. PUF.

Lewenstein, B. V. (1995). From fax to facts: communication in the cold fusion saga. *Social Studies of Science*, **25**, 403–36.

Lewontin, R. (1991). *Biology as ideology: the doctrine of DNA*. New York: Harper Collins.

Lewontin, R. C. (1998). Genes, environment, and organisms. In R. Silvers (ed.), *Hidden histories of science* (pp. 115–140). London: Granta.

Li, X. (1996). *'Good writing' in cross cultural context*. New York: State University of New York.

Littlejohn, A. (1988). How to fail interviews. In A. Littlejohn and M. Melouk (eds), *Research methods and processes*. Lancaster: Lancaster University Dept of Linguistics.

Lock, S. (1988). Structured abstracts. *British Medical Journal*, **297**, 156.

Love, A. M. (1991). Process and product in geology: an investigation of some discourse features of two introductory textbooks. *English for Specific Purposes*, **10**, 89–109.

Love, A. M. (1993). Lexico-grammatical features of geology textbooks: process and product revisited. *English for Specific Purposes*, **12**, 197–218.

Lundquist, L., Picht, H. and Qvistgaard, J. (eds) (1998). *LSP: identity and interface. Research, knowledge and society*. Copenhagen: LSP Centre, Copenhagen Business School.

Luukka, M.-R. (1995). Puhuttua ja kirjoitettua tiedetta. Funktionaalinen ja yhteisollinen nakokulma tieteen kielen interpersonaalisiin piirteisiin. *Jyvaskyla Studies in Communication*, **4**.

Lyons, J. (1977). *Semantics*, vols 1 and 2. Cambridge: CUP.

MacDonald, S.P. (1994). *Professional academic writing in the humanities and social sciences*. Carbondale: Southern Illinois University Press.

Malcolm, I. (1999). Writing as an intercultural process. In C.N. Candlin and K. Hyland (eds) *Writing: texts, processes and practices* (pp. 122–41). London: Longman.

Malcolm, L. (1987). What rules govern tense usage in scientific articles? *English for Specific Purposes*, **6**, 31–44.

Marcuse, H. (1972). *One dimensional man*. London: Abacus.

Martin, J.R. (1998). Discourses of science: recontextualisation, genesis, intertextuality and hegemony. In J.R. Martin and R. Veel (eds), *Reading science: critical and functional perspectives on discourses of science* (pp. 3–14). London: Routledge.

Martin, J.R. and Veel, R. (eds) (1998). *Reading science: critical and functional perspectives on discourses of science*. London: Routledge.

Martin, J. and Christie, F. (eds) (1997). *Genre and institutions: social processes in the workplace and schools*. London: Cassell.

Mauranen, A. (1993). Constrastive ESP rhetoric: Metatext in Finnish–English economics texts. *English for Specific Purposes*, **12** , 3–22.

McKenna, B. (1997). How engineers write: an empirical study of engineering report writing. *Applied Linguistics*, **18** (2), 189–211.

Miller, C. (1984). Genre as social action. *Quarterly Journal of Speech*, **70**, 157–78.

Miller, C. (1994). Rhetorical community: the cultural basis of genre. In A. Freedman and P. Medway (eds), *Genre and the new rhetoric* (pp. 67–78). London: Taylor & Francis.

Milton, J. (1999). Lexical thickets and electronic gateways: making text accessible by novice writers. In C.N. Candlin and K. Hyland (eds) *Writing: texts, processes and practices* (pp. 221–43) London: Longman.

Milton, J. and Hyland, K. (1999). Assertions in students' academic essays: a comparison of L1 and L2 writers. In R. Berry, B. Asker, K. Hyland and M. Lam (eds), *Language analysis, description and pedagogy*. Hong Kong: Hong Kong University of Science and Technology Press.

Moore, J. (1986). Socializing Darwinism: historiography and the fortunes of a phrase. In L. Levidow (ed.), *Science as politics* (pp. 38–80). London: Free Association Books.

Morino, A. I. (1997). Genre constraints across languages: causal metatext in Spanish and English RAs. *English for Specific Purposes*, **16** (3), 161–79.

Mulkay, M. (1976). The mediating role of the scientific elite. *Social Studies of Science*, **6**, 445–70.

Mulkay, M. (1979). *Science and the sociology of knowledge*. London: Allen and Unwin.

Mulkay, M. (1995). Galileo and the embryos: religion and science in parliamentary debate over research on human embryos. *Social Studies of Science*, **25**, 499–532.

Murray, D. (1989). *Write to learn*. New York: Holt, Rinehart and Winston.

Myers, G. (1989). The pragmatics of politeness in scientific articles. *Applied Linguistics*, **10**, 1–35.

Myers, G. (1990). *Writing biology: texts in the social construction of scientific knowledge*. Madison: University of Wisconsin Press.

Myers, G. (1991). Lexical cohesion and specialized knowledge in science and popular science texts. *Discourse Processes*, **14** (1), 1–26.

Myers, G. (1992a). 'In this paper we report ...': speech acts and scientific facts. *Journal of Pragmatics*, **17**, 295–313.

Myers, G. (1992b). Textbooks and the sociology of scientific knowledge. *English for Specific Purposes*, **11** (1), 3–17.

Myers, G. (1998). Displaying opinions: topics and disagreement in focus groups. *Language in Society*, **27**, 85–111.

Myers, G. (1999). Interaction in writing: principles and problems. In C.N. Candlin and K. Hyland (eds), *Writing: texts, processes and practices* (pp. 40–61). London: Longman.

Namsaraev, V. (1997). Hedging in Russian academic writing in sociological texts. In R. Markkanen and H. Schroder (eds), *Hedging and discourse: approaches to the analysis of a pragmatic phenomenon*. Berlin: de Gruyter.

Nash, W. (1990). Introduction: the stuff these people write. In W. Nash (ed.), *The writing scholar: studies in academic discourse*. Newbury Park, CA: Sage.

Nash, W. (1992). *An uncommon tongue*. London: Routledge.

Nystrand, M. (1987). The role of context in written communication. In R. Horowitz and S.J. Samuels (eds), *Comprehending oral and written language* (pp. 197–214). San Diego, CA: Academic Press.

Nystrand, M. (1989). A social interactive model of writing. *Written Communication*, **6**, 66–85.

Odell, L., Goswami, D. and Herrington, A. (1983). The discourse-based interview: a procedure for exploring the tacit knowledge of writers in non-academic settings. In P. Mosenthal, L. Tamor and S. A. Walmsley (eds), *Research on writing: principles and methods*. New York: Longman.

Olshtain, E. and Weinbach, L. (1986). Complaints – a study of speech act behaviour among native and non-native speakers of Hebrew. In M. Papi and J. Verschueren (eds), *The pragmatic perspective: selected papers from the 1985 International Pragmatics Conference*. Amsterdam: John Benjamins.

Orteza y Miranda, E. (1996). On book reviewing. *Journal of Educational Thought*, **30** (2), 191–202.

Palmer, F. (1990). *Modality and the English modals* (2nd edn). London: Longman.

Paltridge, B. (1994). Genre analysis and the identification of textual boundaries. *Applied Linguistics*, **15** (3), 288–99.

Paltridge, B. (1995). Working with genre: a pragmatic perspective. *Journal of Pragmatics*, **24** (4), 393–406.

Pardoe, S. (1999). Respect and the pursuit of 'symmetry' in researching literacy and student writing. In D. Barton, M. Hamilton and R. Ivanic (eds), *Situated literacies*. London: Routledge.

Park, D. (1986). Analysing audiences. *College Composition and Communication*, **37** (4), 478–88.

Passell, L. (1988). Getting out the word: an insider's view of Physical Review Letters. *Physics Today*, **41** (3), 32–7.

Paul, D. and Charney, D. (1995). Introducing chaos (theory) into science and engineering. *Written Communication*, **12** (4), 396–438.

Pennycook, A. (1994). *The cultural politics of English as an international language*. London: Longman.

Perkins, M. (1983). *Modal expressions in English*. London: Pinter.

Porter, J. (1992). *Audience and rhetoric: an archaeological composition of the discourse community*. Englewood Cliffs, NJ: Prentice Hall.

Prelli, L. (1989). *A rhetoric of science: inventing scientific discourse*. Columbia: University of South Carolina Press.

Prior, P. (1998). *Writing/Disciplinarity: a sociohistoric account of literate activity in the academy*. Mahwah, NJ: Erlbaum.

Probst, R. E. (1989). Transactional theory and response to student writing. In C. Anson (ed.), *Writing and response* (pp. 68–79). Urbana, IL: NCTE.

Purves, A.C. (1988). *Writing across languages and cultures: issues in contrastive rhetoric*. Newbury Park, CA: Sage.

Purves, A.C., Quattrini, J.A. and Sullivan, C.I. (1995). *Creating the writing portfolio*. Lincolnwood, IL: NTC Publishing.

Quirk, R., Greenbaum, S., Leech, G. and Svartvik, J. (1972). *A grammar of contemporary English*. Harlow: Longman.

Rampton, B. (1995). Politics and change in research in applied linguistics. *Applied Linguistics*, **16** (2), 233–56.

Rauch, Y. M. (1992). The rhetoric of the probable in scientific commentaries: the debate over the species status of the Red Wolf. *Technical Communication Quarterly*, **6**, 91–104.

Rawlence, C. (1990). *The Missing Reel*. London: Collins.

Redd-Boyd, T. and Slater, W. (1989). The effects of audience specification on undergraduates' attitudes, strategies, and writing. *Research in the Teaching of English*, **23**, 77–103.

Redner, H. (1987). *The ends of science: an essay in scientific authority*. Boulder, CO: Westview Press.

Reynolds, M. and Dudley-Evans, T. (eds) (in press). *Genre analysis: current perspectives, applications and contributions*. Cambridge: CUP.

Richards, S. (1987). *Philosophy and sociology of science: an introduction.* (2nd edn). Oxford: Blackwell.

Rogoff, B. (1990). *Apprenticeship in thinking: cognitive development in social context.* New York: Oxford University Press.

Roper, D. (1978). *Reviewing before the Edinburgh: 1788–1802.* London: Methuen.

Rorty, R. (1979). *Philosophy and the mirror of nature.* Princeton: Princeton University Press.

Rose, D. (1998). Science discourse and industrial hierarchy. In J.R. Martin and R. Veel (eds), *Reading science* (pp. 236–65). London: Routledge.

Rosenblatt, L. M. (1985). Viewpoints: transaction versus interaction – a terminal rescue operation. *Research in the Teaching of English,* **19** (1), 96–107.

Rothblatt, S. (1985). The notion of an open scientific community in historical perspective. In M. Gibbons and B. Wittrock (eds), *Science as a commodity* (pp. 21–75). London: Longman.

Rounds, P. (1982). *Hedging in written academic discourse: precision and flexibility* (Mimeo). Ann Arbor: The University of Michigan.

Sacks, O. (1998). Scotoma: forgetting and neglect in science. In R.B. Silvers (ed.), *Hidden histories of science* (pp. 141–88). London: Granta.

Salager-Mayer, F. (1990). Discoursal flaws in medical English abstracts: a genre analysis per research and text type. *Text,* **10** (4), 365–84.

Salager-Mayer, F. (1992). A text-type and move analysis of study verb tense and modality distribution in medical English abstracts. *English for Specific Purposes,* **11**, 93–113.

Salager-Meyer, F. (1994). Hedges and textual communicative function in medical English written discourse. *English for Specific Purposes,* **13** (2), 149–70.

Salerno, D. (1988). An interpersonal approach to writing negative messages. *Journal of Business Communication,* **25** (1), 41–51.

Samraj, B. (1998). Discoursal variation in abstracts from two disciplines. Paper given at AAAL Conference, Seattle.

Schiffrin, D. (1980). Metatalk: organisational and evaluative brackets in discourse. *Sociological Inquiry: Language and Social Interaction,* **50**, 199–236.

Schröder, H. (1991). Linguistic and text-theoretical research on Language for Specific Purposes. In H. Schroder (ed.), *Subject-oriented texts: Language for Special Purposes and text theory* (pp. 1–48). Berlin: de Gruyter.

Schröder, H. (1995). Der Stil wissenschaftlichen Schreibens zwischen Disziplin, Kultur und Paradigma. In G.Stickel (Stilfragen). Berlin: de Gruyter.

Scollon, R. (1994). As a matter of fact: the changing ideology of authorship and responsibility in discourse. *World Englishes,* **13**, 34–46.

Scollon, R. and Scollon, S. (1995). *Intercultural communication.* Oxford: Blackwell.

Scott, M. (1996). *Wordsmith tools.* Oxford: OUP.

Shapin, S. (1984). Pump and circumstance: Robert Boyle's literary technology. *Social Studies of Science,* **14**, 481–520.

Shaw, P. (1992). Reasons for the correlation of voice, tense and sentence function in reporting verbs. *Applied Linguistics,* **13**, 302–19.

Skelton, J. (1988). Comments in academic articles. In P. Grunwell (ed.), *Applied linguistics in society.* London: CILT/BAAL.

Skelton, J. (1997). The representation of truth in academic medical writing. *Applied Linguistics,* **18** (2), 121–40.

Spack, R. (1988). Initiating ESL students into the academic discourse community: how far should we go? *TESOL Quarterly,* **22** (1), 29–52.

Sperber, D. and Wilson, D. (1986). *Relevance: communication and cognition.* Oxford: Blackwell.

Spinks, S. (1998). Relating marker feedback to teaching and learning in psychology. In C.N. Candlin and G. Plum (eds), *Framing student literacy*. Sydney: NECLTR Macquarrie University.

Steig, M. (1986). *The origin and development of scholarly historical periodicals*. Alabama: University of Alabama Press.

Street, B. V. (1995). *Social literacies: critical approaches to literacy in development, ethnography and education*. New York: Longman.

Sullivan, D. (1996). Displaying disciplinarity. *Written Communication*, 13 (2), 221–50.

Swales, J. (1990). *Genre analysis: English in academic and research settings*. Cambridge: CUP.

Swales, J. (1993). Genre and engagement. *Revue Belge de Philologie et Histoire*, 71 (3), 689–98.

Swales, J. (1995). The role of the textbook in EAP writing research. *English for Specific Purposes*, 14 (1), 3–18.

Swales, J. (1996). Occluded genres in the academy: the case of the submission letter. In E. Ventola and A. Mauranen (eds), *Academic writing: intercultural and textual issues* (pp. 45–58). Amsterdam: John Benjamins.

Swales, J. (1998). *Other floors, other voices: a textography of a small university building*. Mahwah, NJ: Erlbaum.

Swales, J. and Najar, H. (1987). The writing of research article introductions. *Written Communication*, 4, 175–192.

Swales, J., Ahmad, U., Chang, Y-Y., Chavez, D., Dressen, D. and Seymour, R. (1998). Consider this: the role of imperatives in scholarly writing. *Applied Linguistics*, 19 (1), 97–121.

Tadros, A. (1993). The pragmatics of text averral and attribution in academic texts. In M. Hoey (ed.), *Data, description, discourse*. London: HarperCollins.

Tadros, A. (1994). Predictive categories in expository text. In M. Coulthard (ed.), *Advances in written text analysis* (pp. 69–72). London: Routledge.

Taylor, P. (1986). Dialectical biology as political practice: looking for more than contradictions. In L. Levidow (ed.), *Science as politics* (pp. 81–111). London: Free Association Books.

Thetela, P. (1997). Evaluated entities and parameters of value in academic research articles. *English for Specific Purposes*, 16, 101–18.

Thomas, J. and Short, M. (eds) (1996). *Using corpora for language research*. London: Longman.

Thomas, S. and Hawes, T. (1994). Reporting verbs in medical journal articles. *English for Specific Purposes*, 13, 129–48.

Thompson, G. (1996). Voices in the text: discourse perspectives on language reports. *Applied Linguistics*, 17, 501–30.

Thompson, G. and Thetela, P. (1995). The sound of one hand clapping: the management of interaction in written discourse. *Text*, 15, 103–27.

Thompson, G. and Ye, Y. (1991). Evaluation of the reporting verbs used in academic papers. *Applied Linguistics*, 12, 365–82.

Thompson, J. B. (1984). *Studies in the theory of ideology*. Cambridge: Polity Press.

Todeva, E. (1999). Variability in academic writing: hedging. *AAAL Conference*. New York, 6–9 March.

Torfing, J. (1999). *New theories of discourse*. Oxford: Blackwell.

Toulmin, S. (1958). *The uses of argument*. Cambridge: CUP.

Toulmin, S. (1972). *Human understanding*, vol 1. Oxford: Clarendon Press.

UNESCO (1992). *Statistical Yearbook 1992*. Paris: UNESCO.

Ungerer, F. and Schmid, H.-J. (1996). *An introduction to cognitive linguistics.* London: Longman.

Valero-Garces, C. (1996). Contrastive ESP rhetoric: metatext in Spanish–English economics texts. *English for Specific Purposes,* **15** (4), 279–94.

Valle, E. (1997). A scientific community and its texts: a historical discourse study. In B.-L. Gunnarson, P. Linell and B. Nordberg (eds), *The construction of professional discourse* (pp. 76–98). London: Longman.

van Dijk, T.A. (1997). Discourse as interaction in society . In T.A. van Dijk (ed.), *Discourse as social interaction* (pp. 1–37). London: Sage.

Vande Kopple, W. (1985). Some exploratory discourse on metadiscourse. *College Composition and Communication,* **36**, 82–93.

Ventola, E. (1992). Writing scientific English: overcoming cultural problems. *International Journal of Applied Linguistics,* **2** (2), 191–220.

Ventola, E. (1997). Abstracts as an object of linguistic study. In S. Čmejrková, F. Danes and E. Havolova (eds), *Writing v Speaking* (pp. 333–52). Tübingen: Gunter Narr.

Ventola, E. and Mauranen, A. (eds). (1996). *Academic writing: intercultural and textual Issues.* Amsterdam: John Benjamins.

Vygotsky, L. (1978). Mind in society: the development of higher psychological processes. In M. Cole, V. John-Steiner, S. Scribner and E. Souberman (eds), Harvard, MA: Harvard University Press.

Watson, J. (1968). *The double helix.* Harmondsworth: Penguin.

Webber, P. (1994). The function of questions in different medical English genres. *English for Specific Purposes,* **13**, 257–68.

Weimer, W. (1977). Science as a rhetorical transaction: toward a nonjustificational conception of rhetoric. *Philosophy and Rhetoric,* **10**, 1–29.

Whitley, R. (1984). *The intellectual and social organisation of the sciences.* Oxford: Clarendon Press.

Wichmann, A., Fligelstone, S., McEnery, T. and Knowles, G. (eds) (1997). *Teaching and language corpora.* London: Longman.

Wolfson, N. (1989). *Perspectives: sociolinguistics and TESOL.* Cambridge, MA: Newbury House.

Wright, P. (1999). Writing and information design of healthcare materials. In C.N. Candlin and K. Hyland (eds), *Writing: texts, processes and practices* (pp. 85–98). London: Longman.

Ylonen, S., Neuendorff, D. and Effe, G. (1993) Zur kontrastiven Analyse von medizinischen Fachtexten. Eine diachrone Studie. In C. Lauren and M. Nordman (eds), *Special language: from humans thinking to thinking machines.* Clevedon: Multilingual Matters.

Ziman, J. (1984). *An introduction to science studies: the philosophical and social aspects of science and technology.* Cambridge: CUP.

Subject Index

Author Index